S0-BIK-338

For Mrs Lucy G. Speed, from whose pious hand I accepted the present of an Oxford Bible twenty years ago.
Washington, D.C. October 3. 1861   A. Lincoln.

(By permission of the Century Co.)

Abraham Lincoln
Man of God

By

John Wesley Hill, D.D., LL.D.

Chancellor of Lincoln Memorial University

G. P. Putnam's Sons
New York and London
The Knickerbocker Press
1920

COPYRIGHT, 1920
BY
G. P. PUTNAM'S SONS

Printed in the United States of America

To

FRANK A. SEIBERLING

MY HONOURED FRIEND

*This book is dedicated, not merely as an expression
of personal esteem but also, and chiefly, because, in a life
of humble beginnings, he has achieved a notable success
through the observance of Lincoln-like standards of honour;
because in the management of a gigantic business he has
realized an Industrial Republic based on Lincoln-like
conceptions of justice; and because, as patron of Lincoln
Memorial University and as chairman of its Board of
Directors, he has nobly wrought to bring to the youth
of Lincoln's mountain country opportunities of an
education whose purpose and method are responsive to
the Lincoln inspiration.*

To

FRANK A. SEIBERLING

MY HONOURED FRIEND

This book is dedicated, not merely as an expression of personal esteem but also, and chiefly, because, in a life of humble beginnings, he has achieved a notable success through the observance of Lincoln-like standards of honour; because in the management of a gigantic business he has realized an Industrial Republic based on Lincoln-like conceptions of justice; and because, as patron of Lincoln Memorial University and as chairman of its Board of Directors, he has nobly wrought to bring to the youth of Lincoln's mountain country opportunities of an education whose purpose and method are responsive to the Lincoln inspiration.

A TRIBUTE

"I DOUBT whether any statesman who ever lived sank so deeply into the hearts of the people of many lands as Abraham Lincoln did. I am not sure that you in America realize the extent to which he is also our possession and our pride. His courage, fortitude, patience, humanity, clemency, his trust in the people, his belief in democracy, and, may I add, some of the phrases in which he gave expression to those attributes, will stand out forever as beacons to guide troubled nations and their perplexed leaders. Resolute in war, he was moderate in victory. Misrepresented, misunderstood, underestimated, he was patient to the last. But the people believed in him all the time, and they still believe in him.

"In his life he was a great American. He is an American no longer. He is one of those giant figures, of whom there are very few in history, who lose their nationality in death. They are no longer Greek or Hebrew or English or American— they belong to mankind. I wonder whether I will

v

be forgiven for saying that George Washington
was a great American, but Abraham Lincoln
belongs to the common people of every land."

LLOYD GEORGE.

At the unveiling of the Lincoln
statue near Westminster
Abbey in August, 1920.

FOREWORD

Dr. Hill's *Abraham Lincoln, Man of God*, brings Lincoln before us as a man, splendid in his strength of purpose, unshaken by popular clamour, humane, sympathetic, and far-seeing; a man who understood and appreciated the problems of life, the passions and the weaknesses of his fellow-men, strong because of his trials and triumphs; a great leader—so great as to be without jealousy; humble, because of his knowledge and experience, forgetful of self in his desire to best serve his country and mankind.

He stands before us a heroic and earnest figure, as one humbly seeking the inspiration, counsel, and help of the Almighty, praying for guidance from above and giving sympathy, assistance, and leadership to all about him, with unshaken faith in the ultimate success of the Right; as a finite mind seeking the guidance of the infinite.

We see in Lincoln's deep religious nature the effect of his early training, and in those direct appeals to and communions with God we see not

only an abiding faith and trust in God but also
something of the spirit of the revival, the intense
religious emotionalism of those great meetings of
his boyhood out of which came much of definite
conviction, of faith and of trust in God.

As one reads one feels that Lincoln was indeed
"A Man of God."

INTRODUCTION

No new biography of Lincoln is needed to portray his public life. The standard histories give in all detail the great events of his career. But interpretations of his inner life are still in order. Few great men of the past have suffered as much as Lincoln at the hands of the well-meaning and uncritical, the ill-informed and prejudiced.

Charlemagne and Cromwell, Washington and John Marshall, all were children of their time. Only in the light of circumstances which produced them can they be explained. The interplay of heredity and environment on powerful personalities and the compelling reaction of personalities on their surroundings furnish a task beyond the reach of those who lack human understanding and spiritual imagination.

Abraham Lincoln was born amid a somewhat primitive and tumultuous religious upheaval expressed in the powerful preaching of Peter Cartwright and illustrated in the perennial popularity of the camp-meeting. Brought up by parents

whose lives were lived amid such influences,
Abraham Lincoln was from his earliest years
religious. The Bible was the book of books to
him. He prayed so constantly and confidently
as to seem a kind of modern Brother Lawrence
practising the Presence of God. He worked out a
theology in general conformity with the accepted
standards of Christianity. In the darkest hour
of his White House days when personal bereavement was added to national anxiety, he literally
lived on his knees.

Yet even in his lifetime he was often charged
with infidelity. Some too near the trees to see
the woods even wrote books attributing Lincoln's
frequent depression to irreligion. He believed
he was defeated for office in 1841 because of the
report that he was not a Christian. Many still
are blinded by the same delusion.

A book has long been needed to bring discussion
to an end, to set at rest much foolish speculation,
and to convince the most incredulous that Abraham Lincoln, Man of God, was as sincere in his
religious faith as Robert E. Lee or Willliam E.
Gladstone.

This book from the pen of Chancellor John
Wesley Hill of Lincoln Memorial University
seems likely to perform this purpose. For many

years, both in his personal and official capacity, he has been collecting evidence at last massed in this book as challenging as it is interesting. Even the most casual reader will perceive that all of Lincoln's convictions sprang out of his profound belief in God as set forth in the Christian teachings, that his habit of studying both sides of every question and of stating each as strongly as he could was in part responsible for the misapprehensions of some who have held a superficial view of his religious life, and that his intimate friend Noah Brooks writing as early as 1872 a personal letter stated the truth this compelling book illustrates that "any suggestion as to Mr. Lincoln's skepticism is a monstrous fiction, a shocking perversion."

These times as truly try men's souls as Lincoln's times. Problems of today are as grave and complex as the problems to which Lincoln brought as clear a mind and pure a soul as modern times have known. A free people whose freedom has been purchased at a great price must now choose between the merely economic and the spiritually moral, between irresponsible Marxianism so subtle that even the timid who dare not champion it outright are still under its dominion, and Lincolnism calling as loudly today as in the Gettysburg address: "This nation, under God, shall have a new birth of freedom."

We are at the parting of the ways. Is our thought to function in the lowlands of materialism in the days before us, or in the religious highlands where Lincoln lived and died that we might live? That is the supreme question we have now to answer.

In giving Abraham Lincoln his undisputed place among the men of God who have taught us how to find the proper answer to this question, the author of this volume has rendered a service as opportunely patriotic as it is lastingly religious.

Warren G Harding

PREFACE

GOD's heralds have the right of way. Their thoughts and deeds are the richest legacy of humanity. They are lights kindled upon the dome of the centuries illuminating the mental and the moral atmosphere. History is the story of their epochal deeds. Civilization is the lengthened shadow of their exalted souls. Serving most they are the greatest.

Victor Hugo has said: "The summit of the human mind is the ideal toward which God descends and man ascends." From below the world watches them. "How small they are," says the crowd. Through storm and cloud, by scarped cliff and yawning abyss, they ascend until they reach the summit where they catch great secrets from the lips of God.

The centuries are the solemn priests which anoint and enthrone the prophets of God. A saint is a good man dead one hundred years, cannonaded then but canonized now. "A prophet is not without honour save in his own country."

This is true of all the prophets. Stones have been their bread and bed.

Abraham Lincoln was no exception. He was cartooned as a gorilla, denounced as a buffoon, hounded by political malcontents, assailed by seditionists and traitors, and finally sacrificed as a vicarious offering upon the altar of freedom.

What was the secret of his incomparable leadership, his exalted personality? Whence the inspiration by which he mastered the political and social problems of the antebellum days? Whence the light through which he saw the destiny of the American republic? Whence the patience, the wisdom by which he was able to guide the ship of state through the raging storm of a rebellion into the haven of a restored and permanent Union? Who doubts that his inspiration was from above, that his marvellous power came not so much from training, environment, and opportunity, as from the spiritual endowment which dominated his will, quickened his sympathies, fired his faith, fused his fortitude, and steadied and directed his unswerving ambition to keep step with the march of the divine purpose as revealed in the great epoch in which Lincoln towered above the men of his time as the Colossus of the desert towers above all the neighbouring gods standing upright upon their pedestals.

The cause of human liberty came to its supreme
test when the South seceded from the Union. The
destiny of the United States held in solution the
hopes of upstruggling humanity. To this country
the world was looking for answers to questions
involving the capacity of mankind for self-govern-
ment, the possible elimination of the institution
of human slavery from the social order, the effect
of freedom on the development of ideal social and
industrial conditions, and the triumph of human
rights over property rights.

To Abraham Lincoln, the solution of this composite problem of the ages, depended not solely
upon the force of arms and magnetism of brilliant
leadership, but upon the help of the Almighty.
His trust was not in horses and chariots, but in the
King Eternal, and according to his own statements,
it was under divine guidance that he directed one
of the greatest military struggles the world had
ever known to the achievement, against tremendous obstacles, of the conclusive victory that
preserved the Republic and brought an end to
slavery.

Through all these dark and ominous times,
Mr. Lincoln's heart, though often bowed with a
grief such as only he could know, looked to God,
depended upon His guidance, found solace in

prayer, and strength and comfort in the Scriptures.
Let those who will, oppose the affirmation of Lincoln's Christian character and assert that he was
an atheist or sceptic, that he had only a vague
conception of God and professed no belief in religion.   Let those who will, believe that Lincoln
owes his leadership to his master intellect alone
or that he rode to his place of power and dominion
over the hearts of men on the billowing tide of
favouring circumstances.   Let the eccentric, if they
will, attempt to explain away his patience, his
judgment, and vision by reference to the "conjunction of the planets at his birth," "chance," "luck,"
"genius," or any other empty phrase.

In the midst of all such vain attempts, the character of the great emancipator stands out in world
history as the incarnation of qualities so pure, so
spiritual, that the secret is found in but one word—
God.

Up to Lincoln's time, history seemed in large
part to present but a repetition of political and
military short-sightedness, or of crimes perpetrated
in the name of religion and justice.   For this reason the intellectual world stands confounded before Abraham Lincoln's simplicity.   How was it
possible for a mind so simple and direct to wield
an influence so potent?   No one like him had

ever been seen on the public rostrum. Born and
bred in the western wilderness, he had to wrestle
with rhetorical gladiators in the greatest political
arena of the world, and to face, single-handed,
hostile individuals, groups and parties backed
by financial privilege and supported by social
prestige.

The essential religiousness of Lincoln's life is
presented to the Anglo-American people in this
critical time, when every thoughtful person knows
that the problems now before us are as difficult as
those which the martyred President had to solve.
We are in the welter of materialism, the chaos of
indifference to the best. Plans and panaceas in
abundance have failed to allay the world unrest.
A new day must dawn or a darker night settle on
the world. We must have leaders who will touch
those in the dull sleep of materialism with the
finger-tip of divine reassurance and bring them to
their feet with the glad cry: "Arise, shine, for thy
light is come, and the glory of the Lord is risen
upon thee."

For the day in which he lived Abraham Lincoln
did precisely this. In consequence I would write
no biography. This honourable task has been
worthily performed by others from Dr. J. G.
Holland writing while the guard around the great

man's tomb at Springfield was still new at its post,
to Lord Charnwood laying on the casket of his
memory the other day the noble tribute of an
appreciative Englishman.

Phillips Brooks once said that in Lincoln was
"vindicated the greatness of real goodness and the
goodness of real greatness." It is my modest
aspiration to explain and to confirm this obvious
truth in terms as simple as Lincoln himself was
accustomed to employ. Abraham Lincoln was a
man of God. Recalling his frequent reference to
Jesus Christ, it would seem altogether fitting to
indicate that he set a high standard of Christian
manhood; that he drew his inspiration and his
superlative wisdom in state affairs directly from
the source of all wisdom; that in the darkest hours
through which he and his cause were called to
pass he was sustained by an unfailing faith; and
that when he proclaimed to the world that he was
actuated "with malice toward none and charity
toward all," he was exemplifying the spirit of the
Christian religion in which he believed.

A portrayal of the religious life of Lincoln should
be of value alike to the professing and the non-
professing Christian; to the orthodox and to the
liberal; to the thoughtful of no faith at all and to
those vaguely religious who, with Marcus Aurelius,

believe that from the divine principle all things come, in it all things subsist, and to it all things return. Such a portrayal may vividly illustrate that faith and prayer are for the strong, as well as weak, and that to this mightiest man of the centuries they were avowedly the source of inspiration which enabled him to perform his divinely appointed tasks.

There is a divine Providence beyond human ken which shapes the destinies of men and nations, and Lincoln's faith was builded on the Rock of Ages. He believed Providence was directing the destiny of the American Union and the march everywhere of human freedom. He accepted the triumph of his cause as the fulfilment of a divine plan, inevitable as the whirl of the planets in their appointed orbits. His eyes were fixed on higher and surer things than the tumultuous and changing currents of human thought and action, on the pillar of cloud by day, of fire by night, guiding the nation he was leading toward the fulfilment of its appointed mission. The services of other great civil and military leaders of Lincoln's time are not forgotten; but without Lincoln's profound insight, his unfailing patience, his unshakable firmness, and, above all, his faith and serene reliance upon a Higher Power, their efforts would have been in vain.

A candid examination of the evidence will show that the religious element in Lincoln's life was its dominant factor; that his character as a politician and as a statesman was determined by his character as a Christian; and that he drew from the story of the "Man of Sorrows" the conclusion that God rules the world in a personal way.

Abraham Lincoln rose to his position of eminence from beginnings which, to the superficial, gave no promise beyond mediocrity. Born to poverty, nourished on the barest necessities, he obtained the equipment for his life work through heart-breaking self-denials. Julius Cæsar boasted that he was descended from Venus and Anchises, through the great Æneas and the royal Lavinia. Lincoln made no claim to descent from any lofty personage. His ancestors were pioneer stock— brave, hardy, adventurous folk, who developed in the discipline of the wilderness those sterling qualities which had nerved their race to maintain their rights against the king and parliament of England, and, in the New World, against the depredations of the painted savage.

Such ancestry was sturdily human and laid the foundation upon which to build manly character and the Christian virtues. Lincoln descended from men and women who, in their daily life, prayed to God, read His Word, and worshipped Him in devout reverence. From such stock came the typical American whom this book would describe without reserve as a man of God.

J. W. H.

New York City,
October, 1920.

CONTENTS

Abraham Lincoln—Man of God

Abraham Lincoln—Man of God

CHAPTER I

THE BACKGROUND

THE prairies of the Great West were as vast
seas in which the groves, God's first temples, were
like islands. Their rolling waves of summer verdure, their sombre glow of autumn haze, their
angry aspect when swept by raging storms, their
billowing drifts of winter snows, impressed the
pioneer mind with a sense of the infinite.

The frontier communities were saturated with
religious sentiment. Nearness to nature keyed
their souls to spiritual influences. They saw God
in the clouds, heard Him in the winds, read His
providence in the upspringing of verdure, and in
the recurrence of the seasons. Their hardships
chastened them; their common dangers drew them
closer together; their perils and helplessness taught

them reliance upon a Higher Power. They drew their religious faith and fervour from the Puritans of New England, the Cavaliers of Maryland, the Scotch Presbyterians of the Carolinas, and from other types of Christians. Central among them was Methodism, which exerted a wide and deep influence in moulding the rugged religion of the pioneer.

Fortunately, in the intimate association of the wilderness, sectarian and denominational differences lost their strong hold, and tolerance was practised from necessity as well as inclination. The people merged into a brotherhood of mutual helpfulness in spiritual as well as in material things. They met and exchanged ideas and experiences as freely as they exchanged the products of the soil and chase.

As their mode of life brought health and strength, their religious life lent joyousness, instead of Puritanic gloom. Limited in the number of their "meeting houses," the rude school houses were often utilized for worship.

The one big event of the year was the camp-meeting. It attracted, from far and near, multitudes of all classes, the pious and impious, the reverent and profane. Believers and unbelievers found in the camp-meeting the only touch of cos-

mopolitan life that modified the loneliness of the
frontier.

The people made their way to these camps in
vehicles of every description, farm wagons, ox
carts, boats; while some went on horseback and
hundreds travelled on foot. They talked over
neighbourhood affairs, discussed the questions of
the day, and gathered from each other the drift
of national tendencies, the progress of settlement,
and the spread of religious sentiment.

Naturally these exchanges, however, centred in
their exuberant religious life. One who passed his
youth amidst such scenes wrote:

It was a heterogeneous gathering,—humourists who
were unconscious of their humour; mystics who did
not understand their strange, far-reaching power;
sentimental dreamers who did their best to live down
their emotions; old timers and cosmopolitans with a
wonderful admixture of sense and sentiment; political
prophets who could foresee events by a sudden, illuminating flash and foretold them in a quick-spoken,
pithy sentence; theologians educated on the frontier,—
these met and prayed and wrestled in sharp verbal en-
counters that were as educational in their way as were
the discussions in the academic groves of Athens. [1]

It was an unusual people, living in a second
Canaan, in an age of social change and upheaval,
in a period of political and economic strife. There

[1] *The Valley of the Shadow*, Francis Grierson.

was something Biblical in all of this, applied to the circumstances of the day. There was charm in their mode of living, and romance even in the incidents of their surroundings. The religious exercises of the camp-meeting were calculated to quicken the spirit, intensify the faith, and arouse the inward depth of individuals and communities. The meetings were centres for religious fervour. From them radiated spiritual influences which shaped and moulded public sentiment. Under the pointed and fervid preaching, the results were instantaneous and at times astounding. Sinners were "convicted"; skeptics who "came to scoff remained to pray"; unbelievers, convinced of their errors, fell upon their knees, called upon God for mercy, publicly confessed Christ, and touched by missionary zeal, became enthusiastic evangels of the new-found joy.

Their singing was not that of the trained choir. It was the spontaneous outburst of souls attuned to nature and to God. Inspired by love and quickened by a gratitude which overflowed all the ordered laws of song, they poured forth an impetuous Niagara of praise.

Theirs was the music of the heart evoked by the consciousness of "sins forgiven," sweeping heavenward under the urgency of an unction unearthly and divine.

Their prayers, often uttered in rude and blundering phrase, perchance by stammering tongues, were yet sustained by a faith that pierced the limits of time and space and found favour with the Most High.

The distinguishing characteristic of preacher and people was the spirit of independence. No creed formulated by church councils could bind them. No edicts of potentates could fetter their speech. No law of established reputation or of place and procedure could prevent their plain speaking. The prophets among them both foretold and forthtold.

Rude, abrupt, strident, and mandatory, they appeared like John the Baptist, crying in the wilderness, "Repent ye, for the Kingdom of Heaven is at hand."

The preacher of that period was aggressive. His saddlebags were his theological seminary, his Bible and hymn book his library. Like John Wesley, he constructed his sermons as he journeyed, drew his inspiration from nature and nature's God, preached along the bridle paths, in the open fields, on the streets of straggling villages, anywhere he could find a congregation, small or great. The roof of his cathedral was the arching heavens, its walls the forests that fringed the highway.

He was more than a great preacher; he was a
political force.   Peter Cartwright, for instance,
was even nominated against Lincoln for Congress.
The preacher was social guide and mentor.   He was
prodigious in all respects.   In many of the frontier
communities were groups of rowdies who sometimes varied the monotony of the wilderness by
"licking the preacher."   The largest and strongest
of one of these groups was selected to "lick" Peter
Cartwright on his way to keep a preaching appointment.   The bully lay in wait along the roadside.
The revivalist rode up, Bible in hand, evolving his
sermon as he came.   As he neared his destination,
the bully stepped out from the shadow of a tree
and thus addressed Peter: "I have come out here
for to lick ye."   "Wait until I get off this horse,"
Cartwright responded, without the flicker of an
eyelash or the tremor of a muscle.   He dismounted,
laid aside his clerical coat, and said, "Now I am
ready."   The man of the cloth then whipped the
bully until the bully cried, "I have got enough;
let me up!"   But Cartwright was not through
with his antagonist.   "No, I'll not let you up until
you confess your sins and accept Jesus Christ as
your Saviour."   And lying prone on the ground,
with the clergyman on top of him, the bully was
finally converted.   It was related that later he

became a genuine convert and was loyal both to Cartwright and the Christian faith.[1]

Preachers then were militant. They differed in characteristics and in creeds, but they preached the Gospel in a spirit as uncompromising as that of the prophets of old. They were worthy successors of the early disciples of the Master, of whom it was said: "These are the fellows who are turning the world upside down." They turned the religious and political and social conditions of their time not only upside down, and inside out, but also right side up, until the great religio-political principles which are fundamental to human life and liberty, no less than to Christian civilization, were sounded far and near. It was mostly the inspiration that swept from these prairies, breathed by those pioneer preachers and people, that aroused the slumbering conscience of the nation, and finally kindled the flame of liberty on the altar of democracy.

Lincoln's immediate ancestry was of the generation that was perhaps most powerfully affected by this strong, subtle, permeating, spiritual environment. It was said that his mother's family, the

---

[1] Peter Cartwright was in so many essentials a forerunner of Lincoln that a somewhat full discussion of the man is given in the Appendix.

Hankses, were "Great at camp-meetings." It is significant that Herndon, not appreciative of Lincoln's religion, thus accounts in part for Lincoln's mystic temperament. He says that a camp-meeting had been in progress for several days, during which religious fervour ran high. All were there in complete accord, continuing in supplication, awaiting the celestial fire. Suddenly, there was a stir in the camp. Something extraordinary had happened. The multitude who were kneeling sprang to their feet and broke forth into shouts which rang out amid the primeval shades. Presently a young man, who had been absorbed in prayer, began leaping, dancing, and shouting, while to his left a young woman, as though inspired by the example she had witnessed, sprang forward, her hat falling to the ground, her hair tumbling down in graceful braids, her eyes fixed heavenward, her lips vocal with strange, unearthly song, her rapture overflowing until, grasping the hand of the young man, they both began singing at the top of their voices.

The family tradition identifies the couple as Thomas Lincoln and Nancy Hanks, and reports that they were married the following week in a little cabin on the "Rock Spring Farm" in Washington County, Kentucky, by the Reverend Richard Berry, June 12, 1806.

CHAPTER II

GODLY PARENTAGE

To come to its best in every way, character must have a sound physical basis. The father of Abraham Lincoln, though not as tall as his tall son, was five feet ten inches high, weighed 195 pounds, and was so compactly built that it was said no point of separation could be found at any place between his ribs. Thomas Lincoln was equal to any call upon his strength. Habitually inoffensive and peace-loving, once aroused he never failed to give of himself a good account. Until Ida Tarbell wrote her painstaking *Life of Lincoln*, Thomas Lincoln was commonly believed to be shiftless. Now we know that at a time when few indeed made even a tolerable living, Thomas Lincoln at least provided for the bare necessities of his increasing family; and he was a good man, adding to devoutness a jovial and buoyant temperament.

It was a Christian home in which the Christian statesman was brought up. The parents were

church members, at first affiliated with a free-will
Baptist Church in Kentucky and later with the
Presbyterians in Indiana. The home life was
conventionally religious. The family altar was
set up at the beginning and was never down. No
meal began without a blessing even though at
times there was little on the table for which to
offer thanks. One day when potatoes made up
the entire menu, the youthful Abe, with a twinkle
in his honest eyes but no irreverence in his heart,
remarked to his good father, "Dad, I call these
mighty poor blessings."

Good children are apt to have good mothers.
Both in his mother, Nancy Hanks, and later in his
step-mother, Sally Johnston, Lincoln was unusually
fortunate. Both were godly women, and both
passed on to Abe their godliness. They laid deep
and wide the foundations of a Christian manhood
which sustained him amid the changing scenes
and vicissitudes of his epochal career. Nancy
Hanks's forebears early hailed from Plymouth,
though they were not among *Mayflower* folk.
Then they moved to Virginia whence Nancy's
father moved across into Kentucky where on her
father's death, when she was barely nine years old,
she grew up into a sweet-tempered and fair woman-
hood, the centre—as tradition has it—both of

country merry-making and of industrious house-
wifery. Three children came the first three years
of her happy married life, and she lost a little of
her buoyancy and vigour in her conscientious
efforts to meet her maternal responsibilities.
But though such hard circumstances would have
turned ordinary women into slatterns, they simply
brought out the heroically adequate in Nancy
Hanks and made her worthy to bring up her little
children, the second of whom died in early infancy.

When in his later years, his mother, who died
before he reached the age of ten, was but a tender
memory, Lincoln used to say: "All that I am or
hope to be I owe to my angel mother." Nancy
Hanks Lincoln accepted the responsibilities of
motherhood amid the rude hardships of a frontier
life, with a sense of reverence that lifted her above
the dull and deadly routine of the commonplace
and impecunious. A shack alone protected the
little family from the chilly blasts of winter, and
on one side the only doorway was a curtain made
of skins. The sack mattress on which the father
and the mother slept was filled with husks or
leaves, and even into it the little folks from their
rude shake-down on the floor, peculiarly accessible
to the winds, would often crawl for warmth. The
only food they had was sometimes brought down

in the forest by the mother's rifle as well as by the father's, and was supplemented by fish caught in the nearest stream, corn raised from the stubborn soil and turned into Johnny-cake before the open fire by the busy hands of the fond mother whose eyes at the same time were ever on her young.

Hers was a busy life under handicaps, yet mother love was never once forgotten or disowned. No matter what demands were made upon her time and strength she always gave first thought to her children. She taught them to read their Bible[1] and such other books as were available. Abraham Lincoln's earliest recollection of his mother was of sitting at her knee with his sister drinking in the tales and legends that were read or told to them by her.[2]

When Abe was past nine years, and the dreamy haze of Indian summer was in the air, his mother passed away, telling him with dying breath:

" I am going away from you, Abraham, and shall not return. I know that you will be a good boy; that you will be kind to Sarah and your father. I want you to live as I have taught you, and to love your Heavenly Father and keep His commandments."[3]

[1] Phoebe Hanaford, *Life of Lincoln*, p. 20.
[2] Noah Brooks, *Works of Lincoln*, vol. viii., p. 6.
[3] Arnold, *Life of Lincoln*, p. 27.

Though stunned by the blow which had fallen upon him, Thomas Lincoln, in the usual exigencies of pioneer life, made with his own axe and saw the coffin for his loved one, and as the glowing colours of the dying year were lighting up the west, he laid her to rest, who had been his staff of life as well as mother of his children, in a clearing in the woods not far from the cabin she had made to bloom into a Christian home. No minister could then be had. Besides, the custom still persists among the mountain whites sometimes of having the formal burial service long after the interment. The grief-bowed man added, however, to the last sad offices he performed a homely prayer attended by the reading of a Bible passage as he knew that Nancy Hanks would have desired.

Swiftly the long and dreary winter swept down on the wifeless home without a mother. The little family did the best they could. Abe cheered them as he later cheered a nation in its darkest days. He never once forgot the final admonition of his mother to be kind to Sarah and his father. Already religion was coming to its proper place in that great soul; for it was Abe, who when the spring returned and he agreed with his father that the burial service was incomplete without a minister, wrote the letter to a preacher, a long hundred miles

away down in Kentucky, to come as soon as possible
and preach the funeral sermon.

Through the wilderness Parson Elkin made the
journey on horseback and arrived one Wednesday.
Word was sent to all the neighbours for a score of
miles around. By Sunday all were there. For such
a place and time they seemed a multitude. Till
that day never in that region had so many come
together for any purpose whatsoever. As the hour
drew near for service, they grew quiet and medi-
tative. Wherever there was room they found
rude seats on logs and stumps and even on the
ground. The preacher offered prayer. With one
accord the people sang a solemn funeral hymn.
As next he eulogized the saintly woman, recollection mingled with respect and love, and honest
grief was freely poured out for her whom they all
recognized instinctively as the worthiest in that
whole region to be a Christian wife and Christian
mother to the ones who loved her best.

With the service ended, Parson Elkin flung himself into the saddle and headed South again. The
settlers scattered on their homeward way. The
family in quiet stole back to the cabin. Then
when all were gone Abe turned toward the
grave, flung himself upon the cold dead earth,
wept as he had wept when first the clods fell on

the coffin, and prayed and prayed to God to give him strength to live the life his mother would approve.

It was a wretched make-shift year the family spent without the mother. How the children needed her! Abe was turning ten. Sarah, now past twelve, was the best housekeeper she knew how to be. The father, like all normal men, dependent on a woman's touch, was both helpless and depressed. The crude cabin, perhaps, missed its mistress most of all.

Then Sally Johnston came to prove that where there is mother love there is true motherhood. The new step-mother won at once the love and confidence both of Abe and Sarah. Fortunately she brought with her—for measured by the standard of the time she was not poor—a goodly store of well-made bedding, convenient cooking utensils, a mother heart and mother touch that lighted up the cabin and made the father and the children happy as they had never dreamed that they could be again. Abounding in energy, she imparted energy to all. The cabin floors were at last laid. Doors and windows were hung. The cracks between the logs were plastered to keep out the cold. The ticks of husks and leaves gave way to feather beds. The children for the first time in their lives

2

were fitted out with clothes that made them conscious that they were somebody.

Tall, straight, sprightly, a good talker, appreciative, and discerning, honestly and with success Sally Johnston endeavoured to train up the girl and boy as Nancy Hanks had started them. Recognizing the rare promise Abe gave, she sent him off to school a mile and more away. A classmate later wrote, "Abe always was at school early, attended faithfully to his studies, and stood at the head of his classes." When hard times came he sometimes had to stay at home to do the work, to help out with the family expenses, and even to work out among the neighbours as a "hired hand." The conscientiousness which was both a native gift and was developed by his two mothers, supplemented by his reliability and thoroughness, gave him a high value in the labour market, and to his paid duties he was always ready to add his special cleverness in computing interest and even writing letters for the neighbours.

Like Nancy Hanks, Sally Johnston, who long outlived her step-son, bore testimony later to his goodness which grew with the years:

Abe was a good boy, and I can say what scarcely one woman, a mother, in a thousand can say! Abe never gave me a cross word or look, and never refused in fact or appearance to do anything I requested of him. He was a dutiful son to me always . . . the best boy I ever saw, or expect to see.[1]

Lincoln's appreciation in return of his step-mother was as keen as hers of him. He spent the last day before he left Springfield to be inaugurated President in affectionate companionship with her. The first large fee he ever earned from his law practice in his early days at Springfield he voluntarily and joyously devoted with half as much again, which he borrowed from a friend, to the purchase for $750 of a quarter section of land which he settled on her for life, in fee simple. Until his death he cared for her in constant tenderness, calling all that he did "a poor return" for her devotion and fidelity to him.[2]

Thus even before he came into his 'teens, Lincoln had developed a mature sense of responsibility to God which never failed to find expression in reverent obedience to God's laws as he understood them; of responsibility to man in every relationship of life, particularly to his kindly father and his two devoted mothers, alike motherly to him and consecrated to his upbringing in "the fear and admonition of the Lord."

[1] Nicolay and Hay, *Abraham Lincoln, a History*, vol. i., p. 35.
[2] Carpenter, 238, and Curtis, 30.

CHAPTER III

IT was in his eleventh year that the beginning of Lincoln's marvellous mental as well as physical development became obvious.

His craving for education soon marked him as peculiar among his fellows. While not at work or school, he studied at home with an ardour that is now a bright tradition of the Republic. For his mathematical exercises the walls of the cabin were his blackboard, a bit of chalk his crayon. He devoured with avidity every book he could obtain. Fortunately, the few books which found their way into the frontier settlements were mostly works of standard value. In this plastic period of his life, Lincoln appears to have followed in his reading and study the bent given to his nature by the teachings and the posthumous influence of his mother, and also the constant association with his step-mother.

Truth was the fundamental principle on which he based every discussion as he grew in mind and morals. He would not lie, nor permit his political opponents to lie. What is right? What is truth? were tests he always applied to the solution of social and political problems. Finding for himself the answers to these questions, no power could turn him from advocating the right and proclaiming the truth.

An incident is related which shows his native honesty, even in his boyhood days. His step-sister, Matilda Johnston, followed Abe one morning as he went into the forest to clear a piece of land. She was then in her 'teens, and, like the other Johnston children, was fond of Abe. The mother had forbidden Matilda to go away that morning from the cabin, but the girl escaped her mother's watchful eye, unknown to Abe. Slyly creeping through the dense undergrowth, she sprang upon the boy with such sudden force as to bring them both to the ground. In falling, the girl's ankle came in contact with the keen edge of the axe. Abe staunched the blood with strips of cloth torn from his shirt and from her dress. Then turning to Matilda he asked: "What are you going to tell your mother about this?" "I'll tell her that I did it with the axe," she sobbed; "that will be the truth, won't it?" "Yes, that's the truth, but not all the truth," Abe responded.

"Tell the whole truth, Tilda, and trust your mother for the rest."

The same uncompromising spirit of truth and devotion to righteousness was shown at every stage of his career, and never more clearly than nearly forty years later in his Cooper Institute speech on the 27th of February, 1860. In dissecting with merciless logic the threats of the proslavery advocates to destroy the Union if a Republican President was elected, he said:

If slavery is right, all words, acts, laws, and constitutions against it are themselves wrong and should be silenced and swept away. If it is right, we cannot justly object to its universality. If it is wrong, they cannot justly insist upon its extension. All they ask we could readily grant, if we thought slavery right. All we ask they could readily grant, if they thought it wrong. Their thinking it right, and our thinking it wrong, is the precise fact upon which depends the whole controversy.

These pregnant sentences lifted the slavery controversy out of mere sectional and partisan contention to the lofty heights of pure morality. The politicians of the day did not relish this plain setting-forth of truth. Their aim was to confine political discussions to property rights, to economic questions, to industrial conditions, North and South, and thus make the controversy a battle of brains over technical questions, over constitutions, statutes, and vested rights. They also wished to keep the political arena exclusively for technical legerdemain to the end that the common people might be made to believe that the issues were beyond their comprehension. Who, and what, was this Lincoln that he, with a sentence, should brush aside these technicalities, and lift the dominant issue of the time into the exalted sphere of political morality? Who? The man who had learned his morality at his mother's knee, as she thumbed the pages of her Bible and taught her children its sublime truths.

In this, his eleventh year, his personality planted upon a firm moral basis, began an amazing physical development which continued until at his majority he stood six feet four inches in height. The labour to which he was forced by the poverty of his youth toughened his muscles and sinews, and made him a physical giant. His was a physique to match his mind. His power of concentration of thought was so great that often he was literally lost in profound abstraction. His genius for analysis and his ability to state a case with clarity have never been surpassed.

When he was about to begin his debates with Douglas, many of his friends were honestly alarmed. Scarcely one but feared a failure. Hardly, however, had that titanic contest started when opinion at home gradually changed in Lincoln's favour, while in all parts of the country men began to realize that a great man had been called forth by the hour to meet the new emergency. Miss Tarbell has discovered a letter written by a statesman in the East to some friend in the middle East asking: "Do you realize that no greater speeches have been made on public questions in the history of our country; that his knowledge of the subject is profound, his logic unanswerable, his style inimitable?"

Both his physical and mental development were dominated by an imperative spiritual influence. His inherent mystical temperament might, perhaps, have been abnormally developed, had it not been for the practical wisdom of his step-mother. It was she who drew him away from too constant introspection and melancholy, directing his mind toward the acquirement of practical knowledge.

Hazel Dorsey was his first teacher during the few weeks he regularly attended school when in his eleventh year. Owing to the pressing necessities of the Lincoln family, Abe was not again permitted to attend school until his fourteenth year, when Andrew Crawford was his schoolmaster.

This was his last term in school. Study with him was, however, continuous. Having acquired a taste for learning, he pursued it with an eagerness and interest that never lagged.

So insatiable was his thirst for education that he was known to trudge seven miles to borrow an English grammar. Then, stretched upon the cabin floor, before an open fireplace, an ungainly figure clad in coarse garments, he studied his borrowed grammar and his arithmetic. His slate was a wooden scoop-shovel which, when covered with figures, he would shave clean with his father's drawing knife or jack plane. Thus the lad may be said to have scooped knowledge into his capacious head.

Such were the conditions under which the character of Abraham Lincoln gradually unfolded. The eagerness to learn, the love of truth, the reverence for things sacred, the disposition to investigate, his patience under rebuke, his latent humour, which preserved his sense of proportion, his sensitiveness to suffering, the heroism with which his burdensome tasks were borne—all contributed to the formation of a composite man. Withal he was light-hearted, humorous, witty, but never frivolous. Through all, his face was turned toward the light and his pensive eyes looked far down the path of achievement, and with calmness and courage seemed to discern the end.

No reminiscence of this early development in Lincoln's life shows more clearly the interrelation of Lincoln's intellectual and moral life than an article which appeared in *The Independent*, September 1, 1864, from the pen of the Reverend Dr. John Putnam Gulliver, of Norwich, Connecticut. No abbreviation of it will suffice for such a purpose as this chapter has in view. It must be told in full. Dr. Gulliver says:

It was just after his controversy with Douglas, and some months before the Chicago Convention of 1860 that Mr. Lincoln came to Norwich to make a political speech. . . . The next morning I met him at the Railroad Station where he was conversing with our Mayor, every few minutes looking up the track and inquiring half impatiently and half quizzically, "Where's that 'wagon' of yours? Why don't the wagon come along?" On being introduced to him he fixed his eyes upon me and said, "I have seen you before, sir!" "I think not," I replied; "you must have mistaken me for some other person." "No, I don't; I saw you at the Town Hall last evening." "Is it possible, Mr. Lincoln, that you could observe individuals so closely in such a crowd?" "Oh yes!" he replied laughing, "that is my way, I don't forget faces." "Were you not there?" "I was, sir, and I was well paid for going." As we entered the cars, he beckoned me to take a seat with him and said in a most agreeably frank way, "Were you sincere in what you said about my speech just now?" "I meant every word of it, Mr. Lincoln. Why, an old dyed-in-the-wool Democrat, who sat near me, applauded you repeatedly; and when rallied upon his conversion to sound principles, answered, 'I don't believe a word he says, but I can't help clapping him, he is so pat!' Indeed, sir, I learned more of the art of speaking last evening than I could learn from a whole course of lectures on Rhetoric."

"Ah! that reminds me," said Mr. Lincoln, "of a most extraordinary circumstance which occurred in New Haven the other day. They told me that the Professor of Rhetoric in Yale College was in the audience, —a very learned man isn't he?"

"Yes, sir, and a fine critic, too."

"Well, I suppose so; he ought to be, at any rate. They told me that he came to hear me and took notes of my speech and gave a lecture on it to his class the next day; and not satisfied with that he followed me up to Meriden the next evening and heard me again for the same purpose. Now, if this is so, it is to my mind very extraordinary. . . ."

"That suggests, Mr. Lincoln, an inquiry which has several times been upon my lips during this conversation. I want very much to know how you get this unusual power of 'putting things.' It must have been a matter of education. No man has it by nature alone. What has your education been?"

"Well, as to education, the newspapers are correct; I never went to school more than six months in my life. But, as you say, this must be a product of culture in some form. I have been putting the question you ask me to myself, while you have been talking. I can

say this, that among my earliest recollections I remember how, when a mere child, I used to get irritated
when anybody talked to me in a way I could not
understand. I don't think I ever got angry at anything else in my life. But that always disturbed my
temper, and has ever since. I can remember going to
my little bedroom, after hearing the neighbours talk
of an evening with my father, and spending no small
part of the night walking up and down, and trying to
make out what was the exact meaning of some of their,
to me, dark sayings. I could not sleep, though I often
tried to, when I got on such a hunt after an idea, until
I had caught it; and when I thought I had got it, I
was not satisfied until I had repeated it over and over,
until I had put it in language plain enough, as I
thought, for any boy I knew to comprehend. This
was a kind of passion with me, and it has stuck by
me; for I am never easy now, when I am handling a
thought, till I have bounded it north, and bounded it
south, and bounded it east, and bounded it west.
Perhaps that accounts for the characteristic you
observe in my speeches, though I never put the two
things together before."

"Mr. Lincoln, I thank you for this. It is the most
splendid educational fact I ever happened upon. . . .
But let me ask you, did you prepare for your profession?"

"Oh, yes! I 'read law' as the phrase is; that is, I
became a lawyer's clerk in Springfield, and copied
tedious documents, and picked up what I could of law
in the intervals of other work. But your question
reminds me of a bit of education I had, which I am
bound in honesty to mention. In the course of my
law-reading, I constantly came upon the word 'dem-

onstrate.' I thought at first that I understood its meaning, but soon became satisfied that I did not. I said to myself, 'What do I mean when I demonstrate more than when I reason or prove?' I consulted Webster's Dictionary. That told of 'certain proof,' 'proof beyond the possibility of doubt'; but I could form no idea what sort of proof that was. I thought a great many things were proved beyond a possibility of doubt, without recourse to any such extraordinary process of reasoning as I understood 'demonstration' to be. I consulted all the dictionaries and books of reference I could find, but with no better results. You might as well have defined 'blue' to a blind man. At last I said, 'Lincoln, you can never make a lawyer if you do not understand what "demonstrate" means'; and I left my situation in Springfield, went home to my father's house, and stayed there till I could give any proposition in the six books of Euclid at sight. I then found out what 'demonstrate' means, and went back to my law-studies."

I could not refrain from saying, in my admiration at such a development of character and genius combined: "Mr. Lincoln, your success is no longer a marvel. It is the legitimate result of adequate causes. You deserve it all, and a great deal more. If you will permit me, I would like to use this fact publicly. *Euclid*, well studied, would free the world of half its calamities, by banishing half the nonsense which now deludes and curses it. I have often thought that *Euclid* would be one of the best books to put on the catalogue of the Tract Society, if they could only get people to read it. It would be a means of grace."

"I think so," said he, laughing: "I vote for *Euclid*."

As we neared the end of our journey, Mr. Lincoln

turned to me very pleasantly, and said: "I want to thank you for this conversation. I have enjoyed it very much."

"Mr. Lincoln, may I say one thing to you before we separate?"

"Certainly, anything you please."

"You have become, by the controversy with Mr. Douglas, one of our leaders in this great struggle with slavery, which is undoubtedly the struggle of the nation and the age. What I would like to say is this, and I say it with a full heart, *Be true to your principles and we will be true to you, and God will be true to us all!*" His homely face lighted up instantly with a beaming expression, and taking my hand warmly in both of his, he said, "I say Amen to that—Amen to that!"

CHAPTER IV

THE BLENDING OF THE MENTAL AND THE MORAL

In the dome of the Congressional Library at Washington is this inscription from the Prophet Micah: "What doth the Lord require of thee, but to do justly, and to love mercy, and to walk humbly with thy God?" No man in American history—no man in the history of the world—ever more completely filled this measure of a man of God than did Abraham Lincoln. But his growth was gradual in godliness. It had its beginnings in the unquestioning faith in the teachings of his mother, in her Bible reading to him. Then he read the Scriptures for himself—read them as he read everything else, thoughtfully and with discrimination.

The religious beliefs of his early years were saturated with superstitions. Belief in the baneful influences of witches, and in the curative power of wizards was everywhere prevalent. To shoot the image of a witch with a silver ball was believed to break the spell she was supposed to exercise over her victims. The magic divining rod of the water-wizard was followed with implicit confidence, as was the faith doctor, who wrought miraculous cures with strange sounds and with signals to some mysterious power. There were signs, lucky and unlucky, while the phases of the moon were believed to influence the minds of the people, as well as the growth of vegetation. It would have been strange, indeed, had not Lincoln's pensive nature been deeply affected by this atmosphere of superstition. His leaning toward the supernatural manifested itself in his later life when the burden of responsibility for the world's moral progress, if not the fate of civilization itself, seemed to rest upon his shoulders. The fatalistic type of his early religious training was one of the secrets of his never-wavering faith in the ultimate victory of the forces of freedom. While his thinking and his reading gradually broke the spell of the grosser superstitions, they never banished his belief in the significance of visions and dreams.

Lincoln's mystic temperament developed along rational lines, thanks in part to his step-mother's influence, and never turned him aside from the well-surveyed routes his thought travelled to the final goal of his great mission. His reading had much to do in determining the type of his religious

life.   His favourite books were the Bible, Æsop's
Fables, Bunyan's *Pilgrim's Progress*, and Shakespeare's plays, though in addition he read every
book he could borrow within a radius of fifty miles.
Everything was grist that came to his intellectual
mill.   He got hold of a copy of the Revised Statutes
of Indiana, and read it with as much avidity as the
ordinary boy would read a tale of adventure.   Nor
was his reading superficial.   When in the field
plowing, he would stop to read, and then ponder
on what he had read after resuming his labour.
Among other books that fell into his hands was
Weems's *Life of Washington*, a work that added
fuel to the glowing flame of patriotism always
inseparable from his sense of loyalty to God.   One
of his most treasured volumes was a borrowed
book which he damaged, and then "pulled fodder"
for three days to pay for it.

But the Bible was his favourite.   Indeed, it was
the first book he read with interest and appreciation.   Poring over it for hours at a time, his
memory became saturated with its language, his
soul with its spirit, his life with its teachings.   So
familiar did he become with the Scripture phraseol-
ogy, and so imbued with the solemnly grand strain
of thought and feeling that pervades the sacred
pages, that his utterances often breathe the sub-

limity of the prophets, the poetry of Job or the
Psalmist, the sweetness and pathos of the Gospels.
Hence it was that he was enabled, as at Gettysburg, to fire the finest intellects with enthusiastic
admiration and strangely to move and thrill the
hearts of the multitudes. In August, 1920, at the
unveiling of the Lincoln Statue near Westminster
Abbey, Lloyd George said, "I doubt whether any
statesman who ever lived sank so deeply into the
hearts of people of many lands as did Abraham
Lincoln."

In his early teens, Lincoln acquired a facility of
expression, both with tongue and pen, unusual in
one of his years. He began public speaking to his
schoolmates and his fellow-labourers, and wrote
compositions on all sorts of subjects. An essay on
temperance, written in his seventeenth year, so
attracted the favourable attention of Aaron
Farmer, a Baptist preacher of local renown, that
he sent it to an Ohio newspaper for publication.
About this time, too, Lincoln prepared an essay on
the American Government, calling attention to
the necessity of preserving the Constitution and
the perpetuation of the Union. John Pitcher, a
lawyer, who afterward became a judge declared
this composition "a world beater." It is remarkable that, at so early an age, he should have per-

ceived the precise issue upon which he was to wage his battle for human rights, and upon which the political differences that agitated the Republic were to be fought out in the great Civil War.

All these preparatory experiences would, in some natures, have developed a Caligula or a Nero. But Abraham Lincoln was not of the stuff of which tyrants are made; and the time was swiftly approaching when the American people would need a leader, not simply of commanding intellect but also of heart big enough to encompass all the people, and, in return, win all. Lincoln's experiences and his religious training had deepened and intensified his native kindliness of heart until, later in life, it bordered close upon being a fault. He himself appeared to think so.

It was sometimes hard for him to do justice, so dearly did he love mercy. His compassion extended to dumb brutes and was scarcely less in its intensity than his passion for mercy to his kind. When Thomas Lincoln, with his family, moved from Indiana to Illinois, the streams had to be forded, for bridges were not then in fashion. One day, after crossing a river, the family dog was missing. Looking back, they saw him on the opposite side, whining piteously. As the banks were fringed with broken ice, the dog was afraid to make the plunge. To the suggestion that they go on without him, Abe said: "I could not endure the thought of abandoning even a dog." Pulling off his shoes and socks, he waded the icy stream and returned with the quivering animal under his arm. Lincoln declared that the frantic leaps of joy and the other demonstrations of gratitude by the dog were reward enough.

It was this same tender heart, only grown bigger and more tender, to which, when he became President, the mothers never appealed in vain when their soldier boys were under penalty of death. Secretary Stanton often complained that he could never get soldiers shot for desertion if the women succeeded in getting to Lincoln first. A soldier with a grievance, who had been rebuffed by everyone else to whom he had appealed, followed Mr. Lincoln to the Soldiers' Home near Washington. The President, beset by disaster on every hand, and overborne with care, reproved the man and sent him away. After a night of remorse, Lincoln went early the next morning to the man's hotel, begged his forgiveness for treating with rudeness one in sore distress who had offered his life for his country, took him in his carriage and saw him through his difficulties. Secretary Stanton, when told what had been done, apologized to Mr. Lincoln for having rejected the man's appeal. "No, no," replied Lincoln, "you did right in adhering to your rules. If we had such a soft-headed old fool as I am in your place there would be no rules that the Army and the Country could depend upon."

Lincoln's moral preparation for the burdens of responsibilities yet to be thrust upon him was commensurate with his physical growth, his mental development, his tenderness of heart. Grown up under crude environment, subjected to the influences of roughness, coarseness, intemperance, and immorality, endowed with abounding physical vigour and enjoying well-nigh universal popularity among both men and women, from his youth he lived his life clean and wholesome. He shared the sports and pleasures of his youthful contemporaries, yet at no point did he yield to those human weaknesses which impair both the moral stamina and the physical powers.

In after years, when the political tempest was at its worst, when bitterness and hatred reached the white heat of threatened assassination, his antagonists, bent upon his political destruction, searched in vain his whole life through for some moral taint, some scandal, some dishonest act, but found nothing that might not have been proclaimed from the housetops to his honour. He walked humbly with his God.

CHAPTER V

FORTUNATE FAILURES

At the age of twenty-one, Lincoln, with the rest of the family, moved into Illinois. The time had now come to begin life for himself. He had long felt the call to a broader field of activity than the circumstances of his home life afforded, and had often been tempted to break away and strike out for a future of his own. But his sense of loyalty and obligation to his parents had held him from the fulfilment of his longing for a more active life. Being now of age, he could follow the bent of his aspirations.

He did not hesitate to accept the most humble tasks in order to meet his pressing necessities. His great physical strength enabled him to perform the severest kinds of labour, such as cutting cord-wood, working on farms, operating a flatboat, and splitting rails. He did some clerking in a grocery store, and also tried his hand at running a store for himself.

At the outbreak of the Black Hawk War in

1832, Lincoln promptly enlisted at the call of the Governor for troops to put down the uprising of the noted Indian Chief. Though but twenty-three, his popularity led to his election as Captain of the Sangamon County Contingent, and brought him more widely into public notice. The sterling qualities he exhibited, and his considerate treatment of the men under his command, still further increased his growing popularity. But Lincoln was in no battle. He did not take the war seriously. He rather looked upon it as something of a joke and described it later in a semi-humorous vein.

In the same year he stood for election to the Legislature of Illinois, and was defeated, but had the consolation of knowing that, of the entire two hundred and eight votes cast in his home precinct, he received all but three. This was the only defeat he ever suffered at the hands of the people; for in his race against Stephen A. Douglas for the United States Senate he received a majority of the popular vote in the State, though with a majority of the members of the Legislature against him he was not elected.

In this first political campaign, Lincoln, always mindful of religion, issued a circular announcing his platform of principles, in which he declared that all citizens, however poor, should be afforded an opportunity to acquire at least a moderate education, to the end that they might be able "to read the Scriptures and other works, both of a moral and religious nature, for themselves." This doctrine contained the germ that has flowered into the magnificent Public School System, through which every State in the Union offers its youth, not only a moderate education, but also the highest scholastic attainments. This first political output of the future President grew out of the deprivations of his youth and was affected by his early home training.

From his defeat in politics Lincoln turned again to business. But there, too, he promptly failed. His partner, William Barry, in the little country store drank too much, and Lincoln read too much and told too many stories for the good of trade. In consequence, in the spring of 1833 the store's stock was sold to satisfy the creditors; but running true to form, Lincoln took upon himself the responsibility for the firm's debts, the last of which he paid in 1848.

It was in the days that followed at New Salem, where he eked out a bare living for several years as postmaster and surveyor, that a failure overtook him which plunged him into sorrow so profound that for a time his friends feared he would take away his life. The fair Anne Rutledge seemed to have been abandoned by her betrothed. Lincoln, boarding at her father's tavern, essayed the rôle of comforter as he daily sat at table with her or whiled away the evening by her side. It is doubtful that her heart was ever weaned away from her first love, but there is no doubt that Lincoln's sympathy soon turned into genuine affection and they were to be married when Anne fell ill and died. From this grief he never quite recovered. He used to stand beside her grave and tearfully protest: "I cannot bear to have the rain fall upon her." When in the White House he once said, "I really loved that girl"; and there is good reason to believe it was with her in mind he used to quote the verse of Dr. Holmes:

> The mossy marbles rest
> On the lips that he has prest
> In their bloom.

These early failures in public life, business, love, had a large share in the making of the man of God. In place of a Napoleon, a John Wanamaker, or an obscure family man too early wedded, they assured America her Lincoln. They deepened his capacity to feel. They gave him an appreciation success can never give of what in life is really worth while.

They saved him from the temptation high success at last invariably brings to break with God and to overestimate one's own importance. They tempered the fine steel of his strong character so that he could set even Cabinet ministers in their proper place without obtruding on them anything that could be called executive conceit. They helped him to keep close to the deeper things of life, and they make it easier for us to understand how he turned away from the anxieties and worries of high office to seek comfort in the lines he had his young Secretary, John Hay, read to him from *The Tempest:*

> We are such stuff
> As dreams are made on; and our little life
> Is rounded with a sleep.

CHAPTER VI

OMINOUS SHADOWS

SOME natures are endowed with a prescience far above the ordinary. "Coming events cast their shadows before"; but the rare few discern the shadows and rightly interpret them. The footfalls of the march of coming events may be caught only by ears attuned to hear them. Abraham Lincoln made no claim to divination, but he was quick to read and to interpret the signs of the times. As a young man his responsive soul was strangely disturbed, while the multitudes were thoughtlessly at their ease. He dipped far into the future while others made merry with today. At twenty-six Lincoln was at least a score of years ahead of his time.

Even then he sensed the danger that some astute demagogue might take advantage of turmoil and unrest, seize the reins of power, and make himself dictator. Against such usurpation Lincoln would forfend by fortifying the public mind with a conservative democracy that would guide the Nation triumphantly through any national transition, such as, indeed, was already under way. He was firm in the belief that God was at the helm, and that man was but the humble though coöperating agent through whom the Almighty was working out the destiny of mankind. With these thoughts swelling in his mind, when but twenty-eight years old, he made an address before the Young Men's Lyceum of Springfield, on "The Perpetuation of Our Political Institutions," which deserves to be far better known. It shows how this humble prairie lawyer, even then, was thinking far ahead and making ready to lead the people into light. His perception of the trend of events seemed in the circumstances almost preternatural. He said:

In the great journal of things happening under the sun, we, the American people, find our account running under date of the nineteenth century of the Christian era. We find ourselves in the peaceful possession of the fairest portion of the earth, as regards fertility of soil, extent of territory, and salubrity of climate. We find ourselves under the government of a system of political institutions conducing more essentially to the ends of civil and religious liberty than any of which the history of former times tells us.

We, when mounting the stage of existence, find ourselves the legal inheritors of these fundamental blessings. We toiled not in the acquirement or the establishment of them. They are a legacy bequeathed to us by a once hardy, brave, patriotic, but now lamented and departed race of ancestors.

Theirs was the task (and nobly they performed it) to possess themselves, and through themselves us, of this goodly land and to rear upon its hills and valleys a political edifice of liberty and equal rights. 'Tis ours only to transmit these, the former unprofaned by the foot of the invader and the latter undecayed by the lapse of time. This, our duty to ourselves, and our posterity, and love for our species in general, imperatively requires us to perform.

How, then, shall we perform it? At what point shall we expect the approach of danger? By what means shall we fortify against it? Shall we expect some trans-atlantic giant to step across the ocean and crush us at a blow? Never. All the armies of Europe, Asia, and Africa combined, with all the treasure of the earth (our own excepted) in their military chest with a Bonaparte for a commander, could not by force take a drink from the Ohio or make a track on the Blue Ridge in a trial of a thousand years. At what point then, is the approach of danger to be expected? I answer, if it ever reaches us, it must spring up among us. It cannot come from abroad. If destruction be our lot, we must ourselves be its author and finisher. As a nation of freemen, we must live through all time or die by suicide. There is even now something of ill omen among us. I mean the increasing disregard of law which pervades the country, the growing disposition to substitute the wild and furious passions in lieu of the sober judgment of courts, and the worse than savage mobs, for the executive ministers of justice. This disposition is fearful in any community, and that it exists in ours, though grating to our feeling to admit, it would be a violation of truth and an insult to intelligence to deny. I know the American people are much attached to their government. I know they would suffer much for its sake. I know they would endure evils long and patiently before they would think of exchanging it for another. Yet notwithstanding all this, if the laws be continually despised and disregarded, if their rights to be secure in their persons and property are held by no better tenure than the caprice of a mob, the alienation of their affection from the government is a natural consequence, and to that sooner or later it must come.

Here, then, is the one point at which danger may be expected. The question recurs, how shall we fortify against it? The answer is simple: let every American, every lover of liberty, every well-wisher to his posterity, swear by the blood of the Revolution never to violate in the least particular the laws of the country, and never to tolerate their violation by others. As the patriots of '76 did to the support of the Declaration of Independence, so to the support of the Constitution and the laws, let every American pledge his life, his property and his sacred honour; let every man remember that to violate the law is to trample upon the blood of his fathers and to tear the charter of his own and his children's liberty. Let reverence for the laws be breathed by every American mother to the lisping babe that prattles on her lap. Let it be taught in schools, in seminaries, and in colleges. Let it be written in primers, spelling books, and almanacs. Let it be preached from the pulpits, proclaimed in legislative halls, and enforced in courts of justice. In short, let it become the political religion of the nation.

Developing his theme, Lincoln pointed out the logical result that flows from growing lawlessness:

Many great and good men, sufficiently qualified for any task they should undertake, may ever be found, whose ambition would aspire to nothing beyond a seat in Congress, a gubernatorial, or a presidential chair. But such belong not to the family of the lion or the brood of the eagles. What? Think you these places would satisfy an Alexander, a Cæsar or a Napoleon? Never. Towering genius disdains a beaten path. It seeks regions heretofore unexplored. It sees no distinction in adding story to story upon the monuments of fame directed to the memory of others. It denies that it is glory enough to serve under a chief. It scorns to tread in the footsteps of any predecessor, however illustrious. It thirsts and burns for distinction, and if possible it will have it, *whether at the expense of emancipating slaves or enslaving freemen.*

Is it unreasonable, then, to expect that some man, possessed of the loftiest genius, coupled with ambition sufficient to push it to its utmost stretch, will at some time spring up amongst us, and when such an one does, it will require the people to be united with each other, attached to the government and the laws, and generally intelligent, successfully to frustrate his design.

Distinction will be his paramount object, and although he would as willingly, perhaps more so, acquire it by doing good as harm, yet that opportunity being passed and nothing left to be done in the way of building up, he would sit down boldly to the task of pulling down.

Here, then, is a probable case, highly dangerous, and such a case could not have well existed heretofore.

At times Lincoln evinced an almost uncanny foresight as he foresaw that in some way he was to be instrumental, under God, in leading the Nation through the approaching crisis. To him slavery was what he once called "the double-refined curse of God upon His creatures,"[1] for which atonement could at last be made only by its entire destruction. Slavery was legally right in any State that saw fit to adopt it; but it was everywhere and always morally wrong.

When still a young man, Lincoln made his second trip to New Orleans with a cargo of produce. After disposing of the cargo he, with one of his fellow boatmen, sauntered through one of the great slave marts. Here planters were gathered from all parts of the south-west. Black men, women, and children were in rows for sale. The auctioneer cried their good qualities, inviting purchasers to examine them, as though they were horses or mules. If any of the slaves happened to be professing Christians, the fact was in itself regarded as a special asset to enhance the value of the slave upon the block. Again and again the hammer fell. Husbands were separated from wives, parents from children, brothers from sisters. Lincoln witnessed

---

[1] Temple Scott, p. 54, quoting a *Fragment on Slavery*, July 1, 1854.

3

the scene with a horror words could not express. His lips quivered and his voice choked as he turned to his companion and is reported to have said: "If ever I get a chance to hit that thing, I will hit it hard!"

Commenting upon this incident, Dr. Gregg has truly said:

Who was Abraham Lincoln to hit the thing a blow? He was only a boatman, a splitter of rails, a teamster, a backwoodsman. His poverty was so deep that his clothes were in tatters. What position of influence or power was he likely to attain, to enable him to strike a blow? The thing which he would like to hit was incorporated into the framework of society and legalized in half the States composing the Republic. It was intrenched in church and state alike. It was a political force, recognized in the Constitution. It entered into the basis of representation. Was there the remotest probability that he would ever be able to smite such an institution? Why did he utter these words? Why did he raise his right hand to Heaven and swear the solemn oath? Was it some dim vision of what might come to him through divine Providence, in the unfolding years? Was it an illumination of the Spirit, forecasting for the moment the impending conflict between right and wrong, in which he was to play the leading rôle? Was it a whisper by a divine messenger, that he was to be the chosen one to wipe the "thing" from the earth and give deliverance to millions of his fellowmen? Was it not rather the mind and heart and power of God planted by heredity and

early training in the depths of his being and abiding
there with a holy impatience waiting for the clock of
destiny to strike?

The mystic element in Lincoln's nature manifested itself in prophetic visions and expressions
not unsuited to the time but cryptic to his followers. In August, 1837, Mr. Lincoln, with six other
lawyers and two doctors, went in a band wagon
from Springfield to Salem to attend a camp-meeting. On the way Lincoln cracked jokes about the
horses, the wagon, the lawyers, the doctors—
indeed about nearly everything. At the camp-
meeting Dr. Peter Akers, like Peter Cartwright, a
great Bible preacher of his day, then in the fulness
of his powers, preached a sermon on "The Dominion of Jesus Christ." The object of the sermon was
to show that the dominion of Christ could not
come in America until American slavery was wiped
out, and that the institution of slavery would at
last be destroyed by civil war. For three hours the
preacher unrolled his argument and even gave
graphic pictures of the war that was to come.
"I am not a prophet nor the son of a prophet,"
said he, "but a student of the prophets. As I read
prophecy, American slavery will come to an end
in some near decade, I think in the sixties."

Akers's audience was composed mostly of people

from the slave States, and was decidedly pro-slavery. Indeed, there were scarcely enough abolitionists outside of Boston to count. This great sermon was preached within sixty miles of Alton, where a few weeks before Lovejoy had been murdered by a pro-slavery mob. The people surged about the preacher in wild excitement as he denounced slavery and predicted the approaching war. At the climax of his sermon he cried at the top of his voice: "Who can tell but that the man who shall lead us through this strife may be standing in this presence!" Only thirty feet away stood Lincoln drinking in his every word.

That night, on the return trip to Springfield, Lincoln was silent. After some time one of the doctors, an intimate friend, asked: "Lincoln, what do you think of that sermon?" After a moment Lincoln replied: "I never thought such power could be given to mortal man. Those words were from beyond the speaker. The Doctor has persuaded me that American slavery will go down with the crash of a civil war." Then for a few moments he was silent. Finally the solemn words came slowly forth: "Gentlemen: you may be surprised and think it strange, but when the Doctor was describing the Civil War, I distinctly saw myself as in second sight, bearing an important part in that strife." Some there were who believed that, even then, he caught a glimpse of his part in the bloody drama more than a score of years distant, and the fearful tragedy in which it was to end.

The next morning, when Mr. Lincoln came late to his office, his partner, without looking up, said: "Lincoln you have been wanted," then glancing up at Lincoln's haggard face he exclaimed: "Why, Lincoln, what's the matter with you?" Lincoln replied by telling him about the sermon, and said: "I am utterly unable to shake from myself the conviction that I shall be involved in that tragedy."[1]

[1] From Bishop C. H. Fowler's *Patriotic Orations*, also Ida Tarbell's *Life of Lincoln*.

CHAPTER VII

COURAGE MOUNTS WITH OCCASION

LINCOLN displayed courage always moral in the political alliances he formed. Practically, he joined no political party. He was against the party then dominant. The State of Illinois was overwhelmingly democratic and strongly attached to the person and policies of Andrew Jackson. The Jackson majority was intolerant. It controlled the patronage and lived up to the maxim: "To the victor belongs the spoils." The road to preferment was evidently through alliance with the Jackson party. Lincoln's biographers, Nicolay and Hay, write:

It showed some moral courage and certainly the absence of the shuffling politician's policy, that Lincoln, in his obscure youth, when what little social influence he knew would have led the other way, opposed a furiously intolerant majority and took his stand with the party which was doomed to long continued defeat in Illinois.

The fact is, Abraham Lincoln was making for himself, though he was not aware of it, a party

whose sole platform was truth, justice, righteousness, God.

When he first became a candidate for the Legislature, Lincoln issued an address to the voters, in
which in the following words he modestly furnished a keynote to his whole career:

Every man is said to have his peculiar ambition.
Whether it be true or not, I can say, for one, that I
have no other so great as that of being truly esteemed
by my fellowmen by rendering myself worthy of their
esteem. How far I shall succeed in gratifying this
ambition is yet to be developed. I am young and
unknown to many of you. I was born and have
ever remained in the most humble walks of life. I
have no powerful or wealthy relations or friends
to recommend me. My case is thrown exclusively
upon the independent voters of the country, and if
elected, they will have conferred a favour upon me
for which I shall be unremitting in my labour to
compensate. But if the good people in their wisdom,
shall see fit to keep me in the background, I have
been too familiar with disappointment to be very
much chagrined.

In 1836, again a candidate for the Legislature,
Lincoln greatly distinguished himself by singling
out the moral issue from all others and by putting
to confusion his political opponent in "the lightning
rod" speech not popularly known.

There lived, in the most pretentious house in

town, a politician by the name of George Forquer who had long been known as a leading Whig but who now had gone over to the Democrats, and had received from the democratic administration an appointment to the lucrative post of Register of the Land Office at Springfield.

Upon his handsome new house he had lately placed a lightning rod, the first one ever put up in Sangamon County. As Lincoln was riding into town with his friends they passed the fine house of Forquer, observed the novelty, and discussed the manner in which the rod protected the house from being struck by lightning.

There was a large meeting and great curiosity to hear the speaker from New Salem. There were seven Whig and seven Democratic candidates for the lower branch of the Legislature, and after several had spoken it fell to the lot of Lincoln to close the discussion. Forquer, though not a candidate, asked to be heard for the Democrats in reply to Lincoln. He was a good speaker, and his special task was to attack and ridicule the young country-man from Salem.

Turning to Lincoln he said: "This young man must be taken down and I am sorry that the task devolves on me." He proceeded to heap ridicule on the person, dress, and arguments of Lincoln, and with so much success that Lincoln's friends feared the outcome.

As soon as Forquer closed, Lincoln took the stand and one by one demolished his opponent's arguments, ending with these words:

The gentleman began his speech by saying that this young man, alluding to me, must be taken down. I am not so young in years as I am in the tricks and the trades of a politician, but [he went on, pointing to the unfortunate Forquer], live long or die young, I would rather die now, than, like this gentleman, change my politics and with the change receive an office worth three thousand dollars a year, and then feel obliged to erect a lightning rod over my house to protect a guilty conscience from an offended God.

It is difficult to realize the effect produced on the old settlers by these words. They had slept all their lives in their cabins, in conscious security. Here was a man who was afraid to sleep in his own house without special protection from the vengeance of the Almighty. The old settlers concluded that nothing but a consciousness of guilt could account for such timidity.

Forquer and his lightning rod were talked of in every settlement from the Sangamon to the Illinois and Wabash. [1]

[1] Arnold, *Life of Lincoln*.

It is little wonder that a candidate so honest in moral conviction and courageous in its assertion distanced his rivals in that political campaign and won the election to the Legislature by a handsome majority. Nor is it surprising that during his incumbency of that office he approached every issue with the question, "Is it right?"

A tremendous struggle to secure the removal of the capital of the State from Salem to Springfield arose and Lincoln was deeply disturbed by efforts to couple with that movement certain measures to which he was unalterably opposed. In the midst of the contest, a caucus was called for the purpose of dissuading Lincoln from his determination to oppose the capital removal measure until it was dissociated from the schemes to which he objected.

Lincoln stood firm, and past the hour of midnight rose in the caucus and delivered a speech of extraordinary moral earnestness in opposition to the movement as it then was. These were his closing words:

You may burn my body to ashes and scatter them to the winds of Heaven: you may drag my soul down to the regions of darkness and despair to be tormented forever; but you will never get me to support a measure which I believe to be wrong, although by doing so I may accomplish that which I believe to be right.[1]

[1] Tarbell, *Life of Lincoln*, vol. i., p. 139.

Thus, as each occasion offered, Lincoln made his moral attitude increasingly apparent, striking in this instance at the sophistry that "the end justifies the means," declaring his unwillingness to support a measure which he believed to be right by resorting to methods which he knew to be wrong. His independence was natural, the inevitable trend of his mind impelled by moral earnestness. Prone to take counsel with his associates, he nevertheless acted upon the theory that he, and he alone, was responsible for what he did and was, and that he was responsible to God alone. His professional confrères early observed that he seldom, if ever, asked advice as to his line of legal conduct, although there were among his friends capable lawyers who would gladly have aided him. He preferred to work out his cases with his own judgment in the sight of God.

His self-reliance built on God was still more noticeable when later, charged with high public and official responsibilities, he had to deal as President with the strong men he brought into his Cabinet. Each at first thought himself a bigger man than Lincoln. Seward during the first month offered, superciliously, to run the Government. There was perhaps not one but naturally expected to be a little king in his own department without much interference from the crude son of the western prairies. But these Eastern statesmen-scholars soon had their eyes opened to the masterful ability of the Westerner. Seward led the way in recognition of the supremacy of Lincoln in character and ability, as well as in moral and religious principles. Stanton was a little gruff unto the end but he knew that where Lincoln sat, there was the head of the table.

The practical side of Lincoln's religious life was illustrated in his remark to Herndon that his religious code was like that of an old man back in Indiana, who said: "When I do good, I feel good; when I do bad, I feel bad, and that's my religion." Such, also, was the political creed which he wove into his platform utterances and practised all his life. His outspoken, but not obtrusive independence in religious as well as political affairs, sometimes caused him to be misunderstood and subjected him to the charge of scepticism. In 1842 the Washington temperance organization, of which Lincoln was a member, requested him to deliver an address on Washington's birthday. One paragraph of this address, which was delivered in a church, offended the church members who were present, and, as reported by them, aroused the resentment of many church people throughout the country. Speaking of certain Christians who refused to associate with drunkards, even for the purpose of reforming them, Lincoln said:

If these Christians believe, as they profess, that Omniscience descended to take on Himself the form of a sinful man, and as such died an ignominious death, surely they will not refuse submission to the infinitely less condescension for the temporal and perhaps eternal salvation of a large, erring, and unfortunate class of their fellow creatures; nor is the condescension very great. In my judgment, such of us as have never fallen victims, have been spared more from the absence of appetite than from any mental or moral superiority over those who have. Indeed, I believe if we take the habitual drunkard as a class, their heads and hearts will bear an advantageous comparison with those of any other class.

The active temperance propaganda, then in its inception, was not in high favour. Professing Christians of good church and social standing were not averse to the "social glass." Even the clergy were far from being "teetotalers." A young housewife of the period relates that when the clergyman made his pastoral call, she would have considered it a breach of hospitality not to mix up "something warm for him to drink." In the face of public sentiment, Lincoln was not only an abstainer both from liquor and tobacco but publicly advocated the cause of temperance. His address, therefore, was considered radical for that time, and the offended church members affected to regard his reference to the condescension of Christian people as a reflection upon the sincerity of their belief. Those who felt themselves hit retaliated by charging him with skepticism; and when, a few years later, he became a candidate for Congress against the noted Methodist "Circuit Rider," the Rev. Peter Cartwright, he met with strong opposition within the church.

In a letter written in March, 1843, explaining his defeat by Baker for the congressional nomination, Lincoln said:

It would astonish, if not amuse, the older citizens to learn that I, a stranger, friendless, uneducated, penniless boy, working on a flat boat at ten dollars a month, have been put down here as a candidate for pride, wealth, and aristocratic family distinction. There was, too, the strangest combination of church influences against me. Baker is a Campbellite, and, therefore, as I suppose, with few exceptions, got all that church. My wife has some relatives in the Presbyterian churches and some in the Episcopal churches, and, therefore, wherever it would tell, I was set down as either one or the other, while it was everywhere contended that no Christian ought to vote for me because I belonged to no church, was suspected of being a deist and had talked about fighting a duel.

Lincoln, in the days of his omnivorous reading, had devoured the works of Tom Paine,[1] Voltaire, and other French free-thinkers, with the same avidity with which he devoured Weems's *Life of Washington* and the *Revised Statutes of Indiana*. He was, therefore, charged with being a disbeliever in God and in the religion of the day.

A man of Lincoln's intellectual comprehensiveness could read the books of the most powerful skeptics without fear that his faith would be disturbed by disbelief. It was his habit to look on all sides of all questions. Fearless of the consequences, he studied the views of the so-called infidel writers as he studied the opposing side of a law case. His faith in God was so firmly imbedded in his soul that he did not fear its unsettlement even by the widest reading.

In later years in a conversation with Dr. Robert Browne, who was on terms of intimacy with Mr. Lincoln and shared a degree of his confidence, which was given to few men, speaking of Paine's *Age of Reason* he said:

I have looked through it carelessly, it is true; but there is nothing to such books. God rules this world, and out of seeming contradictions, that all these kind of reasoners seem unable to understand, He will de-

[1] See Moncure D. Conway's appreciation of Paine.

velop and disclose His plans for men's welfare in His inscrutable way. Not all of Paine's nor all the French distempered stuff will make a man better, but worse. They might lay down tons and heaps of their heartless reasonings along side a few of Christ's sayings and parables, to find that He said more for the benefit of our race in one of them than there is in all they have written. They might read his Sermon on the Mount to learn that there is more of justice, righteousness, kindness, and mercy in it than in the minds and books of all the ignorant doubters from the beginning of human knowledge.[1]

It is well, however, to note that the charges of infidelity, skepticism, and deism, were launched as "campaign lies." The temperance movement, under the auspices of the Washington Society, assumed a quasi-political aspect, and Lincoln's address that gave offence was used to create prejudice against him in the hope of defeating his political aspirations. The charge, during the Baker–Lincoln contest that he was a deist was absurd precisely as the charge that he was an aristocrat. Notwithstanding the fact that his affiliation with the temperance movement was doing him much political injury, he never faltered but continued to labour zealously in its behalf. He spoke often in Springfield and other places, displaying as Herndon writes, "the same courage

[1] *Abraham Lincoln and Men of His Time*, vol. ii., p. 426.

and adherence to principles that had characterized his every undertaking." Slowly, surely, his moral courage and independence won for him enduring friends.

New Salem, where Lincoln resided as a young man, was known as a "fast" place. It was difficult there for a young man of ordinary moral courage to resist the temptations that beset him on every side. It was considered remarkable in the community that Lincoln retained his popularity with the young men of his own age while refusing to join them in their drinking bouts and carouses. "I am certain," said one of his companions, "that he never drank any intoxicating liquors. He did not even, in those times, smoke or chew."

A pertinent example of the strength of Lincoln's character is found in an incident that occurred when he was making a frugal living by odd jobs of manual labour while yet pursuing his law studies. One of his friends recommended him to John Calhoun, County Surveyor, for the post of assistant. Calhoun was a Democrat and Lincoln a Whig, but the former, for personal reasons, consented to make the appointment. A friend found Lincoln in the woods splitting rails and informed him of the appointment. Lincoln's first inquiry was whether he would sacrifice any prin-

5

ciple or lessen his independence in any degree by accepting the offer. "If I am perfectly free in my political action," said he, "I will accept the appointment; but if my sentiments, or the expression of them, are to be abridged in any way, I would not have it or any other place." Though the appointment would have hastened the realization of his ardent ambition to become a lawyer he stood ready to reject it, if it laid the weight of a straw upon his conscience. Whether the inducement were a petty Assistant County Surveyorship or the Presidency, he was always the same independent, God-fearing man, firm in his faith and therefore resolute to do his duty as God gave him light to see it.

To courage was added a sane tolerance as religious as the tolerance of Gamaliel who put first the will of God in the consideration of all questions. Lincoln's attitude in 1844 in respect to the "Know Nothing" party is noteworthy. He did not believe the political ostracism of foreign-born voters and Roman Catholics was Christian. The riot and bloodshed to which it led in several of the larger cities where the "Know Nothing" party was strong seemed un-Christian. When the movement threatened to sweep the country and place the Proscriptionists in power, Lincoln, with his great heart and mighty intellect, sought by judicious means to check the panic among foreign-born citizens. He introduced and supported a resolution in a meeting at Springfield in June of that year, declaring that, "the guarantee of the right of conscience, as found in our Constitution, is most sacred and inviolable, and one that belongs no less to the Catholic than to the Protestant," and that "all attempts to abridge or interfere with these rights, either of Catholics or Protestants, directly or indirectly, have our decided disapprobation and shall have our most effective opposition." This was the beginning of a campaign against intolerance and disorder which he pursued to the end with unabated zeal. Even at the last Cabinet meeting, the very day the bullet took his life away, Lincoln—says Mr. Welles— "hoped there would be no persecution, no bloody work, after the war was over."

Lincoln lived in all its fulness the Christian faith most of us at best profess.

CHAPTER VIII

LEADINGS OF PROVIDENCE

LINCOLN was far in advance of his day, but he was content to await God's good time—a characteristic attitude of his whole life. This was the measure of his large and growing faith, the secret of his almost limitless patience. Believing that, as the world whirled on its axis and the spheres moved in their appointed orbits, so right would find its proper place in the evolutions in the moral universe. He was, therefore, content to wait, no matter how dark the immediate prospect seemed.

In the Presidential campaign of 1844, in which the gallant, magnetic, and much beloved Henry Clay went down to defeat, Lincoln filled the honourable position of Presidential elector and stumped the state for his party ticket. He was one of Clay's most ardent admirers and read every printed utterance of that brilliant statesman who was moulding, in no small measure, the mental and political type of the Civil War President. Mr. Lincoln, in taking the field for Henry Clay, knew

that the fight was not for that time alone but for
all time—and that many a battle must be fought
before victory would at last be won.

Many of Clay's supporters were deeply depressed by his defeat and believed that, in a sense,
the battle was hopelessly lost.   Some interpreted
his defeat as conclusive evidence that popular
government was a failure.   They could not understand why such a man as Henry Clay, so eminently fitted to carry on the great work for better
government, should have been set aside.   Lincoln,
too, was keenly disappointed—the more so, perhaps, because Clay was of his own native State.
But he did not lose heart.   His faith in the ultimate triumph of the right was unmoved in its
serenity.   He knew, in his soul, that—

> Truth, crushed to earth, will rise again,
> Th' eternal years of God are hers.

Far from abandoning the struggle for the success of his political principles, Lincoln announced
himself a candidate for the Congressional nomination in 1846 to succeed Baker who had been elected
on the Whig ticket in the year of Clay's defeat.
The Democrats placed in nomination the Rev.
Peter Cartwright.   This was the campaign in
which Lincoln was attacked by certain church

influences. Much was made of Lincoln's religious
beliefs—or disbeliefs; but the effect of this crusade
upon the voters of the district in which Lincoln
ran, largely made up of church members and attendants, may be judged by the fact that Lincoln
was elected by a majority of 1511, a much larger
vote than Henry Clay received in the same district two years before. This victory was all the
more signal in view of the "Circuit Rider's"
church following, his well-known oratorical ability,
his personal magnetism and popularity, and his
pronounced adherence to the principles of Andrew
Jackson, then the dominant politico-religious
social power of the commonwealth.

Lincoln's signal triumph over Cartwright was
the verdict of the people, who knew Lincoln best,
upon the charge that he was lacking in sound religious principles. He had been pitted against
a pioneer preacher whose reputation was nation-
wide—a man idealized, if not idolized, by the
rank and file of the professed Christians of the day.
Evidently, they were capable of recognizing the
high character of Lincoln, even if not garbed in
the mantle of formal church membership.

Abraham Lincoln's political course was soon to
be vindicated by the election of Zachary Taylor,
the Whig candidate for the Presidency. The

Whigs had denounced the Mexican War as unnecessary and unconstitutional. Lincoln had joined in this denunciation. In this, as in all issues, he was outspoken, having always the courage of his convictions. The people of his Congressional district did not approve his attitude on the Mexican War, yet such was their confidence in his integrity and ability that they chose him by a large majority to represent them in the halls of Congress.

The anti-slavery forces believed that back of the Mexican War stood the slave power, which sought to use the government for its own selfish ends. They also contended that to prosecute the war was unjustifiable aggression against a friendly power. At the same time they knew that the war was popular with the country inasmuch as it promised the annexation of Texas and the acquisition of other contiguous territory—a potent motive in every country since history began.

The prospect of additional territory, to add to the grandeur of the national domain, dazzled the people for the moment and rendered unpopular those who opposed it.

Lincoln, however, strenuously opposed the war both by voice and by voting for the resolutions against it offered by the Whigs in Congress. But after the war became inevitable and the country was fully committed to it, Lincoln's patriotism constrained him to give it practical support by voting as a member of the Congress for all needed supplies to carry it to a successful issue as speedily as possible. He had satisfied his conscience by protesting against the war; he satisfied his patriotism by supporting measures to place ample men and supplies behind the flag to carry it to final and complete victory.

Zachary Taylor, too, had opposed the War with Mexico; but when the country was swept into it he proved himself one of the heroes of that conflict, manifesting fiery zeal and distinguished courage from the time hostilities began until peace was proclaimed. As Lincoln himself said in a speech in Congress: "When the war had become the cause of the country, the Whigs gave their money and their blood for its prosecution."

At first, many of Lincoln's friends were discouraged by his opposition to the Mexican War. His law partner, Herndon, was gloomy. He wrote Lincoln that he had made a mistake. But Lincoln held to his convictions. He believed that he had done right, and in his magnificent reliance on the right as the safest political course he felt confident that he and his political associates would, in due time, be vindicated.

As it developed, Providence seemed to turn the
war to the political advantage of the party that
had protested against it and then loyally supported
it in a material way on the ground of patriotism.
Their nominee for President had distinguished
himself as an able general and thus made himself
popular with the country. A few days after the
nomination Lincoln wrote, predicting the election
of "Old Rough and Ready." "In my opinion,"
said he, "we shall have a most overwhelming,
glorious triumph. Taylor's nomination takes the
Locos on the blind side. It turns the war thunder
against them. The war is now to them the gallows
of Haman, which they built for us and on which
they are doomed to be hanged themselves."

A little later, in reply to a letter warning him
that his own district was, politically, in bad condition, he wrote that he had just returned from
a Whig caucus, held in relation to the coming
Presidential Election. "The whole field of the
nation was scanned," he said, "and all is high hope
and confidence. Illinois is expected to better her
condition in the race." He ended by advising his
correspondent to keep up good heart and to
continue energetic in the work.

The prediction of disaster to his party in his own
Congressional district was nothing to him in com-

parison with the larger triumph which, as he believed, was coming for the nation. As a matter of fact, although Zachary Taylor was elected in 1848, the Whig candidate for Congress in Lincoln's district, John T. Logan, was defeated. Lincoln, instead of becoming a candidate for re-election, had cheerfully stepped aside in favour of Logan, urging that Logan was the stronger because he had not opposed the Mexican War. Lincoln himself would probably have been elected by reason of the general admiration of his well-known courage in adhering to principle. However, selfishness had no place in his character. He was broad enough to sacrifice himself for the sake of the higher victory.

Lincoln's faith was not a mere theory. It was a productive force. He relied on prayer but he did not believe in supinely waiting for God to answer. He prayed as if everything depended upon God; he worked as if everything depended upon himself. His faith in the outcome of the fight for the right in the Presidential contest of 1848 was the same faith he exercised when, in his prayer for victory at Gettysburg, he told the Lord: "I have done all I can, and now you must help." He was still willing to wait God's own good time, but he wrought with all his might to have things ready when God's time should come.

Lincoln had now become a national figure and was being considered for important official positions. He was quasi-candidate for the office of Commissioner of the General Land Office and was also offered the Governorship of the Territory of Oregon. But Providence was holding him for greater responsibilities when the appointed moment should strike—the moment when God should have need of him to meet a supreme crisis.

CHAPTER IX

THE YEAR OF YEARS

THE year 1848 was one of the most momentous in history. It was a time of hope and fear, achievement and failure. The last king disappeared from France. The first democratic revolution occurred in Germany, and Rome was captured and lost by Garibaldi. Mexico ceded California to the United States, gold was discovered, and the rush of pioneers to the Far West began. The Whigs nominated Zachary Taylor for the Presidency, and the Free Soil Party held a significant convention in Buffalo. There Van Buren was chosen as their Presidential candidate, with the slogan, "No more slave states and no more slave territory"; while at Pittsburgh the cleavage over the slave question in the Methodist Episcopal Church resulted in the organization of the Methodist Church South, an event which thrust religion into the arena of party politics.

In 1848 Horace Greeley, the acknowledged wielder of public opinion in the East, took his seat in the House of Representatives. The spirit of prophecy was moving in the land, and the flame of religious inspiration began to flicker on the altar of liberty. Capitol Hill had witnessed every manifestation of state subsidy and political subterfuge, legal argument, and dialectical parrying.

In the Senate, Daniel Webster, with his Roman mien and eagle eye, offset the Athenian polish and grand manner of Henry Clay. Calhoun, with his trenchant vehemence, and Benton, with his practical realism, passed, or were passing, from public view. One gladiator of the old order remained: Stephen A. Douglas, master of invective, fluent, bold, magnetic, popular. With his pyrotechnic wit, he was already measuring swords with honest Abe, yet to come into his own. From 1848 to 1858 the war went on between liberty and bondage, reason and rhetoric, progress and decadence.

The scene of action now shifted from the National Capital to the prairies of Illinois. Principles opposed opinions. The field of discussion narrowed. A clear road was blazed for the heralds of justice.

The conflict for national liberty, begun by Patrick Henry, gradually changed to the struggle for individual liberty, and for the first time in

America real seership began to exercise a far reaching influence in affairs of State and Nation. From 1776 to 1848 eloquence, persuasion, wit, imagination, legal manœuvre, magnetic personality, charm of manner, social prestige had attracted public attention, swayed parties, and moulded opinion. Webster influenced by the splendour of his eloquence, Clay by his lucid diction, Baker by his extemporaneous outbursts, Wendell Phillips by his relentless arguments, Owen Lovejoy by his impassioned denunciations, Sumner by his scholarship, Seward by his cool logic, Ben Wade by his fearless defiance.

Every phase of sentiment, every shade of opinion, every species of argument, had been forged on the anvil of sectional interest; but until then in the white heat, the hammers of discussion never struck more than detached sparks from the hard iron of party politics.

The Damascus sword of justice, tempered by mercy, was yet unfused and unformed.

At the Washington capital the book of the old order was closing, while in the Far West a prophetic scroll was unrolling as yet inscrutable to all, save to the gaunt, grim man of the prairies. Lincoln, humblest and lowliest of all in that great conflict, was destined for the highest position in the

nation and an immortality of fame crowned by a
holy martyrdom.   Many others had discussed the
political situation from the rostrum and explained
conditions from the pulpit.   Sincere and eloquent,
they halted on the threshold, stumbled over the
question of ways and means, hesitated in the face
of essentials, dissipated vital force in vain and
futile arguments.

The hour had struck for a shuffling of the dry
bones of democracy.   Once for all, the least and
humblest of those engaged in the great conflict was
to dispel the illusion that knowledge is confined to
books, wisdom to schools, and power to patronage.
Once for all, he was to prove the reality of mystical
intuitions and spiritual illumination.   Once for all,
he was to demonstrate the efficiency of spiritual
faith in fundamental affairs, the power of prayer,
and the reign of the Eternal.

In the face of a thousand difficulties and in-
numerable enemies, his thought was growing
more spiritual.   His life and deeds were becoming
a living proof of the shallowness of agnosticism
and the folly of materialism in their constant ex-
emplification of the transcendent power of the
spiritual in solving one of the greatest problems
that ever yet confronted mortal man.

Increasingly his words and deeds were standing

forth as living symbols of the truth that right makes might and that justice will triumph finally over all phases and manifestations of tyranny.

While in 1848 the spirit of individual progress was suppressed in Germany, in America it was just beginning its victorious march towards freedom. The failure of democracy in the Teuton countries cleared the way for Bismarck, the development of materialism, and the temporary triumph of one of the most drastic forms of autocracy civilization has ever known. Without the transcendent words of Lincoln, without his supreme achievements, where today would the political world look for the example that abides, the spirit that illumines? The Kaiser invoked the God of rapine. Lincoln invoked the God of justice and mercy. History has never offered such an antithesis of darkness and illumination, military pandemonium and social progress. The torch which was extinguished in Germany in 1848 was rekindled in America. Religion, in its broad sense, was from this time on, to impose a bond of progressive discipline where license before had ruled. In spite of the division over slavery in the Methodist Episcopal and other Protestant churches, in spite of sectional bitterness and opposition, there would now be one head and one heart, one will, and one conscience, one torch and one illumination.

To enumerate all the events and developments of 1848 would require a volume. Some of the writers who have dealt with the life of Lincoln have either wilfully or unconsciously ignored their mystical import and religious tendency. They have marshalled those transcendent events and occurrences without noting "the Divine Idea" underlying them and throbbing through them. The stages of spiritual progress in the mind of Lincoln were as marked as sign posts separating one country from another. In his mental economy there was no place for guesswork, no time for doing and undoing, no opportunity for mere experimenting, and never in the life of any man were periods of mental and moral progress more precisely and mathematically marked on the highway of time.

Long before 1848 Lincoln's purpose was fixed, but it was not till after 1848 that he seemed to come to the full realization of the social and religious as well as the political import of events. Lincoln did not base his faith on any power in nature, nor on the counsel of individuals or parties when they conflicted with his honest convictions. He stood alone—proof of his absolute trust in a

6

Supreme Ruler of the universe. Other gifted and successful leaders can be described as "practical, common-sense men." Lincoln was so far unlike all "common-sense men" that what he said and what he did had no parallel in the records of any leader. Behind the matter-of-fact, he was sustained by an unfaltering trust, clearly revealed to intuition, yet beyond all definitions the matter-of-fact and obvious can give.

Now, from this year of change and innovation the movement toward the great consummation proceeded without interruption. Midway between that transition year of 1848 and the climacteric year of 1858 the Republican Party was born. Under the blue dome of heaven, on the prairies of Illinois, this pioneer of individual liberty, this prophet of human progress, this man of God entered upon the second period of his God ordained mission.

CHAPTER X

THE GIANT WAKES

For three or four years Lincoln was engrossed in his profession to the practical exclusion of politics. But in May, 1854, he was aroused by the repeal of the Missouri Compromise. This act was to him a call to arms. One of his biographers declares: "He was aroused as he had never been before in all his life." He again entered the arena, and, in accepting invitations to make addresses, he stipulated in every case that he should talk against the Kansas–Nebraska bill. He came back into politics with an earnestness and zeal that surprised even his friends, for he was afire with the great moral issue which had been raised.

Stephen A. Douglas, the author of the bill repealing the Missouri Compromise, was then a commanding figure in the politics of Illinois. By common consent Lincoln was instinctively selected by the opponents of the obnoxious measure as the man best equipped to meet and combat Douglas. When Douglas came to Springfield to speak at the annual State Fair it was announced that Lincoln would answer him the next day. Lincoln's speech was a revelation. The Springfield *Journal* said of it:

It was the profoundest that he has made in his whole life. Lincoln felt upon his soul the truths burn which he uttered, and all present felt that he was true to his own soul. His feelings once or twice came near stifling his utterances. He quivered with emotion. The whole house was as still as death.

This was Lincoln at last aroused by a great moral issue to the fulness of his powers. Before, he had been a political orator of a superior type; now he was as an inspired prophet. The whole man seemed uplifted and transformed. Miss Tarbell says:

He discussed the subject incessantly with his friends as he travelled the circuit. A new conviction was gradually growing upon him. He had long held that slavery was wrong; but that it could not be touched in the States where it was recognized by the Consitution. All that the Free States could require, in his judgment, was that no new territory should be opened to slavery. He held that all compromises adjusting difficulties between the North and the South on the slavery question were as sacred as the Constitution. Now he saw the most important of them all violated. Was it possible to devise a compromise that would settle forever the conflicting interests? He turned over the question continually.

Judge T. Lyle Dickey tells the following story: When the excitement over the Kansas–Nebraska bill first broke out, he was, with Lincoln and some friends, attending court. One evening several persons, including himself and Lincoln, were discussing the slavery question. Judge Dickey contended that slavery was an institution which the Constitution recognized and which could not be disturbed. Lincoln argued that slavery must ultimately become extinct.

After awhile [says Judge Dickey] we went upstairs to bed. There were two beds in our room, and I remember that Lincoln sat up in his nightshirt, on the edge of the bed, arguing the point with me. At last we went to sleep. Early in the morning I woke up, and there was Lincoln, half sitting up in bed. "Dickey," he said, "I tell you, this nation cannot exist, half slave and half free."

This idea had taken full possession of Lincoln. It shaped all his future course. Like a vision in the night it came to him. He grasped it, and made it a reality. As time went on the idea struck its roots deeper. Its full implication grew clearer to him. He saw with a vividness no one else could match that the extinction of slavery was bound up with the preservation of the Union, and yet he set the Union first in order of responsibility. What could be more compelling than these words spoken when the crisis came:

In seeking to attain these results so indispensable if the liberty which is our pride and boast is to endure, we will be loyal to the Constitution and the flag of our Union, and no matter what our grievance, even though Kansas shall come in as a slave State, and no matter what theirs, even if we shall restore the Compromise, we will say to the Southern dis-Unionists, "We won't go out of the Union and you shan't!"

While the repeal of the Missouri Compromise had called Lincoln from his office like a lion from his den, there seems never to have been a time when he was not opposed to it as a moral issue. His first recorded opposition, after he entered upon public life, was early in his legislative career, when he joined with one other member of the State Assembly in a protest against the pro-slavery resolution which had been adopted by that legislative body. While the protest was not radical, its significance was in the declaration that "the institution of slavery is founded both on injustice and bad policy."

Nicolay and Hay, in their biography say: "It may seem strange that a protest so mild and cautious should have been considered either necessary or remarkable." However, it should be remembered that we have travelled far beyond the thought and feeling of those times. If we look carefully into the state of politics and public opinion in the first half of the nineteenth century we shall see much of inflexible conscience and sound reasoning in a protest so simple.

The whole of the North-west Territory had been dedicated to freedom by the Ordinance of 1787; and yet slavery existed in a modified form throughout that vast region wherever there was any considerable population. An act, legalizing a sort of slavery by indenture was passed by the Indiana Territorial Legislature in 1807, and remained in force in the Illinois country after it became a separate territory. Furthermore, an act providing for the hiring of slaves from slave States was enacted in 1814 for the ostensible reason that "mills could not successfully be operated in the territory for the want of labourers and that the manufacture of salt could not be successfully carried on by the white labourers." Coincident with such legislation the most savage acts were passed, from time to time, prohibiting the immigration of free negroes, though the territory was represented as pining for black labour.

In addition those who had held slaves under the French domination continued to hold them and their descendants in servitude even after Illinois had become first a free territory and then a free state. The advocates of slavery argued speciously that the vested property rights of such slaveholders could not have been abrogated by the Ordinance of 1787.

But this quasi-toleration of slavery was not enough for the slave system. The long arm of the oppressor was stretched out to take fast hold upon that territory of the Union which had not as yet been smirched by slavery's loathsome touch. It was not by open, frank advocacy that the pro-slavery power sought to extend its domain, but by all the arts of false logic, by the appeal to the doctrine of vested rights, and by a course of tortuous political intrigue.

And what of the opposition to slavery in the North? The record shows that, for the most part, it operated by the same system of sophistry and evasion, by avoiding that openness and frankness, which alone could have startled the conscience of the nation into a realization of its duty. In the North, fully as much as in the South, the doctrine of dollars, as opposed to human rights, was, almost equally with the South, the guiding principle of all political and economic consideration.

Soon after the adoption of the state Constitution of Illinois which prohibited the holding of slaves "hereafter," there appeared to be a strong undercurrent favourable to the introduction of slavery into the State. Some of the leading politicians, looking to their own personal advancement, began to agitate the question of amending the Constitution so as to permit the enslavement of the negroes.

Another condition tended to sow the noxious seed of slavery in the minds of the people. A strong tide of immigration into Illinois was setting in from Kentucky, Tennessee, and Missouri. As these movers passed through the Illinois settlements they deplored the "short-sighted" policy which had led to the prohibition of slavery in Illinois, and prevented these same settlers from remaining in that beautiful country. They sought to impress upon the people of Illinois a sense of inferiority to slave owners. In 1829 Governor Edwards complained that the people of Missouri were given better mail facilities, presumably because they were regarded by the Federal Government as "gentlefolk, having negroes to work for them," and, therefore, entitled to higher consideration than "us plain, Free State folks, who have to work for ourselves."

An attempt was made in the Legislature of 1822–23 to open the State to slavery. By gross manipulation the pro-slavery forces passed an act providing for a convention to amend the Constitution, but the act had to be submitted to a popular vote and was decisively defeated by the people.

Yet the advocates of slavery did not desist. They sought in every manner and by every device to array public opinion and the social forces against what they stigmatized as "Abolitionism," and to visit with political and social ostracism the opponents of the pro-slavery agitation.

The harsh code directed against the immigration of free negroes remained in force. The feeling was much stronger in central than in northern Illinois, and still more powerful in the southern section of the State. The northern region had been settled largely from New England. But the settlers of the lower counties had come across the line from the border states where slavery was interwoven into the very warp and woof of the social and industrial fabric, and where, politically, it was the all-dominating power, adherence to which was the *sine qua non* of official preferment. How ruthless was the pro-slavery propaganda was shown by repeated acts of mob violence against the advocates of abolition because they stood for making the Declaration of Independence what, it professed to be—the true creed of democracy. By this, and other acts of violence, those who would have fastened the blighting slavery system upon the State of Illinois sought to intimidate their opponents.[1]

The resolution, against which Lincoln protested in the Legislature, denounced the anti-slavery pronouncements of several Northern state legislatures, and declared: "The right by the Federal Constitution." The resolutions in the Illinois Legislature passed the Senate unanimously and went through the House by an overwhelming vote.

There was no reason [say his biographers], why Lincoln should have taken note of these resolutions, more than another. He had only to shrug his shoulders at the violence and untruthfulness of the majority, then vote against them, and go home to his constituents in the flush of his success in procuring the removal of the State Capital to Springfield. But his conscience and his reason forbade him from remaining silent. He felt that a word must be said on the other side, to redress the distorted balance. He wrote his protest and showed it to his colleagues. But none of them dared to sign it, excepting Dan Stone, who was not a candidate for re-election, having retired

[1] See Appendix. The First Martyr.

from politics to a seat on the bench. All the others considered the risk of angering the pro-slavery sentiment too great.

This incident supplies a striking illustration of the method of Lincoln through his whole public life. He never could be hurried. He could be patient beyond the understanding of impetuous men. He could wait patiently even a large fraction of a century until the proper time arrived to strike. Later, when the smoke and the turmoil of the Civil War surged round him, assailed by a storm of bitter criticism, anathematized by the ultra-radicals for not signing the Emancipation Proclamation, he waited even then for the moment when he felt it was God's time for him to act.

Likewise when the Legislature of his State placed itself on the side of oppression, Lincoln knew it was no time for patience and therefore penned his protest in defiance of the powerful and dominant slavery element of his own State. This protest was made when he was only twenty-eight years old. He arrived at a considerable position in the politics and society of the State after a score and more years of singular privation and struggle. Was he to sacrifice everything now by a Quixotic defiance of public opinion? The people of his own county and his most intimate friends were

strongly averse to any public discussion of slavery.
But nothing could restrain him from performing
what he regarded as a simple duty. He took his
political life in his hands rather than remain silent
in the presence of a great wrong. The words of
Nicolay and Hay, with which they conclude their
detailed narrative of this incident, do not
exaggerate its importance:

The young man who dared declare, in the prosperous beginning of his political life, in the midst of a
community imbued with Slave State superstitions,
that he believed the institution of slavery founded
both on injustice and bad policy, attacking thus its
moral and material support, while at the same time
recognizing all the Constitutional guarantee which
protected it, had in him the making of a statesman,
and, if need be, a martyr. His whole career was to
run in the lines marked out by these words, written
in the hurry of a closing session, and he was to accomplish few acts in that great history which God
reserved for him, wiser and nobler than this.

God works through fitting instruments. God
may inspire a weak man, but He seldom does.
Great prophets and leaders have been men of
strength. The Almighty seems to want something
substantial for the foundation of a great achievement. In choosing Lincoln to smite slavery he
added simple goodness to resistless strength.

CHAPTER XI

THE SHADOW OF A MIGHTY ROCK

REARED in the solitude of the wilderness the soul of Lincoln was sensitive, his spirit reverent. He saw more than so many cubic feet of hardness in the rock beneath his feet; more than the cold law of gravitation maintaining the equilibrium of worlds, more than fire mist in the dawn of creation; more than protoplasm as the source of life; more than an abstract God devoid of attributes, who, having started a course of evolution from gas to genius, is an absentee in the affairs of the world. He saw sermons in trees, books in running brooks, and good, which is but another name for God, in everything.

He was never deaf to the call of the Divine. Captain Gilbert J. Green, who was closely associated with Lincoln in early life, gives a striking illustration of Lincoln's appreciation of nature's evidence of God's existence in the words:

When I was a boy about nineteen, one night Lincoln said to me, calling me by my first name "Gilbert, you have to stand at your printer's case all day and I have to sit in the office all day. Let us take a walk." As we walked on the country road outside of Springfield, he turned his eyes toward the stars and told me their names and their distance from us and the swiftness of their motion. He said the ancients used to arrange them so as to make monsters, serpents, animals of one kind or another out of them. "But," said he, "I never behold them that I do not feel that I am looking in the face of God. I can see how it might be possible for a man to look down upon the earth and be an atheist, but I cannot see how he could look up into the heavens and say there is no God." The information and inspiration received that night during the walk I shall never forget. [1]

In September, 1848, when returning from a campaign tour in New England he visited Niagara Falls. After his death there were found among his papers some notes taken evidently to serve in preparation for a lecture which showed how deeply his mind was stirred by this mighty phenomenon of nature.

Niagara Falls! [he wrote] By what mysterious power is it that millions and millions are drawn from all parts of the earth to gaze upon Niagara Falls? There is no mystery about the thing itself. Every effect is just as any intelligent man, knowing the causes, would anticipate without seeing it. If the water moving onward in a great river reaches a point

[1] Chapman, *Latest Light on Abraham Lincoln*, p. 524.

where there is a perpendicular jog of one hundred feet in descent to the bottom of the river, it is plain that the water will have a violent and continuous plunge at that point. It is also plain that the water thus plunging will foam and roar and send up a mist continually in which, during sunshine, there will be perpetual rainbows. The mere physical aspect of Niagara Falls is only this. Yet this is really a very small part of the world's wonder. Its power to excite emotion and reflection is its great charm. The geologist will demonstrate that the plunge, or fall, was once at Lake Ontario, and has worn its way back to its present position. He will ascertain how fast it is wearing now, and so get a base for determining how long it has been wearing back from Lake Ontario, and finally demonstrate from it that this world is at least fifteen thousand years old. A philosopher of slightly different turn will say, "Niagara Falls is only the lip of a basin, out of which pours all the surplus water which rains down on two or three hundred thousand square miles of the earth's surface." He will estimate, with approximate accuracy, that five hundred thousand tons of water fall with their full weight a distance of a hundred feet each minute, thus exerting a force equal to the lifting of the same weight through the same space, in the same time. But still there is more. It calls up the indefinite past, when Columbus first sighted this continent, when Christ suffered on the cross, when Moses led Israel through the Red Sea, nay, even when Adam first came from the hand of his Maker; then, as now, Niagara was roaring here. The eyes of that species of extinct giants whose bones fill the mounds of America, have gazed on Niagara as ours do. Contemporary with the first race of men and older than the first man, Niagara is strong and fresh today as ten thousand years ago. The mammoth and mastodon, so long dead that fragments of their monstrous bones alone testify that they ever lived, have gazed on Niagara, that in that long, long, time, never still for a moment, never dried, never frozen, never slept, never rested.

His reflections on Niagara embraced the whole subject of creation, the existence of God, the mystery and power of the universe, the history, redemption, and fate of man. The question to Job: "Where wast thou when I laid the foundations of the earth?" seems to have been present to Lincoln's mind when he wrote of Niagara as calling up the "indefinite past." The whole fragment is the expression of a soul profoundly imbued with the spiritual theory of the origin and cause of things. The Eternal Power which moves and constantly renews Niagara, and has done so centuries beyond human conception, was to Lincoln a sublime thought—one that stirred his whole being and gave him an outlook far beyond the mere physical expression of this, one of the greatest of the world's wonders.

From this recognition of God in nature it requires but a step to a realization of the divine in the affairs of men. That Lincoln accepted this

7

doctrine Mr. F. E. Chittenden, who was register of the Treasury under President Lincoln, confirms in his *Recollections:* "Lincoln's calm serenity," he says, "at times when others were so anxious, his confidence that his own judgment was directed by the Almighty, so impressed me that I ventured to ask him directly how far he believed the Almighty actually directed our national affairs. After a considerable pause, he spoke as follows:

"That the Almighty does make use of human agencies, and directly intervenes in human affairs, is one of the plainest statements in the Bible. I have had so many evidences of His direction, so many instances when I have been controlled by some other power than my own will, that I cannot doubt that this power comes from above. I frequently see my way clear to a decision when I am conscious that I have not sufficient facts upon which to found it. But I cannot recall one instance in which I have followed my own judgment, founded upon such a decision, where the results were unsatisfactory; whereas, in almost every instance where I have yielded to the views of others, I have had occasion to regret it. I am satisfied that, when the Almighty wants me to do, or not to do, a particular thing, he finds a way of letting me know it. I am confident that it is his design to restore the Union. He will do it in His own good time. We should obey and not oppose His will."

"You speak with such confidence," said Mr. Chittenden, "that I would like to know how your knowledge that God acts directly upon human affairs compares in certainty with your knowledge of a fact apparent to the senses—for example, the fact that we are at this moment here in this room."

"One is as certain as the other," answered Lincoln, "although the conclusions are reached by different processes. I know by my senses that the movements of the world are those of an infinitely powerful machine, which runs for ages without variation. A man who can put two ideas together knows that such a machine requires an infinitely powerful maker and governor; man's nature is such that he cannot take in the machine and keep out the maker. This maker is God—infinite in wisdom as well as power. Would we be any more certain if we saw Him?"

"I am not controverting your position," said Chittenden. "Your confidence interests me beyond expression. I wish I knew how to acquire it. Even now, must it not all depend on our faith in the Bible?" "No," said Lincoln. "There is the element of personal experience. If it did, the character of the Bible is easily established, at least to my satisfaction. We have to believe many things that we do not comprehend. The Bible is the only one that claims to be God's Book—to comprise His law—His history. It contains an immense amount of evidence of its own authenticity. It describes a Governor omnipotent enough to operate this great machine, and declares that He made it. It states other facts which we do not fully comprehend, but which we cannot account for. What shall we do with them?

"Now, let us treat the Bible fairly," continued Lincoln. "If we had a witness on the stand whose general story we knew was true, we would believe him when he asserted facts of which we had no other evidence. We ought to treat the Bible with equal fairness. I decided a long time ago that it was less difficult to believe that the Bible was what it claimed to be than to disbelieve it. It is a good book for us to obey—it contains the Ten Commandments, the Golden Rule and many other rules which ought to be followed. No man was ever the worse for living according to the directions of the Bible."

"If your views are correct," said Chittenden, "the Almighty is on our side, and we ought to win without so many losses. . . ."

Mr. Lincoln promptly interrupted him and said: "We have no right to criticize or complain. He *is* on our side and so is the Bible and so are the churches and Christian societies and organizations—all of them, so far as I know, almost without an exception. It makes me stronger and more confident to know that all the Christians in the loyal States are praying for our success, and that all their influences are working to the same end. Thousands of them are fighting for us, and no one will say that an officer or a private is less brave because he is a praying soldier. At first, when we had such long spells of bad luck, I used to lose heart sometimes. Now, I seem to know that Providence has protected and will protect us against any fatal defeat. All we have to do is to trust the Almighty, and keep on obeying His orders and executing His will."[1]

The genuineness of this interview, when carefully compared with the expression of similar senti-

[1] Chittenden, pp. 448–450.

ments in a conversation with Dr. Robert Browne, finds strong corroboration. Speaking to Dr. Browne of the divine influence upon his life, he said:

"When I set my mind at work to find some way of evading or declining a journey, a speech or service, instead of my own spirit a something stronger says, 'You must go. You must not disappoint these people, who have given you their confidence as they have no other man.'

"I am a full believer that God knows what He wants a man to do, that which pleases Him. It is never well with the man who heeds it not. I talk to God. My mind seems relieved when I do, and a way is suggested, that if it is not a supernatural one, it is always one that comes at a time, and accords with a common-sense view of the work. I take up the common one of making a speech somewhere or other. These come almost every day. I get ready for them as occasion seems to require. I arrange the facts, make a few notes, some little memorandums like these you have seen so often and are so familiar with. I take them, and as far as facts are concerned confine myself to them and rarely make any particular preparation for feeling, sympathy, or purely sentimental thoughts.

"When my plans for the discussion are made, and the foundations are laid, I find that I am done and all at sea unless I arouse myself to the spirit and merits of my cause. With my mind directed to the necessity, I catch the fire of it, the spirit of the inspiration. I see it reflected in the open faces and throbbing hearts before me. This impulse comes and goes, and again returns and seems to take possession of me. The influence, whatever it is, has taken effect. It is contagion; the people fall into the stream and follow me in the inspiration, or what is beyond my understanding. This seems evidence to me, a weak man, that God Himself is leading the way."[1]

These ringing words of faith in the divine are but the highest mark of the great current of spiritual conviction flowing through the life of Lincoln and are therefore clothed with an authoritative import which precludes the possibility of any misgiving as to Abraham Lincoln's trust in a personal God and his ruling presence in the movements of men and nations. Ex-Senator James F. Wilson of Iowa relates an account of a visit which he, with several other gentlemen made upon President Lincoln in June, 1862. Slavery and the war situation were freely discussed. Mr. Lincoln sat quietly in his chair, listening to what different ones had to say. After awhile he arose and stood at his extreme height. Pausing a moment, his right arm outstretched toward the gentleman who had just ceased speaking, his face aglow like the face of a prophet, Mr. Lincoln gave deliberate and emphatic utterance to

[1] *Abraham Lincoln and Men of War Times*, vol. ii., pp. 194–195.

the religious faith which sustained him in the great trial to which he and the country were subjected:

" My faith is greater than yours. I not only believe that Providence is not unmindful of the struggle in which this nation is engaged, that if we do not do right, God will let us go our own way to ruin; and that if we do right, He will lead us safely out of this wilderness, crown our arms with victory and restore our dissevered Union, as you have expressed your belief; but I also believe He will compel us to do right, in order that He may do these things, not so much because we desire them as that they accord with His plans of dealing with this nation, in the midst of which He means to establish justice. I think that He means that we shall do more than we have yet done in the furtherance of His plans and He will open the way for our doing it. I have felt His hand upon me in great trials and submitted to His guidance, and I trust that as He shall farther open the way, I will be ready to walk therein, relying on His help and trusting in His goodness and wisdom."[1]

Whittier was at his best in those formative days of Lincoln's character. His mind moved along the same broad highway up to God, and his marching song could as well have been the marching song of Lincoln:

[1] *North American Review*, December, 1896, p. 667, James F. Wilson.

A marvel seems the universe,
A miracle our life and death,
A mystery which I cannot pierce,
Around, above, beneath.
Now my spirit sighs for home,
And longs for light whereby to see,
And like a weary child has come,
O, Father, unto Thee.

CHAPTER XII

THE WHEAT AND THE TARES

LINCOLN'S protest in the Illinois Legislature against the pro-slavery resolution was the first conspicuous act in the great national drama in which he was to become the principal figure. His faith that the divine purpose would ripen fast and that the truth would ultimately triumph grew stronger with the years. In his manifesto to the electorate during his second candidacy for the Legislature, in 1836, he placed Woman's Suffrage in a moral light:

I go for all sharing the privileges of the government who assist in bearing its burdens; consequently, I go for admitting whites to the right of suffrage who pay taxes or bear arms, by no means excluding females. If elected, I shall consider the whole people of Sangamon County my constituents, as well those that oppose me as those that support me.

This was looked upon as bold and audacious. True, he advocated the limiting of the voting privilege to white persons, but as there was no thought then of extending the suffrage to the coloured race it was not an issue. The characteristic of Lincoln's faith was that it manifested itself along practical lines. "Votes for Women" was a subject little heard of then, though it was beginning to be agitated. Lincoln, in his readiness to enlarge the rights of suffrage so as to include the entire Anglo Saxon race, men and women, was more than half a century ahead of his time. His biographer, Herndon, says:

We need no further evidence to satisfy our minds as to his position on the subject of women's rights, had he lived. In fact, I cannot refrain from noting here what views he in after years held in reference to the great questions of moral and social reform under which he classed universal suffrage, temperance, and slavery. "All such questions," he observed one day, as we were discussing temperance in the office, "must find lodgment with the most enlightened souls who stamp them with their approval. In God's own time, they will be organized into law and woven into the fabric of all our institutions."

Herndon, who is largely responsible for the impression that Lincoln was a sceptic, attributes his rare gifts of foresight to nature. He says: "Nature had burned in him her holy fire, and stamped him with the seal of her greatness." But to Lincoln nature was but another name for God.

While, with prophetic insight, he was always looking to see slavery destroyed, he yet believed in employing rational means. For example, in advocating the election of General Taylor in 1848, he condemned the Free Soilers as practically helping to elect Cass, who was less likely to promote freedom in the territories than Taylor. There was no difference, he claimed, between the Free Soil Party and the Whigs in regard to the exclusion of slavery from the territories. The Free Soilers had but the one plank to their platform, reminding Lincoln of the Yankee pedlar who, in offering for sale a pair of pantaloons, described them as "large enough for any man and small enough for any boy." To their claim to the right and duty to act independently, leaving consequences to God, Lincoln replied: "When divine or human law does not clearly point out our duty, it must be found out by intelligent judgment, which takes in the results of action."

Lincoln was no fanatic, but sought the best means to a desired end, even if it involved delay. So it was with the Emancipation Proclamation. Extremists were ever urging him to take the action sooner than he thought it wise. But he knew that if he issued the Proclamation prematurely he would alienate many loyal men of the

North and also of the Border States who were not yet ready to approve so radical a step. He lived up to the parable of the wheat and the tares. He let the tares grow awhile lest the wheat be harmed by attempting to pluck up the tares. He waited until he could invoke along with the blessing of Almighty God the considerate judgment of mankind before striking the shackles from four millions of men, women, and children held in the bonds of slavery.

Lincoln's common sense illumined by faith in God was evident even to the casual. After his death, one of his fellow lawyers paid him this tribute: "He was wonderfully kind, careful, and just. His love for justice and fair play was his predominating trait. He had an immense stock of common sense and he had faith enough in it to trust it in every emergency."

An incident indicating Lincoln's kindliness of heart and strength of will occurred in 1854. A young negro, the son of a free coloured woman in Springfield, went from his home and hired out as a deck hand on a lower Mississippi steamboat. Though born free, he was subject to the tyranny of the black code prevailing in the slave states, under which he was arrested in St. Louis and kept in prison until his boat left. The authorities then conveniently forgot him. After a given time, established by law, he would have been inevitably sold into slavery to defray prison expenses had not Lincoln, moved by the mother's story, interposed. He, in conjunction with others, went to see the Governor of Illinois who, after a patient and thorough examination of the law, informed Lincoln that the Governor of Illinois had no right or power to interfere. Recourse was then had to the Governor of Indiana, but with like results. Lincoln had a second interview with the Governor of Illinois, but without avail. Lincoln arose, hat in hand, as he said with emphasis: "By the Eternal, Governor, I will make the ground in this country too hot for the foot of a slave, whether you have the legal power to secure the release of this boy or not!"

Having exhausted all legal means to secure the boy's liberation, Lincoln, in pure kindness of heart, drew up a subscription paper, collected funds to purchase the young man's liberty and restored him to his overjoyed mother.

At that time Lincoln was not so poor and friendless as he was when, at New Orleans, he forcibly indicated his determination to hit slavery hard if ever he had a chance at it. He was now a successful lawyer, with enough prominence in politics to receive a majority of the votes of the people of his State for the United States Senate. The place was considered rightfully his due for his services in the movement which gave birth and power to the Republican party, and was destined to stop the further extension of slavery. But he generally yielded to Lyman Trumbull in order to avoid factional division. When he made his New Orleans threat there seemed no possibility of his ever being able to execute it; but the possibilities were not so remote when he declared his purpose to make the ground of the country too hot for the foot of a slave. But in what way, and by what means he should accomplish his purpose had not yet been revealed to him. However, there were the same prophetic stirrings within him that marked his early boyhood, and he held himself then, and at all times, in readiness to obey the summons when called to do his appointed work.

Early in 1855 the "Border Ruffian" outrages began to attract attention. The stories of raids, election frauds, murders, and other crimes stirred the friends of freedom to fever heat. An association was formed in Illinois to aid the cause of Free Statesmen in Kansas. Feeling at the meetings of this association ran so high as to be almost revolutionary. Some of the speakers advocated the employment of any means, however desperate, to defend and promote the cause of freedom. At one of the meetings Lincoln was called on for a speech. The meeting was belligerent in tone and clearly out of patience with the government. Lincoln counselled moderation, less bitterness, and opposed the idea of coercive measures in dealing with the situation. He told them they could better succeed with the ballot than with the bullet:

You can peaceably then redeem the government and preserve the liberties of mankind through your votes and voice and moral influence. Let there be peace. Revolutionize through the ballot box. Restore the government once more to the affections and hearts of men by making it express, as it was intended to do, the highest spirit of justice and liberty. Your attempt, if there be such, to resist the laws of Kansas by force, is criminal and wicked, and all your feeble attempts will be false and end in bringing sorrow on your heads, and ruin the cause you would freely die to serve.

At the same time Lincoln joined in a subscription of money to aid the hard pressed Free Soilers of Kansas. This was the most that sympathizers in other states could do at the time without defiance to the properly constituted authorities. Many of Lincoln's friends were impatient with his moderation, but it was characteristic of him to keep within the law, and to direct public sentiment aright rather than to be led by it into rashness.

After he became President, there was the same bitter complaint of his early conduct of the war; but by refraining from rashness he threw the responsibility for illegal action upon the assailants of the Union, and thus assured the support of intelligent and righteous public sentiment for the Union cause. His heart was set upon preserving our republican inheritance unimpaired, and he realized more clearly than any other man of his time that he could not proceed farther, or faster, than he could carry public sentiment with him without the risk of alienating men who were loyal at heart, and whose support was necessary to success. In his infinite patience and apparent slowness he was guided by true insight into the trend of affairs. When assured of conditions that would require no backward step, he was always ready to move.

His attitude was that of the true progressive, neither reactionary nor unduly radical, but careful, deliberate, and determined. The debate with Douglas, in 1858, revealed Lincoln's prophetic insight. Douglas's acceptance of the Dred Scott decision was inconsistent with his doctrine of

"Squatter Sovereignty." Under that decision the Constitution carried slavery into the territories, but "Squatter Sovereignty" established the right of the voter in a territory to determine whether slavery should exist among them or not. Lincoln claimed that this was equivalent to declaring that the people have a right to drive away that which had a right to remain, and with merciless logic he drove this glaring inconsistency home to Douglas. It was Lincoln's purpose to make Douglas abandon his attitude of indifference to slavery and to compel him to say whether he thought it right or wrong in itself. To this end he framed questions designed to oblige Douglas to admit or deny the abstract right of slavery.

Lincoln's friends remonstrated with him. "If you put these questions," they said, "he will see that an answer giving practical force and effect to the Dred Scott Decision in the territories will inevitably lose him the battle for the Senatorship. He will therefore reply by offering the decision as an abstract principle, but denying its practical application. He will say that the decision is just and right, but that it can be made practically non-effective in any territory by unfriendly legislation." "If he makes that shoot," said Lincoln, "he can never be President." Lincoln's friends replied:

8

"That is not your lookout; you are after the Senatorship." "No, no, gentlemen," said Lincoln, "you do not understand. I am after larger game. The battle of 1860 is worth a hundred of these." There are few, if any, such examples of masterly political strategy. It succeeded because it originated in real faith in God and man. Douglas won the Illinois Senatorship, but lost the Presidency by arousing the distrust and suspicion of the uncompromising pro-slavery vote, especially in the South.

It may be, or it may not, that Lincoln foresaw himself as the Republican nominee for the Presidency in 1860; but his personal interest made no difference with him in his contest with Douglas. He was fighting a battle of principles. He saw that it was necessary to eliminate Douglas as a dominant political factor in order to put an end to the era of nauseating compromise. Douglas was the only man in the country whose adroitness, prestige, and oratorical force could delude the people by juggling with the issues and so prevent the square issue of freedom versus slavery. Lincoln was confident that when these issues were so joined, freedom would triumph. He probably did not believe, any more than other Northern men at the time, that the South would actually fight for

the extension of slavery.   He supposed that, after
being fairly beaten in the battle of ballots, they
would submit to the inevitable.   But he wanted
the issue joined, and was willing to take the risks
even at the sacrifice of his own immediate ambition
to go to the United States Senate.

In the light of subsequent events it seems that
Lincoln was endowed with more than mortal wisdom and that he was God's chosen instrument to
clarify the issues of the inevitable conflict for
which the time was now fully ripe.   When Stephen
A. Douglas was beaten for the Presidency, Lincoln
arose to the full height of his real greatness as a
man, as a statesman, as a patriot.   His popular
vote was 1,375,157—more than a half million
larger than the pro-slavery candidate's—and when
the dreaded conflict came he led this vast army,
with the population it represented, into the fight
for the preservation of the Union.

CHAPTER XIII

THE HOUSE DIVIDED

LINCOLN showed his independence and tenacity of purpose when he wrote his address accepting the nomination for United States Senator at the hands of the Republicans. This is known as "The House Divided Against Itself" speech. It embodied the historic declaration that the Union could not exist "half slave and half free." To his friend, Jesse K. Dubois, Lincoln said:

I refused to read the passage about the house divided against itself to you, because I knew you would ask me to change or modify it, and that I was determined not to do. I had willed it so, and was willing, if necessary, to perish with it. That expression is a truth of all human experience: a house divided against itself cannot stand. I want to use some universally known figure expressed in simple language, that it may strike home to the minds of men, in order to arouse them to the peril of the times. I would rather be defeated with this expression in the speech, and to uphold and discuss it before the people, than to be victorious without it.

It was this singular disposition to speak the whole truth that distinguished Lincoln from his fellows.   He knew that a half truth is often worse than a whole lie.   This he had attempted in his boyhood to make clear to his step-sister.   Skilled politician as he was, his skill lay not in the artistic campaign lie, which may be effective for the moment, but later must inevitably involve its author in difficulty.   His skill grew out of his knowledge that human nature, in the last analysis, adheres to the abstract principle of right, and that men and women the world over can always be aroused to the defence of moral truth when made to understand it.   His political sagacity, therefore, consisted mainly in his faith, which was little short of sublime, in the final verdict of the common people, and "the common people heard him gladly."   His friend and partner, Herndon, more far-seeing than Lincoln's critics, in speaking of the "house divided against itself" phrase, said: "Lincoln, deliver that speech as read, and it will make you President." In the light of subsequent events, Lincoln's utterance on that occasion must be regarded as a flash of inspiration, and his determination to perish with the truth, if need be, as an instance of rare courage, born from above.   To the worldly wisdom of men, his path to the Presidency lay through the United States Senate. It was a supreme moment, therefore, when this backwoods boy grown to manhood, was proposed for the great office of United States Senator. A sorer temptation can scarcely be conceived to barter his convictions to ambition. Lincoln knew that by pandering to the slave sentiment in the State he could probably be elected, and that to tell the truth, the whole truth, and nothing but the truth, would bring defeat.

He recognized that the country must soon be all one thing, or all the other. The North could not remain faithful to anti-slavery, the South to pro-slavery, and the country remain one. He knew this just as he knew that the soul suffers no division in its adherence to spiritual truth. Lincoln could not have been an agnostic, either in religion or in politics, in his love of freedom or his loyalty to the Union. His was a positive nature. He must be either anti-slavery and unionist, or pro-slavery and dis-unionist. If he had not been a positive Christian, he would have been a rank infidel. Hypocrisy was something of which his worst enemies never seriously accused him, The principle that led him to occupy an uncomprising attitude in politics forced him to a like position in religion. It was not his nature to temporize. As fast as he garnered the fruits of his mental and spiritual thought and effort, he brought them into use, adapting his political and social life to them. And the inherent truthfulness that marked his "house divided" address was only his natural and practical religion carried into his secular activities, as true religion should always manifest itself in practical life.

After the repeal of the Missouri Compromise, Lincoln became convinced that the nation could not endure half slave and half free. The Compromise itself, enacted in 1821, was probably the best measure under the conditions then existing. But it could not be finality. The very title of the measure indicated that conflicting views had entered into temporary truce. Inasmuch as these opposing views were based on radically different moral conceptions, it was inevitable that, in time, a conflict must ensue. Nothing is ever settled until it is settled right.

What the result would have been had the South held to the terms of the Compromise, no one can tell. It was the immorality of slavery as an institution, and its inconsistency with the progress of humanity which at last brought on the conflict that ended in the destruction of slavery. However, the slave party rode to its fall by aggressions which impressed the anti-slavery forces, both North and South, with the inevitableness of the conflict. The South was not content to rest upon the laurels it won in the Compromise but continued to plan further extensions of slavery. Not only must it abide in States where human beings were already held as chattels, but the hated institution must be planted in territory then free.

The Southern politicians deliberately sought to nationalize the slavery system. Steadily and stealthily, powerfully but under cover, these pro-slavery leaders planned for the extension of slave territory. It was in the face of this growing and powerful conspiracy that Lincoln hurled his immortal challenge: "This nation cannot exist, half slave and half free."

Other crises in the history of nations have condensed tremendous principle and sentiment into a terse, striking sentence. The French Revolution gave us the words, "Liberty, Fraternity, Equality," which rallied the adherents of a new order and gave them their battle cry. The Revolutionary crisis in this country gave immortality to Patrick Henry's declaration in the Virginia House of Burgesses: "Give me liberty or give me death!" Abraham Lincoln condensed and crystallized American sentiment on the central issue at the threshhold of the Civil War within the compass of nine words: "This nation cannot exist, half slave and half free!" Appealing alike to the scholar, the statesman, the toiler in the field and in the factory, it was another such battle cry as that which summoned men to do and die for the right, and inspired them to the overturning of empires. The sentence did close the door of the United States Senate in Lincoln's face, but it later opened to him the door of the White House.

Lincoln's dictum revealed his capacity to grasp far-reaching and invincible truths, and proved his courage to dare everything in his loyalty to his conviction of right. It showed, further, that he had correctly analyzed the social order, to defend which the slave power was working with all the ingenuity of its able representatives. Lincoln's early training in the wilderness had fitted him to make that analysis. He had lived where every beast of the forest was against every other beast; where one brute tolerated another only when that other could subsist without encroaching upon the natural food supply which he, himself, desired. He knew that, under the law of the forest, the weak were trampled underfoot, and only the strong could survive. He also knew that in the code of the forest there was no clause providing for the

succour of the one that could not contend against
superior strength. To Lincoln, the social condition where slavery obtained was of a kind with the
law of the jungle; its basic principle was as cruel
as that in the wilderness; and the slavery social
order, while boasting of its chivalry, had forgotten
justice—to say nothing of mercy—without which
chivalry is but an empty shell of selfishness.

How gallant, then, Lincoln's challenge, flung to
the country from Springfield, when he accepted the
Republican nomination for United States Senator.
His rival, Douglas, regarded re-election to the
Senate as a great stride toward the Presidency.
Likewise, Lincoln's election to the Senate might
have opened the way for him to the White House.
But his inspiration was wiser than the thoughts
of men. Through his defeat for truth's sake he
aroused the conscience of the Nation and demonstrated the futility of any compromise by which
the slave power was permitted to hold the balance.
Had Lincoln pursued a more politic course by
withholding his celebrated declaration until more
advantageous fighting ground was gained, he
would have acted in accordance with the wisdom
of men; but conscience would not have approved.
He knew in his heart that God hates temporizing
and concealment when vital principle is at stake.

His resolve not to truckle to the prejudices of the
hour was something more than human courage and
wisdom.   It was the manhood of a noble spirit
chosen by Him Who is the arbiter of destiny for
the accomplishment of a great purpose.

It is almost uncanny that at the very time
Lincoln was working out his uncompromising
speech on slavery, Arthur Hugh Clough, both in
England and this country, was setting forth the
principle identical, in verse as memorable as the
prose of Lincoln:

I will look straight out—
See things—not try to evade them.
Fact shall be fact for me, and the truth the truth
    forever.

CHAPTER XIV

THE CLAY AND THE POTTER

THE religious element in Lincoln's character became clearly manifest after the Republican party had come into being. The contest between the old Whig and the Democratic parties had been mainly on economic grounds. There were, of course, economic questions into which the moral element was already entering, as the tariff for example; but there was no question so predominantly a moral question as was that issue of freedom and slavery. Mr. Lincoln's temperament and early religious bias admirably fitted him to deal with moral issues. This became apparent in his speech delivered at Bloomington in May, 1856, before the first Republican State Convention of Illinois.

The new party had been organized upon the issue of the non-extension of slavery. Stephen A. Douglas, and pro-slavery advocates generally, insisted on treating it as a business question, involving only the rights of property. But Lin-

coln saw, behind the property issue, the great
moral question of the right of one human being
holding another human being in bondage, and of
one man eating his bread by the sweat of another's
face. To the argument of Douglas, that the
people of any territory had the right to vote
slavery up or down, Lincoln replied that the
argument would be sound if slavery were conceded
to be right; but that, if slavery were wrong, the
people had no right to extend it beyond the limits
where the Constitution and the ordinances and
agreements made pursuant thereto, already permit
it to exist. In his Bloomington speech, he said:

We have seen today that every shade of popular
opinion is represented here; with freedom, or rather free
soil as a basis, we have come together as in some sort
representatives of popular opinion against the extension of slavery into territory now free in fact as well as
by law. We come to protest against a great wrong
and to take measures to determine that Kansas shall
be free. We, therefore, in the language of the Bible,
"lay the axe to the root of the tree."

He called attention to the fact that Thomas
Jefferson himself a slaveholder, mindful of the
moral element in slavery, solemnly declared that
he "trembled for his country when he remembered
that God was just." And Lincoln asked how any

advocate of the extension of slavery, if slavery was a moral and political wrong, could answer to God for the attempt to spread and fortify it. Further on in his address, he said:

The battle of freedom is to be fought out on principle. Slavery is a violation of the eternal right. We have temporized with it from the necessities of our condition, but as sure as God reigns and school children read, that black, foul lie can never be consecrated in God's hallowed truth. Can we, as Christian men, strong and free ourselves, wield the sledge or hold the iron with which to manacle anew an already oppressed race? "Woe unto them," it is written, "that decree unrighteous decrees, and that have wrought grievances which they have prescribed." Those who deny freedom to others deserve it not themselves, and under the rule of a just God cannot long retain it. There is both power and a magic in popular opinion. To that let us now appeal, and while in all probability no resort to force will be needed, our moderation and forbearance will stand us in good stead when, if ever, we must make an appeal to battle and to the God of Hosts.

If there were no other evidence of Lincoln's Christian character, his Bloomington speech would be sufficient.

Lincoln's reliance upon God for the triumph of moral ideas, as declared in his Bloomington speech, made when there was no thought of him in the public mind in connection with the Presidency, was maintained throughout his official life. When the time came for an appeal to battle, it was always coupled in Lincoln's mind and heart with an appeal to the God of Hosts.

It was the crisis for the fight for freedom which Abraham Lincoln faced when a subservient Congress yielded to the greedy demands of the slave party in the repeal of the Missouri Compromise. Stephen A. Douglas had led the fight for the repeal, and was the one man in the North who joined with the Southern slavery politicians, giving them the political strength essential to the success of the repeal.   Douglas thus gave the South the support in the North, without which it could not have removed the Compromise from the statute books. It was the repeal of the Compromise which convinced Lincoln that further compromise was impossible—that the Nation must now choose between legalized slavery in every part of the country and a country under whose flag every man should be free.   New England anti-slavery forces had been the most powerful in the Nation to that time, but the western prairies were now to take the leadership in the war for human liberty.   Abraham Lincoln and Stephen A. Douglas were the opposing leaders in the conflict and to the victor was to go at last the Presidency.

So far as can be ascertained, Lincoln first gave expression to the conviction that the country must be all one thing or all the other in a private letter of August, 1855, written to George Robertson, of Lexington, Kentucky. In his letter, Lincoln referred to a speech made by Robertson many years before, at the time when Missouri was admitted to the Union. Lincoln wrote:

In that speech, you spoke of the peaceful extinction of slavery and used other expressions indicating your belief that the thing was at some time to have an end. Since then, we have had thirty-six years of experience, and this experience has demonstrated, I think, that there is no peaceful extinction of slavery in prospect for us. The signal failure of Henry Clay, and other good and great men, in 1849, to effect anything in favour of gradual emancipation in Kentucky, together with a thousand other signs, extinguished that hope utterly. On the question of liberty as a principle, we are not what we have been. When we were the political slaves of King George and wanted to be free, we called the maxim that all men are created equal a self-evident truth; but now that we have grown fat and have lost dread of being slaves ourselves, we have become so greedy to be masters that we call the same maxim a self-evident lie. That spirit which desired the peaceful extinction of slavery has itself become extinct with the occasion, and the men of the Revolution. Under the impulse of that occasion, nearly half the States adopted systems of emancipation at once, and it is a significant fact that not a

single State has done the like since. So far as peaceful,
voluntary emancipation is concerned, the condition
of the negro slave in America, scarcely less terrible in
the contemplation of a free mind, is now as fixed and
hopeless of change for the better as that of the lost
souls of the finally impenitent.   Our political problem
now is: Can we, as a nation, continue together permanently, forever half slave and half free? The
problem is too mighty for me.   May God, in His
mercy, superintend the solution.

And God did superintend the solution.   Abraham Lincoln, from childhood to the end of his
wonderful life, was under the direction of this
superintendency.   The progress of events in the
years that preceded the Civil War as well as the
war itself, indicate that the Almighty was directing
affairs and sifting out the agencies through which
the righteous solution was to be obtained.   The
formation of the Republican party, and its early
experiences as a political organization, are conspicuous instances of the divine superintendency.
Both the Whig and Democratic parties had bowed
the knee to Baal.   The slave power had tightened
its grip. Both parties had temporized; but temporizing at such a time was but the strategy by which
the slave party advanced its lines with the purpose of gaining control of the Federal Government
and capturing the country for its system of

9

human slavery. The opposing forces formed the Republican party, and in 1856 nominated the "Pathfinder," John C. Frémont, for the Presidency. It seemed to the Republicans that, unless they succeeded in electing Frémont, the cause of freedom was lost. And yet, how foolish is the wisdom of man as viewed by the God of nations! He knew that the country was not ready for the final test, for the inevitable uprooting of slavery. He knew, and we now know, that it was best for the cause of freedom that the path of the "Pathfinder" did not lead to the White House.

The period of preparation was not yet complete. Public sentiment was not ripe for the elimination of slavery. Had Frémont won, the cause of freedom would probably have been set back many decades. While Lincoln had united his fortunes with those of the new party, it is obvious he realized that the time was not yet ripe. His eyes were looking forward to the contest of 1860, by which time, he believed, public sentiment would be sufficiently powerful to enable the party of freedom to gain control.

The preservation of the Union was the central thought of Lincoln, and around this thought revolved the whole system of his political faith. He had been outspoken in his declaration that the country could not permanently retain the institution of slavery, because he knew that slavery was immoral, and in his mind and heart was the consciousness that no political policy founded on immorality could endure. The Bible was the text book from which he had learned that even an economic policy must be founded upon sound social morality; and the Bible was his ultimate authority, quoted by him over and over again, for the declaration that no policy that comprehended the retention of slavery could be permanent.

Lincoln was firm in the belief that God ordained this Western Republic, founded on the principle of popular government, to be the exemplar of human liberty to endure through the ages. Popular government, therefore, was to him no chimera, no figment of superficial thinkers, no mere sentimental effervescence. Hence Lincoln laid it down as a fundamental and paramount principle that the Union must be preserved at all hazards. To that end he devoted all the powers of his great heart and brain, sustained by the unfaltering faith of his exalted spiritual nature.

How wonderfully Lincoln's thought attuned itself to the Supreme Director of the impending conflict! How unerringly he discerned the Divine purpose, and how accurately he squared his course with the plans of Providence! The leadership of the prairie statesman, viewed from any angle, scrutinized in the light of history, stands forth a striking illustration of a leadership God-led, even in the smallest details.

CHAPTER XV

IT was on the evening of February 27, 1860, that Abraham Lincoln became beyond all peradventure a personality of national proportions. The fame of his victory two years earlier over Douglas had made Republicans in the East eager to see and hear the man. He had taken such high moral ground and there maintained himself against all comers, that the new party had a strong conviction that at least his counsel would be useful in making up the party's policy in the campaign of 1860. Of the score or more of eminent Republicans in the East who joined in sending Mr. Lincoln the invitation to speak at Cooper Institute, only two or three knew him at all and even his name was unfamiliar to the audience in general. Few came that evening expecting to hear anything worth while, and not a few were drawn by idle curiosity or rumours of his uncouthness or power to tell fetching stories. The impression that he made that night has fortunately been recorded by men accustomed to weigh men as well as measures with discriminating accuracy. Major George Haven Putnam says he was but a boy when he first looked on "the gaunt figure of the man who was to become the people's leader" and that he was at once impressed with the outstanding fact that Mr. Lincoln's "contentions were not based upon invective or abuse, but purely on considerations of justice, on that everlasting principle that what is just, and only what is just, represents the largest and the highest interests of the nation as a whole."[1]

The late Mr. Choate awhile before he died pictured Mr. Lincoln's appearance substantially like Major Putnam and other discerning men, who perceived that a new planet had swung into the murky sky of public life, and yet recall his quaintness to an audience made up of the most cultivated men and women in the East. On his long ungainly figure clothes, newly made for the trip, but badly wrinkled on the way, did nothing to relieve the obvious embarrassment of his first moments. "His deep set eyes looked sad and anxious, his countenance in repose gave little evidence"—says Mr. Choate—"of that brain power which had raised him from the lowest to the highest station among his countrymen." When the presiding

[1] George Haven Putnam, *Abraham Lincoln*, 47.

officer, Mr. William Cullen Bryant, presented him, the audience was on tiptoe for a story-telling orator. He disappointed them by dealing seriously with the gravest subject then before America. Everybody soon forgot the obtrusive feet, the clumsy hands, the unruly hair no brush could ever tame, even the harsh and high-pitched voice which as soon as he was safely launched into his theme grew natural and pleasing and winning, as his entire presence became as dignified and nobly graceful as St. Gaudens has represented it in his heroic statue in Chicago.

By sheer simplicity and transparent sincerity, with eyes shining and face glowing with interest in his message, Lincoln played at will upon his audience for an hour and a half. By copious historical proofs and masterly logic he stood there, the mighty man he was, shattering with sledge-hammer blows the barricades of ignorance, venality, and superstition, demolishing the castles of ancient wrong and misinterpretation of the Constitution; and building on the ruins thereof a new and glorious temple founded on divine truth, and dedicated to a democracy in which

> None shall rule but the humble,
> And none but toil shall have.

In the kindliest spirit he protested against the avowed threat of the Southern States to destroy the Union if they could not have their way concerning slavery, and placed the whole subject in a moral and religious light in one of the noblest passages in all his earlier speeches:

Wrong, as we think slavery is, we can yet afford to let it alone where it is, because that much is due to the necessity arising from its actual presence in the nation; but can we, while our votes will prevent it, allow it to spread into the national Territories, and to overrun us here in these free States? If our sense of duty forbids this, then let us stand by our duty fearlessly and effectively. Let us be diverted by none of those sophistical contrivances wherewith we are so industriously plied and belaboured,—contrivances such as groping for some middle ground between the right and the wrong: vain as the search for a man who should be neither a living man, nor a dead man; such as a policy of "don't care" about which all true men do care; such as Union appeals beseeching true Union men to yield to dis-Unionists, reversing the divine rule, and calling, not the sinners but the righteous to repentance.

Then in unconscious illustration that he lived up to his Christian teaching, he turned from the honours men were seeking to heap on him, and making his way through the slums, where it was not safe to go without police escort, he paid a visit on Sunday to the Five Points Mission Sunday School, as thus described by one then teaching there:

Our Sunday School in the Five Points was assembled one Sabbath morning, when I noticed a tall, remarkable looking man enter the room and take his seat among us. He listened with fixed attention to our exercises, and his countenance expressed such genuine interest that I approached him and suggested that he might be willing to say something to the children. He accepted the invitation with evident pleasure, and coming forward, began a simple address which at once fascinated every little hearer and hushed the room to silence. His language was strikingly beautiful, and his tones musical with intense feeling. The little faces around him would droop into sad conviction as he uttered sentences of warning, and would brighten into sunshine as he spoke cheerful words of promise. Once or twice he attempted to close his remarks, but the imperative shouts of "Go on! O! do go on!" would compel him to resume. As I looked upon the gaunt and sinewy form of the stranger, and marked his powerful head and determined features, now touched into softness by the expressions of the moment, I felt an irrepressible curiosity to learn something more about him, and when he was quietly leaving the room, I begged to know his name. He courteously replied, "It is Abraham Lincoln, from Illinois."[1]

[1] See Carpenter's *Six Months in the White House.*

Erastus Corning, President of the New York Central Railroad, heard that speech at Cooper Institute. To him it revealed the keen lawyer as well as the great statesman. Early the next morning he was at the Astor House where Lincoln was staying. "Mr. Lincoln," he said, "I understand that in Illinois you win all your law suits." Laughing softly Lincoln answered, "Oh, no, Mr. Corning, that is not true; but I do make it a rule to refuse cases unless I am convinced the litigant's cause is just." "Mr. Lincoln," came the inquiry, "will you entertain an offer from the New York Central Railroad to become its general counsel at $10,000 a year?" The generous offer was courteously declined and when renewed in writing after Lincoln had returned to Springfield, it was again and finally—after prayerful consideration—refused.

Mr. Lincoln never gave the real reason for resisting a temptation few ever can resist of declining to accept a salary out of all proportion to a lawyer's income in those days. We know only that he had been set on bringing righteousness to rule in the country that he loved, and that even at his mother's knee he had heard the voice of conscience speaking through the Book of Books to him: "Thou shalt wor-

ship the Lord thy God, and him only shalt
thou serve."[1]

[1] This conversation of Mr. Lincoln and Erastus Corning is
reported by Major J. B. Merwin, appointed to the regular army
by Mr. Lincoln in his Presidency.

CHAPTER XVI

THE MAN OF THE HOUR

ABRAHAM LINCOLN was nominated for President by the Republican National Convention held in the Wigwam, at Chicago, May 16 to 18, 1860. The city was thronged with delegates and partisans of their favourites, among whom were Mr. Bates, Mr. Chase, and Mr. Cameron. Judge Wilmot, of Pennsylvania, was chosen temporary chairman, and George Adams, of Massachusetts, permanent chairman, with twenty-seven vice-presidents and twenty-five secretaries. The Convention assembled Wednesday, May 16, and adopted its platform the next day. On the first ballot Lincoln received 102 votes, Seward 173, and the rest of the votes were scattered. The second ballot showed 184½ for Seward to 181 for Lincoln. On the third ballot, Mr. Lincoln had 230, within 1½ of a majority. Vermont had been divided on the first ballot, but cast her full strength, ten votes, in the third for "the young giant of the West," as the delegation chairman announced amid cheers from the Lincoln adherents.

When the third ballot showed Lincoln so close
to the nomination, Mr. Carter, of Ohio, arose and
announced to the Convention that Ohio had four
more votes for Lincoln, giving him the nomination.
Other changes followed until the third ballot, as
officially announced, gave Lincoln 354 votes. On
the motion of Mr. Evarts, of New York, the
nomination was made unanimous. Thus the
backwoods lad of Kentucky, Indiana, and Illinois,
grown to be the central figure in American politics,
was selected candidate for President of the United
States.

The usual committee of notification was appointed to wait upon Mr. Lincoln. Many, if not
most of the members of the committee, believed
Lincoln's nomination to be a mistake. Most of
the Eastern delegates, together with the great
political leaders, were disposed to look upon Lincoln as the creature of a spasmodic sentiment on
the slavery question, destined, even if elected, to
prove that his choice had been a political blunder.
The platform upon which Lincoln had been nominated was so framed as not to permit him to be
carried away by any chimera, even if he had been
the visionary they feared. The platform declared
the preservation of the Union to be the paramount
issue, and assured the people of the South that

there was no intention to deprive them of any property they possessed under the Constitution. This was practically the position upon which Lincoln had conducted his former campaigns; and he was nominated and elected, not as one who was to destroy slavery as an institution, but as one who would not consent to the extension of slavery, and who would, at any cost, preserve the Union.

The Republican platform shows up in its true light when set over against the platforms of the opposition. At first blush, it seems to fall short of the demands of the hour and to be less than might reasonably have been expected as the fighting platform of one who had championed the cause of the black man so often and for so long. The following synopsis will reveal the lines of cleavage between the three leading presidential platforms. The Republicans and Mr. Lincoln believed:

1. That slavery must not be extended into the territories, and that it was the duty of Congress to exclude it therefrom by positive legislation.

2. That it was not right to interfere with slavery in territory in which it then existed.

3. That it was right to protect all persons in the exercise of their constitutional rights. This was meant as assurance to the South that their slaves would not be taken away from them.

The Douglas Democrats believed:

1.   That the people of the territories had the right to decide for themselves whether or not slavery should come among them.
2.   That they had the right to enact legislation, through their territorial legislatures, to make such decisions binding alike upon them and the country at large.

The Breckinridge Democrats believed:

1.   That slavery was sound in morals and in economics.
2.   That the Congress should protect slavery in the territories by specific legislation.
3.   That the Congress should protect slavery in the territories by specific prohibition of territorial legislatures against interfering with it.

Mr. Lincoln faced a great responsibility as the nominee of the Republican party—greater, indeed, than was then supposed.   Shortly after his nomination he wrote George Ashmun, Chairman of the Republican convention, as follows:

"SIR:
I accept the nomination tendered me by the Convention over which you presided, of which I am formally apprised in a letter of yourself and others acting as a Committee for the Convention for that purpose. The declaration of principles and sentiments which

accompanies your letter meets my approval, and it shall be my care not to violate it or disregard it in any part. Imploring the assistance of Divine Providence, and with due regard for the views and feelings of all who were represented in the Convention, to the rights of all the States and Territories and people of the Nation, to the inviolability of the Constitution and the perpetual union, harmony, and prosperity of all, I am most happy to co-operate for the practical success of the principles declared by the Convention.

Your obliged friend and fellow citizen,
ABRAHAM LINCOLN.

To follow Lincoln through the Presidential canvass of 1860 would swell this volume beyond its intended scope. After the most exciting campaign in the history of the country, he was found to be elected by a strong plurality, though the combined vote of all the other candidates was nearly a million in excess of the vote for Mr. Lincoln, who received 1,857,610; Breckinridge, 847,953; Bell, 590,631. In the Electoral College, Mr. Lincoln received all the votes of the Free States except New Jersey, which gave him four and Mr. Douglas three. Mr. Breckinridge received the electoral votes of all the Slave States except Kentucky, Tennessee, and Virginia, which voted for Bell, and Missouri, which voted for Douglas.

What, then, had been achieved by the election of Mr. Lincoln to the Presidency? To the Abolitionists he was not radical enough, and did not forthwith declare his intention to free the slaves.

On the other hand, the slave power knew that Mr. Lincoln's election spelled the doom of their schemes for extending slavery into free territory, and meant the ultimate relegation of slavery into oblivion. Yet Lincoln had never formulated a political programme that comprehended more than the prevention of slavery's extension. He believed that the Federal Constitution preserved inviolate the possession of slaves in the slave States. His cardinal principle was: "Preserve the Union; preserve it free, if necessary; but at all hazards, preserve it."

Mr. Lincoln stood for law and order, for obeying the Constitution and the laws, for faithfulness to any organic or statute law existing; but he also stood for the authority of the general government in all matters pertaining to national affairs, believing that slavery was properly a federal question and that the Government at Washington should take cognizance of it at all times. Therefore, the slave power argued that Lincoln would be in favour of so amending the Constitution as to eliminate slavery altogether. The people south of Mason's and

Dixon's Line insisted upon the rights of the States to regulate slavery and all other affairs that did not affect directly the general government. States Rights had become a sort of fetich with the South; but it was not States Rights *per se* that appealed to them so powerfully. It was their desire to retain slavery; for slavery was the black thread woven into their daily lives, their social relations, their state affairs, and gave a sombre colour to their attitude toward the general government.

Mr. Lincoln's election was the triumph of the theory of a strong central government and an inseparable union of the States, against the Southern theory, held also by many in the North, of a federation of States dwelling together in unity, but each preserving its autonomy, with freedom to depart at any time from the Union. The one involved the idea of the right of the central government to prevent by force, if necessary, any State from leaving the Union. The other involved the idea of a loose federation of States, each having the right to go out at will.

What a momentous day, then, when Abraham Lincoln was named by that Wigwam Convention! What another momentous day when he was triumphantly elected! It was the beginning of a contest that was to settle for all time the

questions in controversy, and to prove that the
Union was "One and indissoluble, now and for
ever."

In the midst of these tremendous happenings,
thrust into the prominence of world politics,
Abraham Lincoln retained his simplicity. Re-
verting to the time when the Committee came to
him in Springfield to notify him of his nomination
for President, the moral power of the man stood
forth when, contrary to custom, he emphasized
his personal abstinence from intoxicants. Frank
B. Carpenter, in his *Six Months at the White
House*, says that, after the ceremony of notification
had ended, Mr. Lincoln remarked to the company
that he presumed good manners would require
that he should treat them to something to drink,
as an appropriate conclusion to an interview so
important and interesting as that which had just
taken place. Opening a door that led to a room
in the rear, he called out, "Mary, Mary." A girl
responded to the call, to whom Mr. Lincoln spoke
a few words in an undertone, closed the door, and
returned to converse with his guests. The maid
soon returned bearing a large tray containing
several glass tumblers and a pitcher, and placed
it on the centre table. Mr. Lincoln arose, and
gravely addressing the company, said:

"Gentlemen, we must pledge our mutual health in the most healthful beverage God has given to man. It is the only beverage I have ever used or allowed in my family, and I cannot conscientiously depart from it on the present occasion. It is pure Adam's ale, just from the spring."

Taking a tumbler, he touched it to his lips and pledged them his highest respects in a cup of cold water. All his guests admired his consistency and good-naturedly followed his example.[1]

[1] In the *Christian Advocate*, February 6, 1919, appears at last the affidavit, documents, and data of the late Maj. James B. Merwin, who died April 5, 1917, concerning the attitude toward prohibition of Mr. Lincoln, his intimate from 1855 to 1865. Lincoln seems to have spoken in 1855 in the interests of prohibition and even to have drawn up the prohibition law passed that year by the Illinois Legislature and submitted to the voters, who failed however to approve it. It is solemnly significant that as Maj. Merwin was talking with the President a few hours before the assassination, Mr. Lincoln said to him according to affidavit: "Merwin, we have cleaned up a colossal job. We have abolished slavery. The next great movement will be the overthrow of the legalized liquor traffic, and you know my heart and my hand, my purse and my life will be given to that great movement. I prophesied twenty-five years ago that the day would come when there would not be a slave or drunkard in the land. I have seen the first part come true."

CHAPTER XVII

PROPHETIC VISIONS

THE cause of freedom having won its first conspicuous victory, its adherents throughout the country were rejoicing. But to Abraham Lincoln, his election to the Presidency was not an occasion for complacency or light-hearted congratulation. The vast responsibility involved in his new relation was so interwoven with the weal of the nation, and, indeed, with the destiny of popular government, that he could not regard it other than a divinely imposed mission requiring patience, sincerity, courage, and dependence for help upon Almighty God. Contemplating the task awaiting him in the White House, fully realizing the weighty responsibility resting on him, it is little wonder that the magnitude of the burden he was soon to bear caused him to be known as "the saddest man who ever occupied the White House."

The mystic element of Lincoln's nature was stirred mightily by his call to the epochal task. Always sensitive to the power of the unseen, it is not strange that, as he stood on the threshold of a future pregnant with perplexity, there came to him a waking vision thus described by Noah Brooks, who writes in his *Life of Lincoln* that he received it from the President himself:

"It was just after my election in 1860, when the news was coming thick and fast all day, and there had been a great 'Hurrah, Boys,' so that I was well tired out, and went home to rest, and threw myself on a lounge in my chamber. Opposite where I lay, was a bureau with a swinging glass upon it, and looking into the glass I saw myself reflected, nearly at full length, but my face, I noticed, had two separate and distinct images, the tip of the nose of one being about three inches from the tip of the other. I was a little bothered, perhaps startled, and got up and looked in the glass, but the illusion vanished. On lying down again, I saw it a second time, plainer, if possible, than before. Then I noticed that one of the faces was a little paler, say five shades, than the other. I got up and the thing melted away, and I went off and in the excitement of the hour forgot all about it, nearly, but not quite, for the thing would once in a while come up and give me a little pang, as though something uncomfortable had happened. Later in the day, I told my wife about it, and a few days later I tried the experiment again, when sure enough, the thing came again, but I never succeeded in bringing the ghost back after that, though I once tried very industriously to show it to my wife, who was worried about it somewhat. She thought that it was a sign that I was to be elected to a second term of office, and that the paleness of one of the faces was an omen that I should not see life through the last term."

Lincoln at different times in his life had received other impressions that he would, some day, be the victim of a tragedy. Mrs. Lincoln had undoubtedly become familiar with the mystic phase of her husband's nature, and worried over the portent. The vision was quite as definite as many that came to the prophets of Holy Writ, giving warning of coming events; but as the Hebrew prophets persisted in the work to which they had been dedicated, whether the omens boded good or ill to themselves, so this seer of the crucial years of the nineteenth century, as God-illuminated as they were, ignored all personal danger and entered fearlessly upon his perilous task.

Lincoln's prophetic insight, so frequently manifested, accounts in large measure for the subtle, intangible, pervasive, ever enlarging influence of his personality upon the minds of men. He has grown more during the years that have followed his martyrdom than any other man in history. Others, prophets and martyrs, have often had to wait for centuries for full recognition; but, even now, while men still live who felt the grasp of his hand, his fame is world-wide.

The thought that appeals specially to the hearts of men is that he was here as a prophet of the Most High on a divine mission, creating an epoch in which he towers as the most conspicuous figure. He belonged to the class of men who have won in consecrated service the crown of enduring fame. It was not his statesmanship alone that keeps his memory great, nor his oratory, nor his gift of boundless common sense, nor even his devotion to the cause of freedom; it was not merely because he was the Chief Executive of the Republic during the stormiest period of its history, and directed it skilfully and successfully through the most terrific civil war ever waged. We must look deeper than his words, deeper than his deeds, to find the real source of his power. In any age, the man who discerns and appropriates the divine purpose projected through history is lifted into immortality through the power, the sweep, the grandeur of that purpose. The purpose which Lincoln grasped and embodied was interwoven with the spiritual texture of his nature and lifted him above the levels of the ordinary.

The career of Abraham Lincoln was the incarnated expression of the divine idea of human liberty and equal opportunity for all, rooted in the ground of common humanity. Throughout his whole career, in the White House no less than in his father's cabin, on the farm, in the humble lawyer's cottage at Springfield, in the courts of law, on the political rostrum, in the halls of legislation, he was ever the plain and unassuming citizen, kindly neighbour, advocate of the poor, counsellor of the widow—always the devout servitor of his fellow man, a Heaven-inspired guide in times of perplexity and peril.

In the order of Providence he came, uncouth and unceremonious—a strange, mysterious man from the tangled forests and interminable prairies of the frontier. He appeared upon the stage of affairs with the simplicity which is the expression of true majesty. In his presence, the most conspicuous men of his time dwindled into comparative insignificance, while he demonstrated the glory of American democracy, and, by his devotion to the Constitution and the flag, preserved the Union and emancipated the slaves, thus making his name the synonym—the enshrined reality, as religious as it is practical—of all the concealed and revealed meaning of Americanism.

CHAPTER XVIII

GUARDING THE CITADEL

MR. LINCOLN was not ignorant of the critical condition into which the country had drifted, nor was he panic-stricken. During the months after his election, and before his inauguration, he studied the situation from every standpoint and took such measures as he could to meet the emergencies he would have to face when clothed with the authority to act. He conducted a voluminous correspondence with trusted men of prominence throughout the country, whose sympathy and co-operation he sought in the solution of the problems which awaited him. His temper, firmness, and determination are sufficiently revealed in his correspondence with Hon. E. B. Washburne, a warm friend of Lincoln's, and Congressman from Illinois. In a letter of December 13, 1860, he wrote:

Your long letter received. Prevent, so far as possible, any of our friends from demoralizing themselves and our cause by entertaining propositions for compromise of any sort on the slavery question.

There is no possible compromise upon it but which puts us under again, and leaves us to do all our work over again. Whether it be a Missouri line or Eli Thayer's Popular Sovereignty, it is all the same. Let either be done, and immediately filibustering and extending slavery, recommence. On that point hold firm as with a chain of steel.

Eight days later, he wrote again to Washburne:

Last night I received your letter, giving an account of your interview with Gen. Scott, and for which I thank you. Please present my respects to the General, and tell him, confidentially, I shall be obliged to him to be as well prepared as he can either to hold or re-take the forts as the case may require, at and after the inauguration.

Thus was Lincoln manifesting the "firmness and determination, without the temper of Jackson," as an intimate friend aptly said. He knew he was succeeding to the office of President, rendered as nearly impotent as plotters in places of power could make it. He was aware that the erstwhile strong arm of the Federal Government was now as weak and helpless as plotting custodians in charge of the public interest had been able to make it. If the Ship of State had not been scuttled and sunk it was through no lack of mean contriving of the plotters.

Lincoln further knew that his life would probably pay the forfeit, if he wrought to stem the tide of secession and to save the Union, which he was already declaring to be his paramount purpose. Yet amid these portentous clouds, even then lurid with the approaching storm, he could calmly say to his friends on departing from Springfield: "We cannot fail, if God shall help us." The man of God was speaking.

Under the weight of all but killing responsibilities, Lincoln's religious character grew day by day. No President ever faced a situation of greater difficulty, of deeper discouragement. "I am driven to my knees," he said, "because there is nowhere else to go." The Ship of State was plunging in a raging storm with hidden reefs on every hand and men's hearts failing them for fear. A deep-laid conspiracy against the Union and also against Lincoln's life was already hatched. His predecessor, a weak and vacillating man, had brought about, with scarcely a word of protest, the disintegration of the army. A majority of Buchanan's cabinet sympathized with the South. The Congress was dominated by men who wilfully betrayed their country by permitting the critical moments to pass without making any provision for the protection of the Union against those who plotted its destruction.

Buchanan refused to permit the strengthening of the forts at Charleston, a measure which might have restrained the South from plunging the Nation into Civil War. During the four months between the time of Lincoln's election and his inauguration, the conspirators resorted to every possible device to overthrow the Government. Lewis Cass, Secretary of State, resigned on December 12, 1860, because President Buchanan refused to fortify the forts of Charleston Harbor. He was succeeded by Jeremiah S. Black, who, as Buchanan's Attorney-General, had handed down the opinion that the Federal Government had not the power to coerce a seceding State.

Howell Cobb, of Georgia, Secretary of the Treasury, and afterwards a general in the Confederate army, "managed to destroy the credit of the Government, and when, on December 10th, he resigned because his duty to Georgia required it, he left the Treasury empty."

John B. Floyd, Secretary of War, and soon to be a general in the Southern army, "before he resigned, partly disarmed the free States and sent the soldiers belonging to the Regular Army so far away as not to be available until the conspirators should have time to consummate the revolution."

Isaac Toucy, of Connecticut, Secretary of the

Navy under Buchanan, scattered the Federal ships to distant seas, and left the Government without a navy.

So bold were the secessionists that they actually planned to prevent Lincoln's inauguration, and to surrender the Capitol and public archives to the insurgents. But for the loyal old General Scott, who had won his spurs a half century before, treason would have had its way, and to oppose it the aged warrior had only a small and questionable army. Buchanan was clay in the hands of Jefferson Davis, Cobb, Toombs, and their disloyal associates. The Government was in the power of conspirators who were plotting its overthrow. Treasonable messages were actually sent back and forth between the desks of high officials. In the Congress and the Cabinet alike, conspirators were boldly carrying on their schemes for the destruction of the Government. No attempt was made to interfere, much less to arrest open and avowed traitors.

A stronger combination of difficulties could scarcely be imagined than that which confronted Abraham Lincoln. The treasury was empty. The trees were yet growing, the iron yet unmined, with which a navy was to be built and armoured. Such army as there was, was widely scattered.

Officers without discipline were set the task of
making a mere mob into an army. Public opinion
in Europe, tampered with by specious arguments
of treason or affected by our home despondency,
was either contemptuously skeptical or actively
hostile. To ensure neutrality abroad there was
on this side the handicap of a Chief Magistrate
hampered at every turn by a reputation still un-
made as national executive, nominal supporters
who doubted his ability, social leaders who ridiculed his manners, and an unscrupulous minority
playing into hostile hands at every turn and greet-
ing every incidental error with "I told you so."

"That a steady purpose and divine aim," wrote
Mr. Lowell in 1864, "were given to the jarring forces
which, at the beginning of the war, spent themselves
in the discussion of schemes which could only become
operative, if at all, after the war was over; that
a peculiar excitement was slowly intensified into
an earnest national will; that the treason of covert
enemies, the jealousy of rivals, the unwise zeal of
friends were made not only useless for mischief, but
even useful for good; that the conscientious sensitiveness of England to the horrors of civil conflict was
prevented from complicating a domestic with a foreign
war; all these results, any one of which might suffice to
prove the greatness of a ruler, were mainly due to the
good sense, the good humour, the sagacity, the large-
mindedness, and the unselfish honesty of the unknown

man whom a blind fortune, as it seemed, had lifted from the crowd to the most dangerous and difficult eminence of modern times.

"It is by the presence of mind in untried emergencies that the native mettle of a man is tested. It is by the sagacity to see, and the fearless honesty to admit, whatever of truth there may be in an adverse opinion, in order more convincingly to expose the fallacy that lurks behind it, that a reasoner at length gains for his mere statement of fact the force of argument.

"It is by a wise forecast, which allows hostile combinations to go as far as, by the inevitable reaction, to become elements of his own power, that a politician proves his genius for statecraft, and especially it is by so gently guiding public sentiment that he seems to follow it, by so yielding doubtful points that he can be firm without seeming obstinate in essential ones, and thus gain the advantages of compromise without the weakness of concession, by so instinctively comprehending the temper and prejudices of a people as to make them gradually conscious of the superior wisdom of his freedom from temper and prejudice—it is by qualities such as these that a magistrate shows himself worthy to be chief in the commonwealth of freedom; and it is for qualities such as these that we firmly believe that history will rank Mr. Lincoln among the most prudent of statesmen and the most successful of rulers."

Thus does Mr. Lowell analyze the situation, divine the forces, and characterize the man of 1861. And then in final explanation of Lincoln's ultimate success he frankly says that Mr. Lincoln was a man of faith.[1]

As though to leave no room to question his supreme test of Lincoln's character, Mr. Lowell some months later, in his "Ode Recited at the Harvard Commemoration," places this wreath on the grave of him who meanwhile had passed out of life:

"Wise, steadfast in the strength of God, and true."

[1] James Russell Lowell, in *The North American Review*, January, 1864.

XIX

AWAKING A CONTINENT

IT is worthy of note that epochal political movements have been preceded by profound and far-reaching spiritual awakenings. Sordidness had come to govern the progress of events in the United States. Property rights had gained the ascendancy. Wealth and money-getting was the prime desideratum. The augmentation of the slave power, chiefly through its masterful statesman, John C. Calhoun had well-nigh achieved the ultimate triumph of the cause of human slavery.

The individual conscience of the average man in the North as well as in the South, seemed corroded by the insidious influences of commercialism. Religion here, as in England before the time of the Wesleys, had become formal, retaining the letter without the spirit.

Lincoln's appeal to the moral sentiment of the nation began slowly to arouse a slumbering Christendom by appealing to conscience, exposing national apostasy, turning the light of truth upon

the monstrous crime of slavery, and condensing
into a few words a moral maxim which demonstrated the impossibility of the continued existence of freedom and servitude under the same
flag.

Silently, like the pervasion of the sunshine in the
springtime, there spread across the land a wave of
moral fervour, a spiritual awakening, a religious
revival such as the nation had never known—an
event which has been strangely overlooked by the
writers of history.   A careful reading of two-score
works upon the events of that time fails to reveal
the full significance of this phenomenal spiritual
awakening in the solution of the vexatious problems of the day.   In fact, the whole nation was
beginning, perhaps vaguely and unconsciously, to
feel the spiritual forces Lincoln had set in motion.
East and West the hearts of men were already
responding to his touch.

In 1857 a small group of business men began a
series of Noonday Prayer Meetings in Fulton
Street, New York.   There was no bishop, no
preacher, no leader.   No Dwight L. Moody was
yet prepared to lend the power of his great name
to the movement.   No one stood forth more
prominently than another.   A company of men,
hitherto absorbed in business down in the storm

centre of the business life of the Metropolis, became strongly convinced that the spiritual life of the Church was rapidly becoming extinct, and that as a result, the nation was losing its virility, its moral vigour and its power. They felt, therefore, that a spiritual awakening was essential to the preservation of America itself.

It is not evident that they realized the relation to the national life of the movement in which they were engaged. Apparently, they thought of their noonday gatherings merely as a means whereby they themselves might be strengthened in religious faith and endowed with renewed spiritual fervour. Evidently, they did not understand that their aspirations were but a part of a religious awakening which was preparing for the mighty conflagration that was to purge the nation of its "sum of all villainies"—the traffic in human slaves. Day after day the noon meetings continued. Soon the room in which they were held was overtaxed. Overflow meetings were arranged. Civic issues were not specially discussed. The slavery question received the same casual consideration as the tariff and the currency. These business men simply besought the throne of grace for help—for the need they felt of the refining fire in their own hearts. Their cry was that of the ancient prophet: "Wilt

Thou not revive us again, that Thy people may rejoice in Thee?"

But a humble lawyer out in the Middle West was seeing farther into the future, lifting up a moral standard to which, as Washington had said before, "the wise and honest could repair," saturating public matters with a spirituality of which no one had perceived that there was need. Deep was calling unto deep. Fire was running to meet fire. Quietly started in New York, the spiritual flame was sweeping from house to house, from church to church, from city to city, from state to state, from ocean unto ocean, gathering in force, augmenting in influence, growing irresistible. Multitudes who knew not God through a vital religious faith joined in the new evangel. Employers excused their employees at early hours that they might attend the meetings; merchants urged their clerks to go; professional men sent their office forces; parents urged their children; colleges and day schools sent their pupils. The churches of all denominations were quickened, from the fervid Methodists to the more formal Episcopalians. Men of all creeds, and many of no creed, joined in the holy propaganda, and with intensified faith and quickened zeal, marched to the inspiring music that had touched the soul of nation and of individual alike and issued the Divine command not to be disobeyed by any soul: "Call nothing common or unclean."

It was out on the prairies of the West that the fire which burns only to refine was sweeping without let or hindrance over human souls. The itinerant preacher who had sometimes in discouragement ridden season after season through the trackless forest, over the still uncharted prairies, was now beginning to see the travail of his soul and reaping satisfaction. The revival of 1857–59 was sensitizing and sharpening the personal conscience of the people as no one could deny and making them to realize the meaning of the words of Emerson: "No greater calamity can befall a nation than the loss of worship." Worship was re-instated; the voice of prayer was heard throughout the land; men called upon God, and He answered, confessed that they were sinners, and He forgave. They acknowledged their heart wanderings and remissness, and He had mercy on them. He put grace into their hearts and a new song on their lips.

It was to hearts now at last awake to spiritual truth that the pioneer preachers appealed as they travelled their circuits and thundered in Buchanan's days against the institution of slavery. They minced no words. They prophesied no

"smooth things." They were warriors, fighting
with their might "the devil and all his works."
When they thought a thing was wrong they denounced it. No rich man in the pew could muzzle
them. Mercenary motives were not theirs. They
were feeders, not fleecers, of their flocks. Through
forests they rode without fear, braving the dangers of swollen streams, tempests, wild beasts, and
savage Indians. They kept step with the Almighty as they wended their way from appointment to appointment, spreading the glad news of
redemption. They scorned the wrath of man.
Peter Akers-like, they held slavery up to view in
the fulness of its gross iniquity. They prophesied
its extinction through the crisis of civil war. They
denounced it as a crime. They called upon the
people to help God sweep it from the land. "Ye
shall know the truth, and the truth shall make you
free," was the burden of their theme, even before
the revival of 1857–59 had ensured the harvest
they had sowed. The work they did in preparation for the cosmic work of Lincoln has never been
appreciated. It is beyond all human estimation.

Who can know what would have ensued when
the shock came of the Civil War but for this
spiritual awakening? There are always those who
say God would have found some other way. But

who that reads history aright can find one instance of an epochal civic regeneration that was not ushered in by a thoroughgoing, heart-stirring religious revival? At any rate, back of Abraham Lincoln was the revival of 1857–59, awakening national conscience, preparing the way for the crisis of 1860, and thus ensuring permanency to the principle of popular government.

What a drama! All unconsciously the actors played their parts. A continent for a stage, acres fertile enough to feed the world, a soil underlaid with boundless stores of mineral wealth, refreshed with rivers like inland lakes and beautified with lakes like rolling seas. For *dramatis personæ:*— money-grabber, personifying sordid commercialism, pushing property rights to the front and human rights into the background; the slave-driver, whip in hand; the crouching negro, driven to his task; the preacher of righteousness, the evangel of freedom; Abraham Lincoln, the impersonation of benign fate, the soul of freedom, the champion of popular government, the man of God. Above all and behind all, "standeth God within the shadow keeping watch above His own," and ruling the mighty drama which, for the freedom and salvation of a world, "He doth Himself contrive, enact, behold."

CHAPTER XX

ON THE WAY IN PRAYER

LINCOLN'S face was now turned toward Washington, where the storm of an incomparable civil strife was soon to beat upon him.

The essential humility of his Christian character found remarkable expression in his farewell speech to his neighbours when about to leave his Springfield home for Washington. He spoke as simply as neighbours speak together over the back fence. None who knew him well could doubt his full appreciation of the magnitude of the task he was about to undertake. At the same time, it was a revelation of his dependence upon God and of his apprehension of the tragedy awaiting him, as indicated by the suggestion that he might never return to them. From the platform of the car he looked for a moment out upon the multitude of sad faces upturned to hear his parting word. Then with hat in hand and gravity upon his sympathetic face he said:

My friends, no one not in my situation can appreciate my feeling of sadness at this parting. To this place and the kindness of this people, I owe everything. Here have I lived a quarter of a century and have passed from a young to an old man. Here my children have been born and one is buried. I now leave, not knowing when or whether ever I may return, with a task before me greater than that which rested upon Washington. Without the assistance of that Divine Being Who ever attended him, I cannot succeed. With that assistance, I cannot fail. Trusting in Him Who can go with me and remain with you and be everywhere for good, let us confidently hope that all will yet be well. To His care commending you, as I hope in your prayers you will commend me, I bid you an affectionate farewell.

While Mr. Lincoln had had some experience in public life, he was without experience in executive office. He was a country lawyer, comparatively unlettered. His association was scant with scholars and statesmen. He knew next to nothing of polite society. His outlook upon life had been from the prairie village and in the main from more than humble surroundings. His confident assumption of a task more difficult than that which had devolved upon Washington was naturally criticized by those antagonistic to his policies. They could not discern his God-given mission. He declared he would succeed only if guided and sup-

ported by the Omniscient mind and the Almighty
arm. By faith, he knew that, with God's help,
he could not fail. It was the same prophetic insight that led him to say to his partner, Herndon,
when they were taking a last look at the office in
which they had worked together so many years,
that he had an instinctive feeling that he would
never return alive.

His feeling of reliance upon Divine aid was
doubtless quickened by the flag which the martyred McKinley said was sent to Lincoln the day
before his departure from Springfield, bearing
upon its silken folds an inscription from the first
chapter of Joshua: "Have I not commanded thee?
Be strong and of good courage, be not afraid,
neither be thou dismayed; for the Lord thy God
is with thee, whithersoever thou goest. There
shall not any man be able to stand before thee all
the days of thy life. As I was with Moses, so
shall I be with thee."

As Lincoln journeyed from Illinois across the
country, he declared all along the route that he
was going forth in the name of the Living God of
Israel. At every railway station the sympathetic,
anxious people in great crowds pleaded that he
speak to them. He always complied, and in every
speech he called upon the people to look to God

for help in that time of peril.   No honest man can follow Lincoln on his trip to Washington, read the speeches he made all along the way, and doubt that he was a God-fearing and God-trusting man. Not even Moses praying, "If Thy presence go not with us carry me not up hence," seemed more dependent in the wilderness on God than Lincoln as he slowly journeyed on to Washington.   At Columbus, Ohio, he said:

I know what you all know, that without a name, perhaps without a reason why I should have a name, there has fallen upon me a task such as did not rest even upon the father of his country.   And so feeling, I turn and look for the support without which it would be impossible for me to perform that great task.   I turn, then, and look to the great American people, and to the God Who has never forsaken them.   We entertain different views upon political questions, but none is suffering anything.   This is a most consoling circumstance, and from it we may conclude that all we need is time, patience, and reliance upon that God Who has never forsaken His people.

To the people of Indianapolis he said:

When the people rise in mass, in behalf of the Union and the liberties of the country, then "the gates of hell cannot prevail against them."

Speaking before the Legislature of New York, Mr. Lincoln assured that body:

In the meantime, if we have patience, if we restrain ourselves, if we allow ourselves not to run off in a passion, we still have confidence that the Almighty, the Maker of the universe, will, through the instrumentality of this great and intelligent people, bring us through this as He has other difficulties of our country. Relying on this, I again thank you for this generous reception.

At Newark, New Jersey, the President-elect said:

I am sure, however, that I have not the ability to do anything unaided by God, and that without His support and that of a free, happy, prosperous, and intelligent people, no man can succeed in doing that the importance of which we all comprehend.

At Trenton, Mr. Lincoln declared:

I shall be most happy indeed, if I shall be a humble instrument in the hands of the Almighty and of this people, as the chosen instrument also in the hands of the Almighty, of perpetuating the object of that great struggle.

At Philadelphia, Lincoln gave utterance to these golden words, suitable as an epitaph to the noblest of God's noblemen:

I have said nothing but that I am willing to live by, and if it be the pleasure of Almighty God, to die by.

Already had been heard mutterings of veiled threats to the effect that Lincoln would not be permitted to reach the Capital alive. So alarming, and so circumstantial, were the reports that Allan W. Pinkerton, the noted detective, was permitted to arrange secretly for a change of programme by which Mr. Lincoln was hurriedly taken from Harrisburg, through Baltimore, to Washington.

Leaving these expressions of confidence in God and devotion to duty to work in the hearts of the multitudes who had heard them on the way, and through them in the hearts of all loyal people of the nation, Abraham Lincoln, after a journey replete with thrilling incidents and threatened tragedy, twelve hours ahead of schedule time, entered the Capital of the nation.

CHAPTER XXI

THE PARTING OF THE ROADS

IN the spirit of reliance on God, breathed by
Lincoln in his Springfield farewell speech, and with
the same devout dependence upon the Almighty,
repeatedly expressed as he travelled to the national
Capital, he arose to deliver his first Inaugural
Address, for which the whole country—the
civilized world, in fact—waited with bated breath.
For that supreme moment he had ample spiritual
as well as intellectual preparation. After reading
the Address that morning to his family he had
sought in prayer the will of God and went forth
from the closet of devotion calmed by communion
with his Heavenly Father.[1]

The devotees of slavery hooted his election, cari-
catured his physical appearance, derided his lowly
birth, impugned his motives, and were at that very
moment plotting, as they had plotted for months,
even years, to destroy the Government consecrated
by the blood of the Revolutionary fathers.

[1] *See* Letter of Rev. N. W. Miner in Lincoln's Scrapbook in
the Library of Congress, p. 52

Who, born of woman, has ever rivalled the wonderful patience and fraternal love that Lincoln evinced for all his countrymen, North and South, by his expressions of friendship, even for those who were berating him, in the closing words of his Inaugural Address.

In your hands, my dissatisfied fellow-countrymen, and not in mine, are the momentous issues of the Civil War. The Government will not assail you. You have no conflict without being yourselves the aggressors. You have no oath registered in Heaven to destroy the Government, while I have the most solemn one to preserve, protect, and defend it. I am loath to close. We are not enemies, but friends. We must not be enemies. Though passion may have strained, it must not break, the bonds of affection. The mystic chords of memory, stretching from every patriotic grave to every living heart and hearth-stone all over this broad land, will yet swell the chorus of the Union when again touched, as surely they will be, by the better angels of our nature.

Mr. Lincoln began at once to construct his administration upon the principles of the Christian religion, and to conduct it in the spirit of obedience to God's Word and love for his fellow-man, of whatever state or station. In forming his cabinet, he invited William H. Seward, his chief competitor for the nomination, to be his Secretary of State;

Simon Cameron to be Secretary of War; Salmon P. Chase to be Secretary of the Treasury; Gideon Wells to be Secretary of the Navy; Caleb C. Smith to be Secretary of the Interior; Montgomery Blair to be Postmaster-General; and Edward Bates to be Attorney-General. When some of Lincoln's friends remonstrated with him as not treating his political followers fairly in rewarding those who sought to take the Presidential nomination away from him, he said both to these protesting friends and to some of the prospective members of the Cabinet:

Gentlemen, the times are too grave and perilous for ambitious schemes and personal rivalries. I need the aid of all these men. They enjoy the confidence of their several States and sections, and they will strengthen the administration.

Appealing to some of them, he further said:

It will require the utmost skill, influence, and sagacity for all of us to save the Republic. If we succeed, there will be glory enough for all.

Mr. Lincoln's trust in God was not a mere passive faith. It was a faith of energetic action. He immediately laid his plans to set in motion every possible force and agency to save the Union. There is little doubt that by the time he had been

12

inducted into the office of President he was fully convinced that civil war was inevitable; but he did his utmost to allay passions and to secure the moderation of the hotheads. In justice to the South, it must be said that, had the wiser counsels of some of the Southern anti-secessionists been followed, and the extremists kept under control, Lincoln would probably have found some way to avoid the terrible struggle that began with the firing on Fort Sumter, and ended only when almost a million men had laid down their lives. When the South made the fatal mistake of forcing war upon the nation, its leaders failed to estimate the stubborn strength of Abraham Lincoln and his masterly ability in statecraft.

Some prominent men of the North made the same mistake in their judgment of Lincoln. They thought of him as a plebeian, a man of too common clay to be equal to the tremendous demands imposed upon him. Although they believed in the theory of a democratic form of government and popular rule, with its corollary of citizen-kingship for the humblest among the people, they feared to put popular government to the test in such a crucial moment. They regarded Mr. Lincoln's election as a risk, as they had regarded his nomination as a mistake.

The Southern leaders apparently believed that they could play a game of bluff sufficiently menacing to cause the North to back down and grant to the slave States the concessions they demanded.

Former President Pierce wrote to Jefferson Davis, January 6, 1860, saying:

If through the madness of Northern Abolitionists, that dire calamity, the disruption of the Union must come, the fighting will not be along the Mason's and Dixon's line merely, it will be within our own borders, in our own streets, between the two classes of citizens to whom I have referred; those who defy the law and scout Constitutional obligation will, if we ever reach the arbitrament of arms, find occupation enough at home.

It is almost unbelievable in these days, with the issues of the Civil War so clearly understood, that one who had been President of the United States should have ever penned a letter so lacking in grasp of the significance of events and so blind to the mighty and eternal forces that were back of the conflict.

Stephen A. Douglas, Benjamin F. Butler, and other contemporaries among the leading men of the country, knew that the fight was to be to the death and rallied loyally to the support of the Union. Mr. Butler went to Washington, consulted with

his former associates among the Democratic
Senators and Representatives, who said: "It
means a separation and a Southern Confederacy.
We will have our independence and establish a
Southern government with no discordant elements." "Are you prepared for war?" asked
Mr. Butler. The reply was: "O, there will be no
war; the North will not fight." "The North will
fight," answered Butler. "The North will send
the last man and expend the last dollar to maintain the Government." "But," said the Southern friend, "the North cannot fight. We have
too many allies there." "You have friends,"
Butler replied, "who will stand by you so long as
you fight your battles in the Union; but the moment you fire upon the flag the Northern people
will be a unit; and you may be sure that if war
comes, slavery ends."

Wrong as Douglas had been on the slavery
question, and opposing the logic of the events of
his times, as in his debates with Lincoln, and
advocating the Missouri Compromise and States
Rights without let or hindrance on the slavery issue, nevertheless he acquitted himself nobly when
war drew near. Having informed the country
where he stood, by an interview which he gave
out through one of the great news agencies, he

started for Illinois to stir up sentiment for the
preservation of the Union, and to impress the citizens of his State with the peril of the situation. En
route, he spoke at Wheeling, West Virginia, and in
Columbus, Ohio. Reaching Springfield, the centre
of the Lincoln–Douglas debates, he made a speech
before the Illinois Legislature great alike in its
magnanimity, after his own life—defeat and utter
repudiation by both the Northern anti-slavery
party and the Southern pro-slavery party, and
in its structure and meaning. Among the abounding epigrams of this speech were:

"So long as there was hope of a peaceful solution I
prayed and implored for compromise. I have spared
no effort for the peaceful solution of these troubles. I
have failed, and there is but one thing to do, to rally
under the flag."

"Shall we obey the laws, or shall we adopt the
Mexican system of warring on every election?" "Forget party. Remember only your country." "The
shortest road to peace is the most tremendous preparation for war." It is with a sad heart, and with grief I
have never before experienced, that I have to con-
template this fearful struggle." "It is our duty to
protect the government and the flag from every
assailant, be who he may."

Mr. Douglas returned to his home in Chicago
and repeated his appeal in the Wigwam where

Lincoln had been nominated. He referred to the conditions in the South, resulting from a conspiracy to "wipe the United States from the face of the earth," and said the conspiracy had been hatching for years. His last slogan was one worthy of his eloquence and prominence: "There can be no neutrals in this war, only patriots and traitors."

The seceding States organized a government with Jefferson Davis, of Mississippi, as President, and Alexander H. Stephens, of Georgia, as Vice-President. Davis had been educated at West Point, and was Secretary of War under President Pierce. Stephens was the ablest of the Southern leaders. He was, at first, against secession—as, indeed, were many other wise Southerners—but when the Confederate government had been formed, he laid down, in an address before the Georgia Legislature, the "moral basis of the so-called Confederacy."

Our new government is founded upon exactly the opposite ideas, [he declared]. Its foundations are laid, its cornerstone rests upon the great truth that the negro is not equal to the white man, that slavery, subordination to the superior race, is his natural and normal condition. This, our new government, is the first in the history of the world founded upon this great physical, philosophic, and moral truth. This truth has been slow in the process of its development, like all other great truths in the various departments of science. It is even so amongst us. Many who hear me, perhaps, can recollect well that this truth was not generally admitted even within our day. The errors of the past generation still clung to many as late as twenty years ago. Those at the North, who still cling to these errors with a zeal above knowledge, we justly denominate fanatics. All fanaticism springs from an aberration of mind, from a defect in reasoning. It is a species of insanity.

Of the sincerity of Alexander H. Stephens there can be no doubt. He was typical of the finest brain and heart in the South. He was conscientious in his conviction that slavery was indeed a divine institution. He believed that God had planned from the beginning the separation of the sons of men into wandering tribes, later into races, to evolve diverse tongues and customs and physical characteristics; that in the divine plan it was decreed that the black man was formed to fit into the scheme of slavery; that his mental traits were suited to it· and that his emotional nature was such as to make him happy and content as a bondman, his whole being attuned to sing the songs of the plantation in the spirit of loyalty to "Ole Marse an' Missus."

Here was a moral attitude to which Lincoln had referred in his Cooper Institute address when he said:

All they ask we could readily grant, if we thought slavery right; all we ask they could readily grant if they thought it wrong. Their thinking it right and our thinking it wrong is the precise fact upon which depends the whole controversy. Thinking it right as they do, they are not to blame for desiring its full recognition as being right; but thinking it wrong as we do, can we yield to them, can we cast our votes with their views and against our own? In view of our moral, social, and political responsibilities, can we do this?

It was the joining of the issue between these two forces—one represented by Lincoln, the other by Stephens—which made the struggle of the Civil War so terrible. Each was conscientious; each believed his cause right; each had approached the crisis by evolutionary stages. Slowly the issue had developed, until from the human standpoint, nothing could have obviated or postponed the clash and carnage of war. Perhaps no one was more thoroughly informed upon the issue involved than Lincoln. He was familiar with every aspect of the slavery question. His grandfather had been a slave owner, and he was born into the atmosphere of slavery. As a lad, like all Southern white boys, he played with the "Pickaninnies," knew the tenderness and devotion of the negro "Mammy," as well as the proverbial patience and the sage wisdom of the coloured "Uncle." It is even hinted by biographers that Lincoln's father left Kentucky for Indiana partly because he could never be anything more than "poor white trash," if he wrought on his farm with his own hands without the help of slaves. He had nothing with which to buy slaves, and there was no prospect of material improvement in his financial condition.

However that may be, it is certain that Abraham Lincoln knew the South, its traditions, its social fabric, and understood the peculiar difficulties which Southern men of heart and conscience had to face. Therefore it was that he proposed the gradual emancipation of the slaves, and that the Federal Government appropriate money to reimburse the holders of the slaves, and thus carry the South through its period of change rather than suddenly break up its social-industrial system.

President Lincoln cherished this plan for many months after entering the White House. He discussed it with his Cabinet, with other men of prominence, and argued for it as the one measure that would accomplish what he believed was right, namely, the freedom of the black man, while maintaining fair dealing with the slave owner. In other words, it would be but justice, which was, to his thought, the very essence of Christianity.

Emancipation by purchase, however, was not possible. Passion was at such height that the North was not willing to acknowledge any element of justice in Mr. Lincoln's proposal. The people of the North refused to concede that slavery had become a national, rather than a sectional sin. Mr. Lincoln's plan for the peaceable adjustment of the slavery question failed because the point had been reached at which inflamed passions would not listen to counsels of moderation.

The Southern States, by resolutions of secession, had determined to depart from the Union. But from Mr. Lincoln's point of view, their resolutions were void, as every State was an integral part of the Union, and had no power to separate from it. There was even more than that in Mr. Lincoln's view of the Union. He, and other statesmen, believed that the United States was so far from being a confederacy that it was not competent to discuss the departure of one of the States; that the Union which, after the failure of the association of the Colonies under the Articles of Confederation, had been made so absolute that to consider seriously the departure of one of the States, was to endanger the integrity of the entire governmental structure.

The opposite view in the South was that each

State maintained its autonomy, was only one of several States which had voluntarily entered the Union, and had the right at any time to go out and remain an independent sovereignty, or join with other States in the formation of a new confederacy. With the hotheads on both sides in the ascendancy, the war was inevitable. As Seward had declared, it was "an irrepressible conflict."

On April 15, 1861, President Lincoln issued a proclamation calling a special meeting of Congress, in which he referred to the secession movement in the slave States of South Carolina, Georgia, Alabama, Mississippi, Florida, Louisiana, and Texas, announcing that he had called out seventy-five thousand militia from the several States to maintain order and enforce the Federal laws, and summoned Congress to take such measures as "in their wisdom the public safety and interest may seem to demand."

Forsythe, of Alabama, and Crawford, of Georgia, had gone to Washington, March 12th, as commissioners from the seven seceding States to treat with the Federal Government. By Mr. Lincoln's direction, Mr. Seward, Secretary of State, refused to receive them, on the ground, as Mr. Lincoln stated, that it "could not be admitted that the States referred to had in law or fact withdrawn." Mr. Seward's communication was written March 15th, but was withheld from publication until the 8th of April, when it was delivered. The issue was now joined. The refusal of the Secretary of State to receive the distinguished commissioners of the South was something in itself not calculated to pacify the ruffled feelings of the boasted chivalry of the slave States.

Lincoln directed that provisions and munitions be forwarded to Fort Sumter, in Charleston Harbor. General Beauregard, of the Confederate Army, telegraphed the Confederate Secretary of War that he had been notified that the supplies would be sent, either peaceably, or by force. Beauregard was instructed to demand the surrender of the fort, which he did on April 11, 1861. The demand was refused by Major Anderson, in command. Negotiations followed, and Major Anderson finally agreed to evacuate the fort by noon April 15th. Beauregard had demanded the evacuation by the 12th, and now notified Major Anderson at half past three, April 12th, that the Confederate batteries would open fire in an hour from that moment.

The war was on. A bombardment of thirty-three hours followed, every shot resounding through the land. The question whether or

not there was to be war was answered; there
was war.

The South sprang quickly to the support of the
seven seceding States. Other States which had
refused to join the movement now passed ordinances of secession and threw their resources
into the Southern cause. With equal promptness
the North responded to the call to arms, ninety-
five per cent. of the people above Mason's and
Dixon's line endorsing Lincoln's call. The issues
that had disturbed the country so long were now
to be decided by the fearful arbitrament of a
fratricidal war.

With brother arrayed against brother, with
hatred swelling into rage, Mr. Lincoln still manifested his reliance upon the Almighty and encouraged his fellow-citizens to face the situation
with stout hearts because God was with the
Union. Mr. Lincoln, in his message to Congress,
met again in special session July 4, 1861, after out-
lining the course the Government should pursue,
said:

And having thus chosen our course, without guile
and with pure purpose, let us renew our trust in God
and go forward, without fear, and with manly hearts.

CHAPTER XXII

THE ENCIRCLING GLOOM

AMID the multiplying difficulties and discouragements Mr. Lincoln encountered in his purpose to preserve the Union, his faith in God never wavered. Indeed, it seemed to strengthen with the increasing weight of the burden under which he laboured. In his first message to Congress, December 3, 1861, he said:

In the midst of unprecedented political troubles, we have cause of great gratitude to God for unusual good health and most abundant harvests.

He closed his message with these trustful words:

The struggle of today is not altogether for today. It is for a vast future, also. With a reliance upon Providence all the more firm and earnest, let us proceed with the great task which events have evolved upon us.

In his message to Congress, December 1, 1862, he declared:

Since your last annual assembling, another year of health and bountiful harvest has passed, and while it has not pleased the Almighty to bless us with the return of peace, we can but press on, guided by the best lights He gives us, trusting that in His own good time and wise way, all will be well.

He closed the same message with this high appeal to patriotism, humanity, and religion:

Fellow-citizens, we cannot escape history. We of this Congress, and of this administration, will be remembered in spite of ourselves. No personal significance or insignificance can spare one or another of us. The fiery trial through which we pass will light us down with honour or dishonour, to the latest generation. We say we are for the Union. The world will not forget that we say this. We know how to save the Union. The world knows we know how to save it. We, even we here, hold the power and bear the responsibility. In giving freedom to the slave, we assure freedom to the free. Honourable alike in what we give and what we preserve, we shall nobly save or meanly lose the last best hope of earth.

Then, referring to his proposed offer of compensated emancipation which he was willing, even then, to tender to the Southern slave owners, he added: "The way is plain, peaceful, generous, just, a way which, if followed, the world will for ever applaud and God must for ever bless."   Lincoln longed for a righteous peace. Knowing the havoc and horror, the barbarism and waste of war, he exhausted every agency at his command in an effort to obviate such an unspeakable calamity. He counted the money that compensated emancipation would cost as nothing, if it would but stop the effusion of blood and save the Union; but it seemed that God hardened the hearts of the slave owners, as He did the heart of Pharaoh, who refused to let the people of Israel go. The bloody work had to go on until, to use Lincoln's words in another utterance, "every drop of blood shed by the lash" was "paid by another drawn by the sword."

The difficulties which beset the Lincoln administration arising from the jealousy or unfriendliness of the foreign powers were, perhaps, the most perplexing and the most menacing. They added to Lincoln's burden of anxiety at a time when, through reverses to the Union Army, his spirits were sorely depressed. During the latter part of 1862, and early in 1863, one general after another, whom he had placed in command of the Army of the Potomac, failed to win conclusive victories against the enemy. Frightful losses were suffered by the Union troops, which sent a wave of discouragement over the loyal section of the country, while there were unfriendly verdicts at the polls which sent the iron into Lincoln's soul.

Fighting for the extension of human freedom, Lincoln must have been deeply grieved by the attitude of such enlightened statesmen as William Ewart Gladstone and Lord John Russell. England's boast had been that when a slave set his foot upon her soil his fetters fell off, perforce, through the spirit of liberty abiding there. Therefore, Lincoln looked to England for sympathy in a struggle which meant, as any intelligent man could see, the establishment and maintenance of freedom if the Union were preserved. And yet, even from the beginning of the Rebellion, the conclusion could not be avoided that the sympathies of the ruling British statesmen of the time were with the Southern Confederacy. Gladstone declared that Jefferson Davis had "founded a nation." Lord Russell used his influence at all times to promote schemes of intervention, ostensibly in the name of peace, but really to assure the division of the American Republic into two hostile governments. The moneyed classes of England, whose business suffered and whose incomes were curtailed because of the war, were plainly against the North from the start. To them, the supply of cotton was more important than the life of a great nation speaking the same language and cherishing similar institutions and traditions.

Slavery was the blot upon the principles of Magna Charta, which were incorporated into our fundamental law. The triumph of the Union promised to erase this blot, while the triumph of the Rebellion would have deepened and extended it. It was political jealousy and sordid commercialism that arrayed the dominant classes of England against the North. It is, however, to the credit of the common people of England that, although many of them were thrown out of employment and reduced to direful straits for the want of cotton to supply their mills, they, for the most part, stood by the cause of freedom in America.

When Henry Ward Beecher was sent over to England to stem the tide of adverse opinion, the effect of his splendid oratory upon the masses was so great that the sinister designs of the British Government were checked. At first Mr. Beecher encountered much hostility. In addressing a mass meeting in Exeter Hall, Manchester, he stood for thirty minutes, unawed and unmoved in the face of a howling mob. Finally, when order was partially restored, one of the angry throng shouted:

"Why haven't you Yankees put down the Rebellion in sixty days, as you said you would?" To which Mr. Beecher flashed back the answer: "Because we are fighting Americans, and not Britishers."

Henry Ward Beecher was an intimate friend and adviser of Abraham Lincoln, though, while editor of *The Independent*, he severely criticized some measures of Lincoln's administration. His visit to England did much to arouse the sympathies of the English masses in favour of the Union and freedom as against secession and slavery. His lecture tour of the British Isles wielded an immeasurable influence in behalf of the cause for which he spoke, and deserves to be listed as one of the most potent forces exerted abroad for the preservation of the American Union. His magnetism and skill as an orator, and his known devotion to the cause of anti-slavery, gave him authoritative utterance, which was heard throughout England and felt throughout the civilized world.

There is reason to believe that the sympathy of Queen Victoria and her noble husband were with the North, even when her ministers were hostile. It was largely owing to the influence of the Queen and her Consort, that the British Government did not officially recognize the Southern Confederacy. Nevertheless, the British Government aided and abetted the Rebellion by permitting Confederate cruisers to arm in their harbours and go forth to prey upon American commerce.

Among the bitterest enemies of the American Union at that time was Napoleon III, Emperor of the French. He had ambitions for the restoration of French influence in America that had been lost in the conquest of Canada by England, and by the cession of the vast Louisiana Territory to the United States by the first Napoleon. While the Emperor did not expect to regain these lost possessions, his ambition seems to have been to overthrow the Mexican Republic and erect on its ruins a monarchy to be ruled by some European royal personage of his own selection. That accomplished, the next step was to have been the annexation of Mexico to France, or at least its domination by France.

But Napoleon III knew that the American Union, undivided, rendered his ambitious scheme impossible. He, therefore, laboured incessantly through the earlier years of the war to induce the other European powers to join him in intervention, or in the recognition of the Southern Confederacy as an independent nation. Fearing the success of the Union cause, Napoleon, in 1862, invited the governments of England and Russia to enter with France into a joint proposition to the United States for mediation between the National Government and the seceders. By the direction of President Lincoln, the Secretary of State instructed all representatives and ministers of the United States abroad to make known the fact that such suggestions from foreign powers could neither be received nor discussed. Nevertheless, the French Government pressed the point, and desisted only when the English and Russian governments, convinced of the firm attitude of President Lincoln and Secretary Seward, rejected the Emperor's overtures.

The Emperor, notwithstanding the failure of his efforts for joint mediation, did not abandon his scheme. He felt that his own situation in regard to Mexico was desperate if he could not either conciliate the United States or destroy its formidable power. He, therefore, caused his Minister Drouyn de l'Huys to address a dispatch to Monsieur Mercier, the French Ambassador at Washington, under date of January 9, 1863, suggesting a conference between Commissioners of the United States and of the Confederacy, with a view to the settlement of the questions at issue by compromise.

This overture reached the President on February 3, 1863. It was immediately following the terrible disaster to the Union forces at Fredericksburg, and preceding the disheartening calamity at Chancellorsville. All the great European Powers, except Russia, had assumed an attitude of veiled hostility, although they halted at direct intervention. The insidious suggestion came at the darkest hour of the Civil War, and a weak and timid administration might have been tempted to listen to the Emperor's wily proposal as a way out of a hopeless tangle of difficulties. But Lincoln saw that to yield to the plan would be a virtual surrender of the national authority.

Lincoln and his Cabinet were moved by this unfriendly suggestion no more than they had been by previous hints at active interference. Secretary Seward, following the direction of his Chief, denied in reply that his government was at all disappointed. He declared that it was bearing itself cheerfully in all vicissitudes, in unwavering confidence of an early and complete triumph of the national cause. He pointed out that, amid the alternation of victories and defeats, the land and naval forces of the United States had steadily advanced, reclaiming from the insurgents the forts and other strategic points that had been treacher-

ously seized before hostilities actually began, that
much of the territory included by the insurgents
in their projected exclusive slaveholding dominions
had already been re-established under the flag of
the Union, that the rebels retained entire only the
States of Georgia, Alabama, and Texas, half of
Virginia, North Carolina, and Mississippi, two
thirds of South Carolina, and one third of
Arkansas and Louisiana.   Continuing, he said:

The national forces hold even this small territory
in close blockade and siege.   This government, if required, does not hesitate to submit its achievements
to the test of comparison, and it maintains that in no
part of the world and in no time, ancient or modern,
has a nation, when rendered all unready for combat
by the enjoyment of almost eighty years of unbroken
peace, so quickly awakened to the alarm of sedition,
put forth energies so vigorous and achieved success so
signal and effective as those which have marked the
progress of this combat on the part of the Union.[1]

The firmness of Lincoln, his confidence, and hope-
fulness when the outlook was darkest, his sublime
faith in the ultimate triumph of righteousness, had
their inspiration in his unwavering reliance upon
an over-ruling Providence.   His clinging faith
in the justice of Almighty God, and his habit of

[1] The Proclamation of March 30, 1863.

prayer, held him steadfast through the darkest hours of the momentous struggle. It was in fact the next month that Lincoln called the entire nation to join him in prayer to God for[1] "the restoration of our now divided and suffering country." Others far and near might waver and lose heart. Lincoln in the face of every difficulty steadily maintained: "If God is with us, we cannot fail."[2]

[1] The Proclamation of March 30, 1863.
[2] Nicolay and Hay: Vol. x, 149, footnote.

CHAPTER XXIII

THE FOUR LONG YEARS

STILL under the blight of the worst war the world has ever known it is difficult for us who live today to realize that Abraham Lincoln, through all those crucial years which we have been describing, was making ready for a task as much bigger than any which had gone before as the World War out-classes all other wars of history. The soul as well as mind had to be prepared; for they were brothers who fought against each other in the Civil War. Besides mental and military efficiency there were needful prayer and faith and love. Victory in arms had to be followed, if there was to be a re-united country, by Christian magnanimity.

It has been worth while to trace in some detail the spiritual growth of Lincoln, if only to realize that it took a man of God to keep through all those dreadful years a spirit sweet and wholesome, finding just before he died expression in his purpose: "to strive on to finish the work we are in; to bind up the nation's wounds; to care for him who shall have borne the battle; and for his widow and his orphan—to do all which may achieve and cherish a just and lasting peace among ourselves, and with all nations."

What was the work to which Lincoln brought in 1861 a soul as Christian as his mind was clear and fertile? In the actual service the one side had some 2,778,304 men; the other 700,000 men operating to advantage on interior lines and always near the base of their supplies. The North lost all told about 500,000 men. The Southern loss in its totality is more difficult to estimate, but was at least 133,821. The twenty-two States that proved loyal to the Union had a population of 22,000,000; the seceding States included 5,500,-000 whites and 4,600,000 blacks. Of her population the North furnished for potential use in the ranks 4,600,000 soldiers or 45 per cent. of her fighting population, the South 1,150,000 or 90 per cent. of her fighting men.[1] In material resources, manufactures, transportation facilities, the balance was favourable to the North. Precisely because of this preponderance of strength, the North had to be led by a man of God in order

[1] These statistics are in general familiar to students. The article in the *Encyclopedia Britannica* supplements them.

to win victories without bitterness; to reconstruct without retaliation.

Until the last Lincoln hoped that war might be averted or at least snuffed out at the beginning. But the shot fired on Sumter was heard in New England, which Butler had accurately predicted would be solid for the Union; in the Northwest, which the South was sure, against the facts, would be so slow in coming in at all that secession would meanwhile grow into a hard reality; even in California, which both North and South mistakenly believed would remain neutral. The Border States were naturally divided, but Lincoln's policy of firmness mingled with unbroken patience saved Delaware and Missouri outright, ensured the carving at the proper time of West Virginia out of old Virginia, and made Maryland and Kentucky minister with considerable consistency to the support of the undivided Union.

Before the war was three months old, Lincoln was able in sincerity and confidence to exhort: "Let us renew our trust in God and go forward, without fear, and with manly hearts." He called for 75,000 volunteers; almost four times as many answered, forerunners of the myriads later to respond: "We are coming, Father Abraham." The too hastily improvised battle of Bull Run turned into a disgraceful retreat back to Washington. But the first year ended with the North settling grimly down to the big work on land and sea, the 3000 miles of Southern coast in large part blockaded, Southern commerce strangled, save for isolated privateers, and Hatteras and Port Royal both in Northern hands.

With the opening of 1862 preparations began on a gigantic scale for the complete conquest of the South. On the one side McClellan and on the other Joseph E. Johnston were training to the finest point such fighting men as had never shed each other's blood before. Spring found Forts Henry and Donelson in the hands of Grant, and Shiloh, at first apparently a drawn battle, ended in the death of the gallant Albert Sidney Johnston and the headlong flight of Beauregard, still proudly mindful of Bull Run. Then Stonewall Jackson swept up the valley of Virginia, scattering on either hand Frémont, Banks, McDowell, making for himself a reputation to outlast all time, opening the way for the noble Lee to come into his own as Southern chief *par excellence*, and helping rob the painstaking McClellan of the golden fruits of what seemed for a time like victories, but turned to ashes in his hands as midsummer found him foiled in reaching Richmond, though this was his second trial.

For a time Tennessee appeared to be the centre of the war, and Rosecrans deserved the great victory he won at Corinth. Then as autumn opened, Pope and Buell were in ill-repute, and Lee, encouraged by his success at Second Bull Run, crossed over into Maryland, to be checked at Antietam by McClellan, and unwittingly to furnish the occasion Lincoln had awaited to announce the Emancipation Proclamation.

When the winter opened, the North began that general offensive which was maintained in spite of some reverses till the end of 1865. McClellan, curiously unable to use with despatch the magnificent army he had wonderfully trained, saw Lincoln, after quaintly suggesting he would like to borrow it, try man after man who could fight as well as plan and drill, march and countermarch. Burnside, excellent in charge of a division, lost Fredericksburg in December, and was replaced by Hooker, able but too talkative, who won no spurs the next spring at Chancellorsville, where Jackson got his mortal wound. With Lee well upon the way to water his horses in the Delaware, Lincoln sent the scholarly Meade to check him in July at Gettysburg, where, as at Antietam, the fatal failure to follow up Lee in retreat prolonged the war.

More and more the eyes of the observant were turned toward the Southwest where the silent Grant was not always winning victories as at Vicksburg, but never ceased to fight. He made the most of what he had. He never offered an excuse. He never talked. He fought. Gradually he won the complete confidence of Lincoln, who without underestimating the good work of Thomas and Rosecrans, both first-class fighting men, gave Grant supreme command in the West and finally, on March 9, 1864, placed him at the head of all the Union forces of the land.

The last year is a story quickly told. The month of May found Grant pressing back the enemy in the Wilderness. Beaten a month later at Cold Harbor, Grant fought on to Petersburg. Though not always winning victories, Grant wore Lee down by constant hammering, and put a chill into the Southern heart. Sheridan swept clean the Shenandoah Valley. Sherman brought to a successful end his campaign against Atlanta, and as the year closed, reached the sea. Grant was tightening his grip on Lee. The Southern star was fast declining. With scarcely any chance to make even a running fight, Lee at last with dignity laid down his arms at Appomattox, and on April 9, 1865, the war was near an end, with Lincoln giv-

ing God the glory and—as Justice Harlan says—
wearing a new "expression of serene joy, as if
conscious that the great purpose of his life had
been achieved."

CHAPTER XXIV

ARMS AND THE MAN

WITH the brief summary of the Civil War before us in the chapter which precedes this, it would seem worth while to observe Lincoln as month after month he dealt with some of the representative problems the War brought to him, sometimes in such complexity or massiveness as almost to break his spirit. But never quite; for Lincoln as perhaps no other man in history, save Cromwell, was "sustained and soothed by an unfaltering trust" in God and man alike.

The time has come not so much to contend for Lincoln's Christian faith as to portray it; not to attempt to prove by laws of logic Lincoln's confidence in that best in the average man which was never broken, as to flash a light along the way of those four years that will, with but little comment, show Lincoln in relationship with God and also with human beings, trusting them when they yielded to the worst, revealing to his associates traits in the mass of men they often doubted that

men had at all, even calling his erring brothers
in the South back to that normal relationship of
human fellowship in words in his first Inaugural
as true as they are tender:

We are not enemies but friends. We must not
be enemies. Though passion may have strained, it
must not break our bonds of affection.

There is one passage in the first Inaugural not
so well known as it ought to be; for it proves even
to the most reluctant that from the first Lincoln's
trust in God and trust in man went side by side
through all those years of bitter bloodshed: "If
the Almighty Ruler of Nations, with His eternal
truth and justice, be on your side of the North, or
on yours of the South, that truth and that justice
will surely prevail by the judgment of this great
tribunal of the American people."

The Battle of Bull Run was the first hard military test of Lincoln's twofold faith. The test was
not of his choosing. The South was farther on
in preparation for the war. Northern editors, in
fact Northern sentiment was clamouring for the
taking of Richmond and the immediate ending of
the war, not foreseeing that wars are not won by
the unprepared unless, like the Allies and America
in the World War, it is possible at first to fight

14

indeterminate battles while preparations are in steady progress for the final issue. The uninformed up North staked all on that one first big battle.

It was June of 1861. The Army of the Potomac was encamped on Arlington Heights in plain view of the Capitol shimmering in the radiant sunlight of the early summer. The White House was gleaming through the lovely foliage where the birds were still busy making nests. Within, the President was dealing with his usual despatch with the details the hour brought, while visitors were coming in and out with ordered regularity. From the observation balloon, hanging over the Potomac, the biggest army ever mustered on our soil was in plain sight. It was, however, only drilling. Neither in Washington nor near was excitement evident.

But as July came in, Beauregard was evidently massing his men at Bull Run, throwing up breastworks, cutting down trees, and disposing his army so as to await attack from McDowell leading the Northern troops. As the 21st drew near, the inevitable crash was the common talk in Washington. Victory seemed so sure to non-combatants that as McDowell moved forward he and his men were followed by the fashionable and curious,

eager to see the "Rebels" thrashed.   By the 21st
the shock of battle had begun.   The earth re-
sounded with such a crash of contending armies as
was plainly heard in Washington.   There was at
first confusion on both sides.   Regiments were
scattered.   Jackson got his prefix of "Stonewall"
because he seemed to be among the few who stood
steady.   Straggling and uneven lines proclaimed
the amateurishness of the fierce fighting.

The South, however, was clearly losing out.   Up
and down their lines the despairing note was
struck: "We are beaten."   The Southern regiments began to melt away.   The stream of fugi-
tives fled faster toward Manasses from the front.
Suddenly—even unexpectedly—Southern re-en-
forcements came by the thousands.   With a wild
yell they plunged, with flashing sabres, into the
very thick of the contest.   The Union forces
faltered, fell back, plunged in a mad, panic-
stricken rout toward Washington, trampling under
feet the heat-exhausted and footsore observers
who had paid their money to come out to see a
victory, not to be dust-choked that hot Sunday
in a disgraceful and disheartening defeat.

By midnight, horror-stricken, haggard, worn,
some of them arrived at the White House to explain.   All day long in prayer and meditation

Lincoln had been receiving the reports and was not unprepared for the outcome, which he accepted with fortitude and resignation.[1]

Now he was lying on his office sofa, listening to the tales of woe, estimating the result at its full value, unconvinced by the voluble and the incompetent that Bull Run after all was nothing but a panic of teamsters and sightseers. To one vindicator of the day he dryly answered: "Ah, I see, we whipped the enemy and then ran away."[2]

Lincoln was far more concerned to have the country recognize that war at last had come and that the country must stand by him, no matter what mistakes might be made by this man or that, no matter what reverses might occur; and that his fellow-countrymen should with him put their trust in God Almighty while they used their resources to the utmost in the winning of the war. The very next day after Bull Run he called McClellan, whose victories in what is now West Virginia had thrilled the country, to Washington, to take command of the demoralized remnant of Bull Run and wipe out the disgrace. Then a little later he called

[1] Mr. Henry C. Whitney in his *Life on the Circuit with Lincoln* says Lincoln's favourite prayer in many a crisis was the Gethsemane prayer of Jesus Christ: "Father if it be possible, let this cup pass from me."

[2] Tarbell, ii., 57.

the entire nation to its knees in prayer that "we
may be spared farther punishment, though most
justly deserved; that our arms may be blessed and
made effectual for the re-establishment of law,
order, and peace throughout the wide extent of
our country."

Already plain people were discovering the big
heart of the man.   He began to do his little nameless acts of kindness on the sly.   The boy who
came along on crutches was apt, if no one was
looking, to have a gold piece thrust into his hand.
The sad and troubled face Lincoln singled out of
every crowd and touched it with the finger-tip
of Christlike uplift and encouragement, and put
gladness in the place of gloom.   Before the year
was over people everywhere began to identify his
interests with their own, to think of his country as
their country, and to call him "Father Abraham."

When he wanted men upon the battlefield they
came because he called.   His war became at last
their war.   They fought for him as well as for home;
as many a Copperhead discovered to his discom-
fiture when—like the false king in *Hamlet*—he was
trying to pour poison into the ears of public opinion
which he thought was not awake.   Children as well
as adults would fight at a drop of the handkerchief
for the man in Washington who understood every-

one and interpreted to all their inmost feelings. *Who's Who* tells us that a now famous University President was ten years old when Lincoln was assassinated, and to one of his old students he once said: "The only fight I ever had in my boyhood was the morning word came of the killing of Mr. Lincoln. I was on my way to school, out in the Middle West. A bigger boy said, 'he was glad old Abe was dead.' I dropped my books and went for him and licked him, too, big as he was."

Already Lincoln was having troubles in the inner circle and dealing with them wisely, patiently, and with a Christlike spirit. What a bother Frémont was! He had been the idol of the North. No Presidential nominee except Blaine and Roosevelt has ever so awakened popular enthusiasm as Frémont awoke it in 1856. Lincoln's appointment of Frémont early in the war to command the Department of the West was the most popular he ever made. But Frémont was in almost every sense a failure. He did not know his place. He would take no hint to resign. Lincoln tried honestly to help him to make good, and when at last Frémont had to go, he showed a delicacy and a long-suffering so utterly misunderstood that Mrs. Frémont, the strong-minded daughter of Senator Benton, called on Lincoln at midnight with the threat that Frémont could set up—if he would—an independent government of his own.

McClellan was almost as difficult as Frémont. He could fight, but he never would unless he was quite sure that he would win; and even if he won as at Antietam, he was not apt to follow up and thus both lost the fruits and let the war drag on. Never was man's patience tried more than Lincoln's under the delays McClellan was habitually, confidently, egotistically explaining even in insulting terms to Lincoln. The contempt he showed for Lincoln everybody understood; but never once did Lincoln show resentment in return. He thought only of his country's welfare. He wanted not personal deference from McClellan; he wanted him to fight. "I will hold McClellan's horse if he will only bring us success," was the familiar summing up of Lincoln's Christian humility in all his dealings with McClellan.

Cameron violated the outstanding policy of the administration and naturally encouraged the arming of the slaves. But in removing him Lincoln, always fair, took the sting away by making him our Minister to Russia. Then in choosing Stanton for the place vacated, he picked a man who had humiliated him a while before and even after taking office rarely showed until the last the consideration one always owes to the chief who has made possible his elevation to high office. For Stanton's personal opinion of him, Lincoln cared nothing. The one fact ever in his mind was that Stanton was able and loyal to the cause, that the country trusted him, that he could and did administer the War Department with integrity and exceptional ability. Stanton might tell others Lincoln was a fool. Lincoln's comment waived aside all personal implications and kept the patriotic motive always actuating him in the foreground, once humorously saying: "Stanton is usually right."

The mistakes Lincoln made in his selection of assistants would have cost him his position had he not been chosen for a four years' term. Frémont had to go and then McClellan. The choice of the self-depreciating Burnside was a grave mistake as Fredericksburg made clear. Hooker had admirable qualities, but he indulged in ambitious dreams, reported to Lincoln, of becoming a dictator, and yet Lincoln appointed him only to see him fail at Chancellorsville as Meade later, after winning Gettysburg, let Lee slip through his hands and recoup himself for what then seemed an indefinite continuation of the war. Lincoln was simply feeling round for the right man at a time

when we had no training-school for big warfare
except war itself.   He never thought of anything
except the preservation of the Union.

But he always trusted God.   He never counted
himself sufficient for the gigantic tasks before him.
When men reported to him Chase's plots to get
into the White House, he amazed informants by
saying frankly that if Chase could do the "hard
job" better, and the people wanted Chase, he was
willing to give way to Chase.   His one concern
was to do God's work in God's own way, and never
in the Civil War was this more evident than when
the *Merrimac* seemed about to finish up its work
in Hampton Roads and then to steam up unhin-
dered to repeat the destruction which had earlier
overtaken Washington in the War of 1812.

The conflict had been dragging on for a whole
year.   The North with its wooden vessels still
had problems on the sea.   The Confederates
captured the *Merrimac* and then converted it into
the first ironclad in history.   The naval experts
around Lincoln were worried beyond self-control.
They foresaw her throwing shells into the White
House and battering down the walls of the Capitol.
Everybody lost his head but Lincoln, and his
reply comes ringing down the years: "The Almighty will prevent her.   This is God's fight.

You do not take into account our little *Monitor* and her commander. The *Monitor* should be in Hampton Roads now. She left New York eight days ago. She may be the little stone in the sling of Almighty God that shall smite the *Merrimac* Philistine in the forehead."[1]

The *Monitor* was. John Ericsson, her inventor, had months before won Lincoln's hearty approval of his plan. Naval experts were not sure. Built in New York, launched in undue haste, without a trial trip, the *Monitor* made her way to Hampton Roads slowly and with difficulty. Sunday morning, March 9, 1862, at two o'clock, she hove to beside the *Minnesota*, which the *Merrimac* after sinking the *Cumberland* and wrecking the *Congress* the day before, had badly damaged. At daybreak the *Merrimac*, all unsuspecting, came lumbering along to finish her fell work. A little speck emerged from out the shadow of the *Minnesota*, and the naval duel then began which closed one chapter and opened another in war on the sea. The story is familiar. The *Merrimac* now lost all power to alarm the North. The blockade of the Southern ports was ever afterwards effective and the real danger that Europe would recognize the Confederacy was forever gone. Some called it a coin-

[1] Crittenden's *Personal Recollections of Lincoln.*

cidence. Lincoln said outright "the *Monitor* was my inspiration." He was a simple Bible Christian. He read the Book constantly with Cruden's Concordance ever on his table to help him understand. He was not merely familiar with such stories as David and Goliath but he could repeat from memory whole chapters from the Psalms, Isaiah, and the New Testament.[1]

Mystic though he was, watchful for the hand of God at every turn of war, Lincoln used his native common sense, always consecrated to his country's welfare. Nothing could have been more clever than his handling of the case of Vallandigham. He sent him South to stop his mischief-making, at a time when the South no more wanted him than England wanted Benedict Arnold in the Revolution, and packed him off to Canada. When rumours came to Lincoln that Grant might possibly want the Presidential nomination in 1864, he was glad to get the word in exactly the right way that Grant wanted no change in the Executive. When in April, 1865, Jefferson Davis slipped away from Richmond and someone remarked to Lincoln that Davis should be hung, the President replied precisely, Charles Sumner says, as the Master would reply: "Judge not that ye be not judged."

[1] Trevena Jackson's *Lincoln's Use of the Bible.*

Some years before the war, Lincoln had known and admired the eloquent prairie preacher, Reverend James F. Jacquess. He regarded him as wise, sagacious, and "God-fearing." When in the Civil War Jacquess won both a Colonelcy, and from Rosecrans the remarkable tribute, "He is John Brown and Chevalier Bayard rolled into one," Colonel Jacquess suffered not in Lincoln's estimation. We have his story from the man who heard it in detail from James R. Gilmore, Jacquess' boon companion. As the Presidential campaign opened up in 1864, the Peace Party in the North was unwittingly strengthening the Southern cause and raising false hopes in the mind of Jefferson Davis. First with the approval, unofficial, of course, of Rosecrans, then of Lincoln, whose native shrewdness saw the point, Colonel Jacquess— later with Mr. Gilmore—went on a peace mission to Davis which, because Davis insisted on recognition of the independence of the South, when it was reported in the North, killed the Peace Party and re-elected Lincoln. Lincoln trusted Jacquess because he had been powerfully moved in earlier years by Jacquess' preaching. In fact, Jacquess, then an old man, told the Rev. E. L. Watson in Minneapolis in 1894, that Lincoln had been definitely converted to Christianity in 1846

in Jacquess' presence and repeated the story at a
reunion of the 73d Regiment of Illinois Infantry,
September, 1897, in Springfield.   Perhaps that is
why Lincoln said in letting Jacquess go on his
mission in 1864:

God selects His own instruments and sometimes
they are queer ones; for instance, He chose me to steer
the ship through a great crisis.

The test of man's belief in God is man's love for
his fellows.   "He that loveth not his brother
whom he hath seen, how can he love God whom he
hath not seen?"   Lincoln never had a more en-
gaging friend than Edward D. Baker.   Far back
in the forties they had become friends in the politics of Illinois.   Lincoln secured for Baker the
nomination for Congress in 1844.   Later Baker
became United States Senator from the new State
of Oregon and was one of the small group Lincoln
called into intimate consultation at Springfield,
after his nomination, for the Presidency.   As
Mr. Lincoln arose at the Inauguration exercises in
1860, his good friend, Senator Baker, introduced
him to the throng.

In a little while Baker exchanged the Senatorship for a Colonelcy in the army, and on October
21, 1861, he was killed at Ball's Bluff.   Charles

Carleton Coffin, who knew whereof he spoke, gave later his deliberate conviction that probably no other of "the many tragic events of President Lincoln's life ever stunned him like that un-heralded message which came over the wires on that mournful evening of October 21, 1861." As Mr. Lincoln left the room his head was bowed, the tears rolled down his furrowed cheeks, his breast heaved with emotion. As he stepped into the street, it looked for a moment as though he would collapse. With both hands pressed to his heart, he staggered on, not even returning the salute of the sentinel before the White House door. He interpreted the friendship of God in terms of human friendship. To be on terms of close friendship with God and man alike is to be the kind of Christian He pictured who once said: "Greater love hath no man than this that he lay down his life for his friend."

CHAPTER XXV

SIFTING THE EVIDENCE

THE charges by Col. W. H. Layman and supported to some extent by Judge William H. Herndon, were that Lincoln was in fact an infidel, and that, "in his morbid ambition for popularity, he played a sharp game on the Christian community by adjusting his religious sentiments to his political interests."

In 1873, the Rev. J. A. Reed, pastor at the time of the First Presbyterian Church at Springfield, Illinois, prepared a lecture refuting the charges of Colonel Layman and Judge Herndon. This lecture was published substantially as delivered, and repeated hundreds of times. No one has ever been able to controvert the evidence adduced by Dr. Reed touching the religious faith and character of Abraham Lincoln. In preparing his lecture Mr. Reed took the pains to procure letters from men who were quite as intimate with Lincoln as were Layman and Herndon. The world is indebted to Mr. Reed for his original research, made within the decade after Mr. Lincoln's death, when the facts were fresh in the minds of men then living.

Mr. Reed makes the point at the outset that even Layman admits that there did come a time in Mr. Lincoln's life at Springfield when, notwithstanding his alleged skepticism, he began to affiliate with Christian people and to give his personal presence and support to the church. Layman could account for this alleged change only by accusing Lincoln of double-dealing in regard to religion, a charge so at variance with Lincoln's well-known love of frankness and sincerity that it falls to the ground with its own weight of falsehood.

Layman and Herndon themselves are loud in their praise of Lincoln's singular conscientiousness and integrity. They seek to draw a line between the secular and the religious. They make him secularly a man almost perfect, yet capable of deceiving his friends by concealing from them his skepticism—which would have been hypocrisy. Judge Herndon writes:

Lincoln was justly entitled to the appellation "Honest Abe." Honesty was his pole star; conscience, the faculty that loves the just and right, was the second great quality and forte of Lincoln's character. He had a deep, broad, living conscience. His great reason told him what was true and good, right and wrong, just and unjust, and his conscience echoed back the decision, and it was from this point he spoke, and wove his character and fame among us.

Layman shows that Lincoln scorned everything deceitful, that he would not even undertake to plead a bad case before a jury. Layman quotes Lincoln's fellow-lawyers as saying that, for a man who was for a quarter of a century both a lawyer and a politician, Lincoln was the most honest man they had ever known; that he could not reason falsely; that if he attempted he failed; that in politics he would never try to mislead; and that, at the bar, when he thought he was wrong he was the weakest lawyer they ever knew. Therefore, the allegations that Abraham Lincoln practised deception in regard to his religious views have but to be stated to suggest their own refutation and are in fact refuted out of the mouths of the men who make them.

Mr. Reed in his lecture shows that Lincoln, during his life in Springfield, attended church, delivered Sunday-School addresses, speeches before the Bible Society, and evinced in every way the conduct of a man who was leading a Christian life. He also showed that the principal persons whose testimony is given by Layman and Herndon to establish the charge of Lincoln's hypocrisy in religious matters were falsely quoted. Two, who stand first on the list of such inaccurately quoted testimony, are John T. Stuart, a former member of Congress and Lincoln's first law partner, and Col. James H. Matheny, a lawyer of Springfield and an intimate friend of Lincoln's. In answer to Mr. Reed's inquiry, the following letter was received:

SPRINGFIELD,
December 17, 1872.

REV. J. A. REED,
Dear Sir:

My attention has been called to a statement in relation to the religious opinions of Mr. Lincoln, purporting to have been made by us, and published in Layman's *Life of Lincoln*. The language of that statement is not mine. It was not written by me, and I did not see it until it was in print. I was once interviewed on the subject of Mr. Lincoln's religious opinions, and doubtless said that Mr. Lincoln was in the earlier part of his life an infidel. I could not have said that Dr. Smith tried to convert Lincoln from infidelity so late as 1858, and could not do it. In relation to that point I stated in the same conversation some facts which are omitted in that statement, and which I will briefly repeat: that Eddie, a child of Mr. Lincoln's, died in 1848 or 1849, and that he and his wife were in deep grief on that account; that Dr. Smith, then pastor of the First Presbyterian Church of

Springfield, at the suggestion of a lady friend of theirs, called upon Mr. and Mrs. Lincoln, and that first visit resulted in great intimacy and friendship between them, lasting until the death of Mr. Lincoln and continuing with Mrs. Lincoln till the death of Dr. Smith. I stated that I had heard at the time that Dr. Smith and Mr. Lincoln had much discussion in relation to the truth of the Christian religion and that Dr. Smith had furnished Mr. Lincoln with books to read on the subject, and among others, one that had been written by himself some time previously, on infidelity, and that Dr. Smith claimed that after this investigation Mr. Lincoln had changed his opinions and had become a believer in the truth of the Christian religion; that Mr. Lincoln and myself never conversed on the subject, and I had no personal knowledge as to his alleged change of opinion. I stated, however, that it was certainly true that up to that time Mr. Lincoln had never regularly attended any place of religious worship, but that after that time he rented a pew in the First Presbyterian Church, and that his family constantly attended the worship in that church until he went to Washington as President. This much I said at that time, and can now add that the Hon. Ninian W. Edwards, the brother-in-law of Mr. Lincoln, had within a few days informed me that when Mr. Lincoln commenced attending the Presbyterian Church, he admitted to him that his views had undergone the change claimed by Dr. Smith. I would further say that Dr. Smith was a man of very great ability and that on theological and metaphysical subjects, had few superiors and not many equals. Truthfulness was a prominent trait in Mr. Lincoln's character and it would be impossible for any intimate friend of his to believe that he ever aimed to deceive, either by his words or his conduct.

Yours truly,

JOHN T. STUART.

The second important witness cited by Mr. Reed is Colonel Matheny, who wrote:

SPRINGFIELD,
December 16, 1872.

REV. J. A. REED,
Dear Sir:

The language attributed to me in Mr. Layman's book is not from my pen. I did not write it, and it does not express my sentiments of Mr. Lincoln's life and character. It is a mere collection of sayings gathered from private conversations, that were only true of Mr. Lincoln's earlier life. I would not have allowed such an article to be printed over my signature as covering my opinion of Mr. Lincoln's life and religious sentiments. While I do believe Mr. Lincoln to have been an infidel in his former life, when his mind was as yet unformed and his association principally with rough and skeptical men, yet I believe that he was a very different man in later life, and that after associating with a different class of men and investigating the subject, he was a firm believer in the Christian religion.

Yours truly,

JAMES H. MATHENY.

Lincoln's final attainment of complete belief in Jesus Christ as the divine Son of God finds ample proof in the report by Newton Bateman, Superintendent of Public Instruction for the State of Illinois. Mr. Bateman occupied a room in the Capitol adjoining, and opening into, the Executive Chamber. The door between the two rooms was frequently open during Mr. Lincoln's receptions, and the two men saw each other nearly every day. This was during Mr. Lincoln's Presidential campaign in 1860. Often when Mr. Lincoln was tired he would close the door against all intrusion and call Mr. Bateman in for a quiet talk.

On one of these occasions Mr. Lincoln took up a book containing the result of a careful canvass of the city of Springfield, showing the candidate for whom each citizen had declared his intention to vote at the approaching election. This was toward the close of October, within a few days of the election. Calling Mr. Bateman to his side, he said: "Let us look over this book. I wish particularly to see how the ministers of Springfield are going to vote." As the leaves were turned, one by one, Mr. Lincoln frequently asked if this one or that one were not a minister, or an elder, or a member of such and such a church, and sadly expressed his surprise on receiving an affirmative answer. After they had gone through the book, Lincoln closed it and regarded in silence for some moments a pencil memorandum which lay before him. At length he turned to Mr. Bateman, his face full of sadness, and said:

Here are twenty-three ministers of different denominations, and all of them are against me, but three. And there are a great many prominent members of the churches, a very large majority of whom are against me. Mr. Bateman, I am not a Christian; God knows I would be one, but I have carefully read the Bible and I do not so understand this Book, [drawing from his bosom a pocket New Testament]. These men well know [he continued] that I am for freedom in the territories, freedom everywhere as far as the Constitution and laws will permit, and my opponents are for slavery. They know this, and yet, with this Book in their hands, in the light of which human bondage cannot live a moment, they are going to vote against me. I do not understand it at all.

Here Mr. Lincoln paused for long minutes, his features surcharged with emotion. He then arose and walked up and down the room in an effort to retain, or regain, his self-possession. Stopping at last, he said in a trembling voice, his cheeks wet with tears:

I know there is a God, and that He hates injustice and slavery. I see the storm coming, and I know that His hand is in it. If He has a place and work for me, and I think He has, I believe I am ready. I am nothing, but truth is everything. I know I am right, be-

cause I know that liberty is right, for Christ teaches
it, and Christ is God.   I have told them that a house
divided against itself cannot stand, and Christ and
reason say the same, and they will find it so.   Douglas don't care whether slavery is voted up or down,
but God cares and humanity cares, and I care, and
with God's help, I shall not fail.   I may not see the
end, but it will come, and I shall be vindicated, and
these men will find that they have not read their Bible
aright.

Much of this was uttered as if he were speaking
to himself, and with a sad and earnest solemnity
of manner impossible to describe.   After a pause,
he resumed:

Doesn't it appear strange that men can ignore the
moral aspects of this contest?   A revelation could not
make it plainer to me that slavery or the Government
must be destroyed.   The future would be something
awful, as I look at it, but for this rock on which I
stand [alluding to the Testament which he held in his
hand] especially with the knowledge of how these
ministers are going to vote.   It seems to me as if God
had borne with this thing, slavery, until the very
teachers of religion have come to defend it from their
Bible and to claim for it a divine character and sanc-
tion, and now the cup of iniquity is full and the vial of
wrath will be poured out.

His last reference was to certain prominent
clergymen of the South, and Lincoln went on to

comment on the atrociousness and essential blasphemy of their attempts to defend American slavery from the Bible. The conversation was continued for a long time. Everything he said was of a peculiarly deep, tender, and religious tone, and was all tinged with a touch of melancholy. He repeatedly referred to his conviction that the day of wrath was at hand, and that he was to be an actor in the terrible struggle which would issue in the overthrow of slavery, though he might not live to see the end. He repeated many passages in the Bible, and seemed especially impressed with the solemn grandeur of portions of Revelation, describing the wrath of Almighty God. In the course of the conversation, he dwelt much upon the necessity of faith in the Christian's God, as an element of successful statesmanship, especially in times like those which were upon him, and said that it gave that calmness and tranquillity of mind, that assurance of ultimate success which made a man firm and immovable amid the wildest excitements. After further reference to a belief in divine Providence and the fact of God in history, the conversation turned upon prayer. He frequently stated his belief in the duty, privilege, and efficacy of prayer, and intimated in unmistakable terms that he had sought in that way the

divine guidance and favour.   As the two men were
about to separate, Mr. Bateman remarked:

"I had not supposed that you were accustomed
to think so much on this class of subject; certainly
your friends generally are ignorant of the sentiments you have expressed to me."

He replied quickly: "I know they are.   I am
obliged to appear different to them; but I think
more on these subjects than upon all others, and I
have done so for years, and I am willing that you
should know it."

This remarkable conversation as set forth in
Holland's *Life of Lincoln*, furnishes a golden link
in the chain of Mr. Lincoln's religious history.
It flashes a strong light upon the path he had
already trod, and illuminates every page of his
subsequent record.   Men have wondered at his
abounding charity, his love of man, his equanimity
under trying circumstances, his patience under
insult and defamation, his delicate consideration
of the feelings of the humble, his apparent in-
capacity for resentment, his love of justice, his
transparent simplicity, his truthfulness, his good
will toward his enemies, his beautiful and unshaken faith in the triumph of the right.   There
was undoubtedly something in his constitution that
favoured the development of these qualities.   But

those best acquainted with human nature will hardly attribute the combination of excellencies exhibited in his character and life to the unaided forces of his constitution. The man who carried what he called "this Rock" in his bosom, prayed and thought more on religious subjects than on all others, had an undying faith in the Providence of God, drew his spiritual life and his many virtues from above.

Some who have claimed that Lincoln was an agnostic have sought to break the force of this Bateman interview by boldly denying its authenticity; but Bateman himself would never put out a denial, though often urged to do so. In response to a direct question from Isaac T. Arnold, author of *Life of Abraham Lincoln*, Mr. Bateman replied, "The interview as published by Holland is substantially correct." There is ample internal evidence of the truth of the story. Bateman and Lincoln were known to be very intimate friends and much in each other's confidence. The utterances ascribed to Mr. Lincoln are known to be in keeping with his life and character. He was not a man to parade his own virtue or morality or to make public display of his religious convictions. It is possible in estimating such a personality to overestimate chronology.

The point is, the sweep of Lincoln's life was toward a complete faith in God perfectly illustrated only in the life and works of Jesus Christ.

Bishop Charles H. Fowler, in his *Patriotic Orations*, quotes the Rev. Dr. Newell Dwight Hillis as saying:

I have a woman in my congregation who is the daughter of the Presbyterian minister in whose church Mr. Lincoln worshipped during the war. She says: "Mr. Lincoln frequently came to our house in the evening, stopped at our door, and said to my father, Doctor, you must pray tonight. One night he called at half-past one, called my father up and said, Doctor, you must come down and go to my room with me. I need you. My father went and found Mr. Lincoln's room strewn with maps, where he was marking out the movements of troops. He said to my father, 'There is your room. You go in there and pray, and I will stay here and watch.' My father heard him repeatedly praying for the Army. Three times he came to my father's room and fell down on his face on the floor by his side and prayed mightily to God to bless the boys about to die for the Republic, and to save the Republic."

Mr. Herndon, with the evident purpose of reenforcing his contention that Mr. Lincoln was a disbeliever, addressed a letter to the Rev. Dr. Smith, whose relations with Mr. Lincoln and his family while he was pastor of the First Presby-

terian Church of Springfield, has already been
mentioned, and received the following reply:

EAST CAINO, SCOTLAND,
24th January, 1867.

W. H. HERNDON, Esq.,
Sir:

Your letter of the 20th of December was duly
received, in which you ask me to answer several questions in relation to the illustrious President, Abraham
Lincoln. With regard to your second question, I beg
leave to say it is a very easy matter to prove that
while I was pastor of the First Presbyterian Church
of Springfield, Mr. Lincoln did avow his belief in the
divine authority and inspiration of the Scriptures.
And I hold that it is a matter of greatest importance,
not only to the present but to all future generations of
the great Republic and to all advocates of civil and
religious liberty throughout the world, that this
avowal on his part and the circumstances attending
it, together with very interesting incidents illustrative
of the excellence of his character in my possession
should be made known to the public.

My intercourse with Abraham Lincoln convinced
me that he was not only an honest man, but pre-
eminently an upright man, ever seeking, so far as was
in his power, to render unto all their due. It was my
honour to place before Mr. Lincoln arguments designed to prove the divine authority and inspiration of
the Scriptures, accompanied by arguments of infidel
objectors in their own language. To the arguments
on both sides, Mr. Lincoln gave a most patient and
searching investigation. To use his own language,

he examined the arguments as a lawyer who is anxious to reach the truth investigates testimony. The result was the announcement by himself that the argument in favour of the divine authority and inspiration of the Scriptures was unanswerable. I could say much more on the subject, but as you are the person addressed, for the present I decline. The assassin Booth, by his diabolical act, unwittingly sent the illustrious martyr to glory, honour, and immortality, but his false friend has attempted to send him down to posterity with infamy branded on his forehead, as a man who, notwithstanding all he suffered for his country's good, was destitute to those feelings and affections without which there can be no excellency of character. Sir, I am, with due respect,

Your obedient servant,
JAMES SMITH.

And the most convincing fact cited by Dr. Smith was contained in a postscript to this letter, in which he avers that shortly after becoming a member of his congregation in Springfield, Mr. Lincoln delivered, before the annual meeting of the Bible Society of Springfield, an address the subject of which was to inculcate the importance of having the Bible placed in the possession of every family in the State. In his address, Mr. Lincoln drew a striking contrast between the Decalogue and the moral codes of the most eminent lawgivers of antiquity, closing with these words:

It seems to me that nothing short of infinite wisdom could by any possibility have devised and given to man this excellent and perfect moral code. It is suited to man in all conditions of life, and includes all the duties they owe to their Creator, to themselves and to their fellow-man.

Some may conclude that Lincoln was converted to a theological belief in the divine authority and inspiration of the Scriptures by Dr. Smith's argument. But long before he had ever seen Dr. Smith he had given evidence of the most convincing nature of his ingrained belief in the essential principles of Christianity. His earlier relations to God were obviously more a religion of the heart, while his later studies of the evidence supporting religious belief added to the emotions of the heart the approval of a trained intellect. Under pressure from Herndon, Mr. Bateman for a time remained silent concerning his reported interview with Mr. Lincoln. But his ultimate reaffirmation was that his first report was substantially correct, and Dr. Barton in his *Soul of Lincoln* admits that "the incident had a basis in fact."

After Lincoln's first inaugural address as President, his pastor in Washington was the Rev. Dr. Gurley, a sound and orthodox minister of the Gospel. Dr. Gurley was Lincoln's friend and spiritual adviser during the most trying period of his life.   He was with Mr. Lincoln during the hours of his personal and family bereavement, as well as when his heart was burdened with the affairs of the Nation.   Dr. Gurley delivered Lincoln's funeral oration in the City of Washington, in which he said:

Since the days of Washington, no man was ever so deeply and firmly imbedded and enshrined in the hearts of the people, as Abraham Lincoln; nor was it a mistaken confidence and love.   He deserves it all. He merited by his character, by his acts, and by the whole tone and tenor of his life.   His integrity was thorough, all pervading, all controlling, and incorrupt-ible.   He saw his duty as the chief magistrate of a great and imperilled people, and he determined to do his duty, seeking the guidance and leaning on the arm of Him of Whom it is written: "He giveth to the faint, and to them who have no might He increaseth strength."   Never shall I forget the emphatic and deep emotion with which he said, in this very room to a company of clergymen who had called to pay their respects to him in the darkest days of the civil conflict.   "Gentlemen, my hope of success in this struggle rests on that immutable foundation, the justice and goodness of God, and when events are very threatening, I still hope that in some way all will be on our side."

In conversation with Mr. Reed, Dr. Gurley, when his attention was called to the rumour of Lincoln's infidelity, then being circulated by Herndon, said:

I do not believe a word of it. It would not have been true of him while he was here, for I have had frequent and intimate conversations with him on the subject of the Bible and of the Christian religion, when he could have had no motive to deceive me, and I consider him sound, not only in the truths of the Christian religion, but on all the fundamental doctrines and teachings; and more than that, in the later days of his chastened and weary life, after the death of his son Willie and his visit to the battlefield of Gettysburg, he said, with tears in his eyes, that he had lost confidence in everything but God, and that he now believed his heart was changed and that he loved the Saviour.

Noah Brooks, one of Lincoln's biographers and an intimate friend, had frequent conversations with the President on social and religious matters. Brooks was accredited by some with knowing more of the secret inner life and religious views of Lincoln than any other man. He reports several instances in which Lincoln put himself on record as a whole-hearted Christian believer.[1] The following letter by Mr. Brooks is illuminating:

NEW YORK,
December 31, 1878.

Rev. J. A. REED,
  My dear Sir:
  In addition to what has appeared from my pen, I will state that I have had many conversations with

[1] *Harpers' Magazine*, July, 1865.

Mr. Lincoln which were more or less of a religious character; and while I never tried to draw anything like a statement of his views from him, yet he frequently expressed himself to me as having a blessed hope of immortality through Jesus Christ. His faith seemed to settle so naturally around that statement that I considered no other necessary. His language seemed not that of an inquirer, but of one who had a prior settled belief in the fundamental doctrines of the Christian religion. He said that after he went to the White House, he kept up the habit of daily prayer. Sometimes he said it was only ten words, but those ten words he had. There is no possible reason to suppose that Mr. Lincoln would ever deceive me as to his religious sentiments. In many conversations with him, I absorbed the firm conviction that Mr. Lincoln was at heart a Christian man, believing in the Saviour, and was seriously considering the step which would formally connect him with the visible church on earth. Certainly any suggestion as to Mr. Lincoln's skepticism or infidelity, to me who knew him intimately from 1862 to the time of his death, is a monstrous fiction, a shocking perversion.

Yours truly,
NOAH BROOKS.

To the Hon. C. H. Deming, of Kentucky, Mr. Lincoln said that the article of his faith was contained in the condensed statement of both law and gospel: "Thou shalt love the Lord thy God with all thy heart, with all thy strength, and with all thy mind, and thy neighbour as thyself."

16

When Lincoln seriously contemplated the issue of the Emancipation Proclamation in the autumn of 1862, the Rev. Byron Sutherland, of Washington, D. C., quotes Lincoln as saying:

I believe we are all agents and instruments of Divine Providence. I hold myself in my present position and with the authority invested in me, as an instrument of Providence. I am conscious every moment that all I am and all I have are subject to the control of a higher Power, and that Power can use me or not use me in any manner and at any time as in His wisdom might be pleasing to Him.

The Rev. Dr. Miner, pastor of the First Baptist Church of Springfield, visited Lincoln and his family in Washington a short time before the assassination. He tells of a conversation he had with Mr. Lincoln, so deeply engraven on his mind that he never could forget it. Dr. Miner was convinced that Lincoln showed his faith both by his words and his acts. His conversation indicated that he was doing his duty, as he saw it, and daily looking to God for help in time of need. "Like the immortal George Washington," writes Dr. Miner, "Lincoln believed in the efficacy of prayer, and it was his custom to read the Scriptures and pray."

These specific proofs of Mr. Lincoln's firm belief in the Christian religion, and of the orderly development from the simple faith of his emotional childhood to the tested knowledge of his mature manhood, are not more convincing than those heretofore presented, but are offered to the students of Lincoln's life, and to the defendant of his faith, as a condensed statement covering the entire range of his career, from the prairies of Illinois to the Capitol of the nation. Let the student of Lincoln's life divest the subject of all argument and controversy, and consider simply what Lincoln was, what he said and did, and the conviction will be irresistible that he saw God, first in the works of nature, and then as his own personal Comforter and Guide, and finally as the Nation's Leader during the tempestuous days of the Civil War.

That Mr. Lincoln at times had doubts does not mean that he was an infidel. That he sometimes went afield in the fog of puzzling questions does not indicate confirmed skepticism. What student, even in a divinity school, passes through his period of quest for truth without being harassed with doubts that try his soul? What faith is worth the having in times of stress that has not been tested as by the refiner's fire?

He fought his doubts, and gathered strength,
He would not make his judgment blind,
He faced the spectres of his mind
And laid them; thus he came at last
To find a stronger faith his own;
And power was with him in the night,
Which makes the darkness and the light
And dwells not in the light alone.[1]

[1] Tennyson's *In Memoriam.*

CHAPTER XXVI

A TEACHER UNTAUGHT OF MEN

LINCOLN'S religious evolution kept pace with his mental growth, the outcome of a deep delving into the fundamental truths of life. And as he studied, he sought to find, not the mere doctrinal forms of ecclesiastical life as formulated in orthodox theology, but rather the practical principles, applicable alike to religion and to all other concerns of life.

But Lincoln was no more orthodox in his political and economic beliefs than in his religious faith. He no more accepted the formulated statements of previous political parties than he accepted the formulated doctrines of denominations. Mr. Lincoln believed in, and practised, the things in orthodoxy that were simple, substantial, and humane; but with profound insight, he never failed to separate the essential from the non-essential, the transitory form the permanent. As he was largely instrumental in the creation of a political party that conserved all the sound principles already formulated by political parties, and, in addition, incorporated new and even startling political doctrines, so would he, had that been his province, have conserved all the essential truths of religion contained in the creeds of the churches and, with them, combined other great spiritual ideas as yet unexpressed in any formal articles of faith. And as his political doctrines were so sound and sensible that they are now appropriated by parties of all shades of political belief, so the religious faith of Abraham Lincoln, had he ever formulated it, would have commanded the respect of Christian organizations of all types.

No man ever lived who was more devoted than Lincoln to obedience to properly constituted authority; and yet, all unconsciously, he was, in a large measure, a law unto himself, *sui generis*, no less in politics and letters than in religion. He knew practically nothing of the writings of the distinguished group of American men of letters contemporary with himself, such as Bryant, Poe, Hawthorne, Emerson, Lowell, Whittier, Holmes, Longfellow, and Thoreau. It is certain that he was not at all familiar with their works during the formative period of his career, and if he read them later in life he gave scant evidence of it in his

utterance. These men of letters, breathing the
same literary atmosphere, undoubtedly helped
to mould and influence one another. They were
men of technical literary education, widely read,
and masters of style. Their workmanship, though
varying greatly, conformed in the main to certain
literary standards. The literary children of the
period, they became the literary parents of the
succeeding generation. Their writings were original, brilliant, elevated in thought, rhythmic, ethi-
cal and founded on well-known classic models.
He did not come under their influence, read their
books, imitate their style, or borrow their colouring.
He had no conscious literary models, nor the inspiration of learned associations. While an Emerson was profiting by the personal acquaintance of
Lowell, while the melancholy Hawthorne was
basking in the sunny smiles of Holmes, Lincoln
was sitting on a soap box in a cross-roads grocery,
talking with carpenters and farmers, and then returning to his crude home to read his Bible. While
the New England masters of a nation's literature
were hearing the erudite sermons of preachers,
who themselves were acknowledged masters of
literary style, Lincoln was listening to the frontier
preachers whose camp-meeting sermons aimed at
immediate spiritual results; himself, the while,

delving to the bottom of things and discovering truth at its very source.

Lincoln had not the advantage of a knowledge of foreign languages. What he knew of English construction he gained from study of only a few books, and that without the aid of instructors. But such works as he was able to obtain—the Bible, Shakespeare, Bunyan—were something more than classics. They reached down to the roots of things. The language they employed was not for show, nor yet to gratify a fastidious literary taste, but for the revelation of the hidden truths of Nature, the heights and depths of human emotion—language that touched the soul as with divine fire. From such books, and from his own experience, Lincoln drew his inspiration and built up a style all his own, which was at once classic and something more—a style as perfect as an example of pure English as Homer is of ancient Greek. A high literary authority declares that one of Lincoln's speeches is known wherever the English language is known and spoken, and is recognized as a classic "by virtue of its unique condensation of the sentiment of a tremendous struggle into a narrow compass of brief paragraphs, and by virtue of that instinctive, felicitous style, which gives to the largest thought the beauty of perfect simplicity."

The beauties of Irving and Thoreau, even the deep spiritual insight of Emerson and Whittier, are tame beside the profound feeling, large vision, clear expression, and persuasive eloquence of the two inaugural addresses. While the purely literary authors were dealing with intellectual and moral theories, Lincoln was grappling with actual conditions, which he handled as exhaustively and fearlessly as an imaginative writer marshals and commands the fictitious children of his brain. Without gloss or deception, he laid bare the vital issues, and forced the Nation to face them by the sheer power of his presentation.

Lincoln's life squared with his utterances. How many there are who work themselves into heroic moods in the quiet of the study and easily picture what they would do when facing severe tests; but who would, in actual practice, fail to meet these very tests, even to their own satisfaction. Lincoln, when subjected to such tests as few men ever underwent, was found equal to the emergencies. He met them in the spirit of one who, knowing his ground and believing in the triumph of the right, went steadfastly forward to the goal of his Christian ambition.

Ralph Waldo Emerson, describing the Cooper Institute speech in New York, says:

He was equal to the occasion. When he spoke, he was transformed. His eyes kindled; his voice rang; his face shone and seemed to light up the whole assembly; and for an hour and a half he held his audience in the hollow of his hand. His style of speech and manner of delivery were severely simple.

What Lowell has called the "grand simplicities of the Bible," with which he was familiar, were reflected in his discourse. With no attempt at ornament or rhetoric, without parade or pretence, he spoke straight to the point. If any came, expecting the turgid eloquence or the ribaldry of the frontier, they must have been startled by the earnest and sincere purity of his utterances. It was marvellous to see how this untutored man, by mere self-discipline and the chastening of his own spirit, had outgrown all meretricious arts and found his way to the grandeur and strength of absolute simplicity.

It has been said that Lincoln acquired his education in such an unusual way that he might be able to speak for his time and to his time with perfect sincerity and simplicity, to feel the moral bearings of the questions which were before the country, to discuss the principles involved, and to apply them so as to clarify and convince. This was self-education. But how are we to account for the temperamental and spiritual quality of soul as embodied in his words, and in his words translated into deeds? When we attempt to answer that question we shall err if we look for the source of

Mr. Lincoln's power entirely in the mode of his education, hard and disciplinary as it was. We must rather look for it in his spiritual inheritance, for there was something more in him than the quality we call genius. Genius accounts for much, but it does not always work out in the courage, the moral elevation, and the devotion to duty which made Lincoln both a hero and a martyr. In Lincoln, all is harmonious and consistent—deed answering to word. When he spoke for the Nation he so loved, his lips were as though touched with a live coal from the altar. He seemed to be of the same fibre with the prophets of Holy Writ and it may be said, without irreverence, that he was a "priest after the order of Melchisedec, without beginning or end of days," combining the kingly and priestly functions essential to the service of his Nation and his time.

The concluding sentence of his Cooper Institute speech, "Let us have faith that right makes might, and in that faith let us to the end dare to do our duty, as we understand it," voiced the faith in which he lived and in which he died. Though dead, he yet speaketh, even as never while he lived; though dead, he remains enshrined in the hearts of the people a living example, as an incentive to higher Christian citizenship, and to the belief in the unity and justice of the divine purpose "toward which the whole creation moves."

Why was it that this product of the prairies, unlettered and unknown, arose to such heights of moral vision and statecraft? Why was it that he who knew so little of literature could compel the eulogia of the Nation's literary masters? Why was it that this son of an humble frontier settler could rise above the clouds that blind the eyes of ordinary men and see the course a mighty Nation must take to preserve its existence and keep alive the hope of human freedom?

Ask God Who, in creating a continent, upraises a mighty mountain range above the plains, and above the mountain peaks one that towers above all the rest, penetrates all clouds and forever reflects the light of the fleckless skies upon the crags and plains below; and Who, once in a century, raises up a man whose towering personality rises above the common multitudes that throng the hills and vales, as the mountain above its fellows, and for all times sheds the light of his achievements and his glory upon the world, to inspire even those who tread the humbler walks of life that they, in their sphere, may make their lives sublime.

CHAPTER XXVII

THE COMPLETE CHRISTIAN

CLEARED of the charges made by Layman and Herndon, and repeated since by many that Lincoln was at heart a skeptic, and possibly an infidel, no matter what he may have seemed to some in private words and public utterances, there remains a task which unperformed still leaves the subject open to discussion. It is not enough to remind the reader that only those see who have eyes to see, only those hear who have ears to hear. Even a casual reader of Herndon's extraordinary oration on Lincoln will perceive that Herndon's instinct was to explain all the phenomena of personality without resort to religious faith, and however intimate Lincoln may have been with his law partner, he was dealing with a man who, like Darwin, born the same year as Lincoln, had developed his great intellectual gifts at the expense of his spiritual genius and without Darwin's awakening at last to his loss of power to be moved, as when a young man he stood in the gorgeous loneliness of a Brazilian forest and heard voices whispering of the Creator.

Of one thing Herndon was certain—that Lincoln was honest in all things, that he never, even in the stress of politics, sacrificed his love of thinking and speaking what appeared to him to be the truth. In consequence it would seem necessary to make clear the Christianity of Mr. Lincoln by telling out of his own mouth the story of his attitude toward Christian fundamentals. This, too, can be done without intrusion on ground dedicated to those elements and incidents illustrative of his greatness as a "human," who would have been great at any time, in any place, inside Christianity like Lincoln, or outside like Marcus Aurelius.

Abraham Lincoln was brought up in a Christian home. No boy ever received more definite Christian training than that given to him by Nancy Hanks and Sally Johnston. He knelt at the family altar. He went to church. He was swept by the emotions kindled at camp-meetings. He heard great revivalists like Cartwright and Akers. There never was a time when he was not interested mind and heart in Christian preaching and in Christian experience. His old friend, Billy Brown, said in 1896:

I never knew anybody who seemed to me more interested in God, more curious about Him, more
anxious to find out what He was drivin' at in the world
than Mr. Lincoln. I reckon he was allus that way.
The Bible was the whole thing, and there ain't any
doubt he knew it pretty near by heart, knew it well
before he could ever read.[1]

If he was slow in committing himself unreservedly to the Christian theology of his day it
was partly because he took a larger view of God's
loving kindness as described by Jesus than some
who were laying more stress on the wrathful
Jehovah of the Old Testament. In his early
manhood he wrote a paper often cited as proof he
was no Christian, which really was such a tribute
as Brooks or Beecher later might have paid to
Love Divine expressed in God's relationship to
man.

Tom Paine, who was no atheist, may have held
him back from full committal to the theology men
commonly associated with the Bible. To a mind as
acute as Lincoln's and accustomed from the first
to see all round a subject, Voltaire came with a
challenge to be sure he was right before he went
ahead. *Volney's Ruins*, not so widely read as Paine

[1] Ida M. Tarbell: "In Lincoln's Chair"—in *The Red Cross
Magazine*, February, 1920, p. 7.

or Voltaire, made peculiar appeal to Lincoln's cosmic and historic sense, till then dormant. For the first time he learned the world had been doing business longer than 6,000 years, that civilization had developed again and yet again only to pass away, that one set of men after another had come along, thought out their religions in the light they had, built up their theologies on such foundations as they found, talked and acted, lived and died, and given way to others who had in turn beat against the bars of limitations set by circumstances.

Lincoln was our first great soul to reconcile the quarrel between realist and idealist, to be practical as well as theoretical. He considered all the evidence. Though he was too honest to plunge rashly into any temporary system of man-made theology, he was early won to the Bible as the Book of God and tried to shape his life by it, and gave himself at last without reserve to it. "Tell your mother," he wrote Mary Speed as early as 1841, "that I have not got her 'present' (an Oxford Bible) with me, but I intend to read it regularly when I return home." A little later, from the pulpit of the First Presbyterian Church on invitation, he addressed the Springfield Bible Society on the importance of placing the Bible in

every family in the State.   Others might speculate
about the Bible; Lincoln read it every day.   Even
in recent years men who were with him in the
White House have given us glimpses of that man
of God on his knees in some great crisis, with his
Bible on the chair before him, seeking help from
the Hills.

He carried the New Testament ever in his
pocket.   He could repeat from memory whole
chapters of it as well as other passages.   To a
deputation of coloured people from Baltimore calling on him in 1864 he described the Great Book
as "the best gift God has given to man.   All the
good Saviour gave to the world was communicated
through this book.   But for it we could not know
right from wrong.   All things most desirable for
man's welfare, here and hereafter, are to be found
portrayed in it."   To Chittenden, the keen and
cultivated lawyer from Vermont, he committed
himself as unreservedly as to the less tutored
negro and in fact closed the subject for all time in
the words: "I decided a long time ago that it was
less difficult to believe that the Bible was what it
claimed to be than to disbelieve it."[1]

He approached from so many points of view and
brought to the consideration of Nature a mind so

[1] Johnson, see *Index;* also Chittenden's *Recollections*, p. 450.

17

acute and fair, that in reading his state papers, his speeches, his letters, and his reported conversations, God is designated in almost fifty different ways, all leading up to St. John's thought of Him as Love, or as Lincoln said to Mrs. Gurney on September 4, 1864, "Our Father in Heaven."

If some still doubt that Lincoln thought of Jesus Christ in terms of our historic Christianity, they must be those who forget that he lived when thoughtful men were in revolt against the mechanical view of the Trinity, which came to its fulness in the days of Jonathan Edwards, was then carried on the wave of the Great Awakening to the Middle West and through the Cumberland Gap to the South-west, and served as framework for the evangelism brought to young Lincoln's very door.

If Lincoln's contemporaries, like Channing and Bushnell in New England, were at that very time breaking with the intellectual formalism of the religion of their day, they were still holding to its spiritual reality. Channing would not use the language of the formalists but he did assert that "Jesus was what He claimed to be, and what His followers attested. Nor is this all. Jesus not only was, He is still the Son of God, the Saviour of the world."

Bushnell's logic seemed to shatter the cold metaphysics of the Trinity as it had been stereotyped by the merely intellectual, but at the very time Lincoln was working his way through to a belief in all the spiritual realities the Bible teaches, Bushnell was saying, "My heart wants the Father; my heart wants the Son; my heart wants the Holy Ghost—and one just as much as the other. My heart says the Bible has a Trinity for me, and I mean to hold by my heart."

Then came Phillips Brooks, entering on his ministry as Lincoln's work was near its end, and making it indubitably clear that heart as well as head is necessary to the understanding of the Bible, saying in his every sermon: "This old faith of ours after all is true, more deeply and more largely true than we have lately thought it. Doctrines are to be studied with the heart as well as mind. Even doubts may have their place in swinging great truths out into the brightest light." It is strange, perhaps providential, that it was in the sermon on the death of Lincoln, which won for Phillips Brooks his widest reputation, that unwittingly he said the final word in explanation of the complete Christianity of Lincoln:

In him goodness and intelligence combined and made their best result of wisdom. For perfect truth consists not merely in the right constituents of character, but in their right and intimate conjunction. You are unable to tell whether in the wise acts and words which issue from such a life there is more of the righteousness that comes of a clear conscience, or of the sagacity that comes of a clear brain.

If more than once Lincoln hesitated to proclaim himself a Christian as in a conversation with Josiah Grady in 1847 or 1848 and when he was leaving Springfield, he took pains in one case to deny he was an infidel, and in the other to indicate by implication that his ideal of a Christian was so lofty that he hesitated in sheer modesty to proclaim himself to be what he thought only better men could hope to be. "God, be merciful to me, a sinner" was more his state of mind than "Lord, I thank thee that I am not as other men."[1]

All the while he was trying to be like Jesus. He once said to a friend: "I have read the beatitudes of Jesus. I have sometimes thought I might claim the benefit of the one that pronounces a blessing upon those who hunger and thirst after righteousness."[2] He habitually referred to Jesus as "our Lord." He accepted literally both the

[1] In a letter to Reverdy Johnson, dated July 26, 1862, and published by Nicolay & Hay, he says, "I am a patient man, always willing to forgive on the Christian terms of repentance and also to give ample time for repentance."

[2] Johnson's *Lincoln*, p. 172.

Temptation in the Wilderness and the Miracles. He never faltered in adherence to the orthodox explanation of the Atonement.[1] Some of his speeches and even proclamations are scarcely more than elaborations of the words of Jesus Christ. The keynote of his more than famous victory over Douglas in debate was simply the quotation from Jesus: "A house divided against itself cannot stand."

The time came, however, when he wanted men to know without further question that like St. Paul, "For him to live was Christ": for just before his death Mr. Lincoln solemnly remarked to a good friend: "When I left Springfield I asked the people to pray for me. I was not a Christian. When I buried my son, the severest trial of my life, I was not a Christian. But when I went to Gettysburg and saw the graves of thousands of our soldiers, I then and there consecrated myself to Christ."[2]

Not often did he speak about the Holy Spirit, but when he spoke he left no room to doubt that when men grow in goodness they do not grow by chance; they grow under the fostering care of

[1] Even in referring to the wounded on the battlefield, Lincoln once inquired if there "isn't something in Scripture about the 'shedding of blood' for the remission of sins."—Carpenter, p. 319.

[2] *Lincoln's Memorial Album*, O. H. Oldroyd, p. 366.

God's Holy Spirit. In references to the Holy Spirit his writings abound. No theologian has ever more confidently explained the Holy Spirit's place in human life than when Mr. Lincoln, after the victories at Gettysburg and Vicksburg, called his people to invoke the influence of the

Holy Spirit to subdue the anger which has produced and so long sustained a needless and cruel rebellion, to change the hearts of the insurgents, to guide the counsels of the government with wisdom adequate to so great a national emergency, and to visit with tender care and consolation throughout the length and breadth of our land all those who, through the vicissitudes of marches, voyages, battles, and sieges, have been brought to suffer in mind, body, or estate, and finally to lead the whole nation through the paths of repentance and submission to the Divine Will back to the perfect enjoyment of union and fraternal peace.

Some still wonder why he never joined a church. Is the day never to dawn when all will understand that Abraham Lincoln was absolutely honest with himself and with the church? He had spent his life among people who believed church membership signified a certain grade of other-worldliness which he never thought he had quite reached, when certainly the vast majority of church members were supposed to understand as well as to believe all the details of evangelical theology. Lincoln's

mind worked slowly.   He would never urge it on.
He wanted time to think, to read, to pray, before
he took a step which seemed to him a virtual assertion that he held the full-orbed faith.   He was
troubled that the various denominations differed
radically as to what they held to be essentials.   He
had heard some sermons which caused him to declare it blasphemy for a preacher to "twist the
words of Christ around so as to sustain his own
doctrine."   He was afraid that some of the theology of the day conflicted with "the true spirit of
Christ."   Yet all the time he regularly attended
church, first in Springfield and then in Washington, and in 1864 wrote his old friend, Joshua
Speed, "I am profitably engaged reading the Bible.
Take all of this Book upon reason that you can
and the balance upon faith and you will live and
die a better man."

The death of Willie and the countless graves he
found at Gettysburg in 1863 seemed to sweep his
heart along toward church membership in spite
of any hesitations the head still entertained.   He
developed the habit of talking out his inmost feelings to the spiritually-minded whom he met.
Carpenter[1] reports his statement to a woman
representing the Christian Commission, "that it

[1] Page 187.

has been my intention for some time at a suitable opportunity to make a public religious profession." To Noah Brooks and his beloved Pastor, Dr. Gurley, he spoke to the same purpose. Then when he was setting his house in order for the peace that followed war, death interrupted all his plans. Though he had not after all joined church,

> Never to the mansions where the mighty rest,
> Since their foundations, came a nobler guest.

CHAPTER XXVIII

THE CHRIST-LIKE STORY-TELLER

IDIOMS, maxims, argument, even illustrations are not always adequate to sink truth deep into all types of mind. Some minds are too clever, some too dull, some too introspective and some too detached to apprehend truth presented in conventional form. But everybody understands a story. Everybody likes a well-told story with a moral which requires no afterword. The *Fables of Æsop*, the *Arabian Nights*, the *Canterbury Tales* of Chaucer are as acceptable today as when they were first told.

He who spake as never man spake was habitually a story-teller. He couched much of his teaching in story form most easy to the understanding of plain people, most stimulating to the thoughtful, most arresting to those engrossed in "the cares of this world, and the deceitfulness of riches, and the lusts of other things." He called his stories parables, and many scholars have gone far afield in giving them an esoteric meaning or in making them a stalking horse for strange or foolish doctrine. But his parables are nothing more than word pictures of a real or an imaginary scene, a probable or improbable occurrence. They are—as in the parable of the Prodigal Son or the Ten Virgins—artistic presentation of a central thought with the details so skilfully grouped around it as to float the truth itself into the mind by way of the imagination as well as of the understanding.

It was largely by this use of the story, that Jesus could give free play without loss of dignity to His sense of mirth and wit, that He could make use at times of irony and sarcasm, and scintillate with raillery and repartee. When He wanted to describe the Father's joy at the return of the prodigal he made to ring out from the parable the sound of music and dancing. When He exhorted His disciples to be happy in the midst of all their tribulations, He bade them leap with joy. In the simile of the camel and the needle's eye there is biting irony.

Was there ever sarcasm more cutting than when he told His hearers who were Jews to take no thought for the morrow, which was the habit of the Gentiles? Did ever raillery go home more quickly than in His pertinent remark about plucking out the beam from your own eye before you try to find the tiny mote in some other's eye? But it was Herodian and Scribe and Pharisee who learned at last that they had no mind, however highly trained and polished, to match the mind which taking all of them in turn smashed their plans and put their intellects to rout in that resistless thrust of repartee: "Render therefore unto Cæsar the things which are Cæsar's: and unto God the things that are God's."

There have been since Jesus' day men who have made successful use of story-telling to re-enforce their arguments. There has been none in the same class as Lincoln. Like St. Paul he was himself in the best sense all things to all men that he might save some; nay more, that he might save the Union. He had so meditated on the words of Jesus Christ that he had caught His secret of tempering justice with mercy, of loving all though some he did not like, of ministering to the needs of suffering ones as well as binding up the wounds of every battlefield.

In all his story-telling he was quaintly self-unconscious. He was merely feathering the arrow of the truth he had thought out that he might lodge it without failure in the most elusive mind or hardest heart. As for the report too long circulated that Lincoln had a penchant for the disbursement of the questionable story, that hoary lie is at last laid low. Brought up amid frontier conditions, accustomed to the sights and sounds of the comparatively primitive, his stories ordinarily reflected the environment of the days before he went to Washington as the parables of Jesus have for their setting the hills and dales, the villages and plains of Palestine.

Fortunately we have Lincoln's own veracious explanation made to Colonel Silas W. Burt of the place of story-telling in his scheme of things.

I believe [he said] that I have the popular reputation of being a story-teller, but I do not deserve the name in its general sense, for it is not the story itself, but its purpose or effect that interests me. I often avoid a long and useless discussion by others, or a laborious explanation on my own part, by a short story that illustrates my point of view. So too, the sharpness of a refusal or the edge of a rebuke may be blunted by an appropriate story so as to save wounding feelings and yet serve the purpose. No, I am not simply a story-teller, but story-telling as an emollient saves me much friction and distress.

Lincoln never went to college. He never ran the risk of growing merely learned. He sharpened at home his wits till none could outmatch them. He developed a sense of the fitness of things the merely academic could not dull or stultify. But he always kept close to the commonplace. He always understood plain people and believed that they come first in any democratic country.

> The colour of the ground was in him, the red earth;
> The tang and colour of the primal things—
> The rectitude and patience of the rocks;
> The gladness of the wind that shakes the corn;
> The courage of the bird that dares the sea;
> The justice of the rain that loves all leaves;
> The pity of the snow that hides all scars;
> The loving kindness of the wayside well;
> The tolerance and equity of light
> That gives as freely to the shrinking weed
> As to the great oak flaring to the wind—
> To the grave's low hill as to the Matterhorn
> That shoulders out the sky.

"He once condemned for its tediousness," said a noted literary man at a dinner in New York, "a Greek history; whereupon a diplomat took the President to task. 'The author of that history, Mr. President,' he said, 'is one of the profoundest scholars of the age. Indeed it may be doubted whether any man of our generation has plunged more deeply into the sacred fount of learning.' 'Yes, or come up drier,' answered Lincoln."

Mr. Lincoln was as fond of framing his retort in language of the Scriptures as Jesus was in quoting the Old Testament. The Secretary of the Treasury in Lincoln's second term, Hugh McCulloch, once with some awe presented to the President a delegation of New York bankers with the preliminary undertone: "These gentlemen have come on to see about our new loan. As bankers they are obliged to hold our national securities. I can vouch for their patriotism and loyalty; for, as the good Book says, 'Where the treasure is there will the heart be also.'" To which Mr. Lincoln quickly answered: "There is another text, Mr. McCulloch, I remember that might equally apply—'Where the carcass is, there will the eagles be gathered together.'"

Lincoln believed no duty was more constant than to keep accessible to the people. No matter how busy he might be, he was always seeing callers. They came to his receptions in such numbers and shook his hand so vigorously that he was often almost lame and came to the signing of the Emancipation Proclamation with a hand so tremulous that at first he was not sure he could affix a signature that would be legible. People came at all hours. Sometimes they roamed at will over the whole house. One man with a Sunday morning engagement on getting no response to the ringing of the doorbell, walked in unannounced, even went upstairs, knocked at the President's private room, and when admitted was informed by Mr. Lincoln: "The boys are all out this morning." The aristocratic Charles Sumner had to seek the President downstairs and when he found him polishing his boots, in astonishment protested: "Why, Mr. President, do you black your own boots?" Looking up for but a moment Mr. Lincoln returned more vigorously to his task with the apt reply: "Whose boots did you think I was blacking?" Far more than St. Paul he had to suffer fools gladly, and in many a stated conference it was his appropriate story that enabled him to refuse requests without offence at a time when for the Nation's good no more enemies must be made by the executive than was absolutely necessary.

In the *Odyssey* we are told that Ulysses, in bringing together the materials for the building of his bed around the olive tree, "bored them all." No President perhaps was ever more beset by men who "bored them all" than Mr. Lincoln. Yet he had to listen patiently even to Robert Dale Owen's long and tiresome manuscript on an abstruse subject and to avoid committal of himself when pressed for an opinion, sought refuge in the safe and solemn generalization: "For those who like that sort of thing that is the sort of thing they like."

Once when the Cabinet seemed broken into halves and Lincoln could not train with either without danger of disruption of the government, he waited till he had in his pocket the resignation of a representative of each group and then jocosely said: "Now, I can ride easily; I have a pumpkin on either side my saddle."

He took no special credit to himself for his renomination for the Presidency in 1864, but assumed that the party leaders had concluded "that it was not best to swap horses while crossing the river, and have further concluded that I am not so poor a horse that they might not make a botch of it in trying to swap."

Before he had thought through all the incidental issues of the time, in fact before he went to the White House, he was once asked for an opinion on the tariff and replied with a story passed on in the nineties by an aged man who heard him tell it:

When I was a clerk in a grocery store in New Salem, down in Menard County, a man came in and said to the storekeeper: "I want a nickle's worth of ginger snaps." When they were laid out on the counter, the customer changed his mind and said, "I'll have a glass of cider instead." He drank the cider and turned toward the door, his bill unpaid. "Here, Bill," said the storekeeper, "ain't you goin' to pay me for that cider?" The reply came back, "Didn't I give you the ginger snaps for it?" "Well then pay me for the ginger snaps." "But I never ate your ginger snaps," was the quick answer. The storekeeper grudgingly admitted that Bill had told the truth, but added he had lost something, somehow, in the deal. So it is [said Mr. Lincoln] with the tariff. Somebody loses; but I do not know as yet just who it is.

To a man in public office a certain type of woman is perhaps most difficult to deal with. She is "more dangerous than the male." She has been the undoing of more than one man able to get on with men. Lincoln's lambent wit was his safeguard, as when the haughty woman came with challenge in her eye and theatrically exclaimed: "Mr. President, you must give me a colonel's commission for my son. Sir, I demand it not as a favour, but as a right. Sir, my grandfather fought at Lexington. Sir, my uncle was the only man who did not run away at Bladensburg. Sir, my father fought at New Orleans; and, sir, my husband was killed at Monterey." Mr. Lincoln never blinked an eye but drily and yet courteously answered: "I guess, madam, your family has done enough for the country. It is time to give someone else a chance." The interview was at an end.

Friends unwittingly and enemies with malice prepense and deliberation meticulous were ever

18

trying to take Jesus unawares or "entangle Him in His talk" or commit Him to a course which would perhaps have saved His life but would have led His mission into a *cul de sac*. His usual escape was through a flashing or bewildering reply or an apt and blistering story that brought immediate silence and finality.

Lincoln's method was precisely similar and out of the multitude of stories that come floating into memory these two seem adequate: When Mr. Gilmore was having his last interview with the President before starting with Jacquess in 1864 on that trip to Richmond which killed the Peace Party and ensured Lincoln's re-election, he hesitated with his hand upon the door knob hoping that the President would have some word to say that would ensure his personal success as well as his official safety. Mr. Lincoln read his mind and sent him off with these words ringing in his ears: "All I can do for you is to give you a pass through the lines and pray for you."

As the famous "peace" conference held February 3, 1865, on board the *River Queen* in Hampton Roads, between the President and Secretary Seward representing the Union and the Confederate Commissioners, Stephen Campbell, and Hunter, drew to its close, Mr. Hunter urged in historical justification of the recognition of Jefferson Davis's power to make a treaty the correspondence which took place between King Charles I and his Parliament. Mr. Lincoln's face took on that indescribable expression which those who knew him best associated with his hardest hits as he replied: "Upon questions of history I must refer you to Mr. Seward, for he is posted in such things; and I don't pretend to be bright. My only distinct recollection of the matter is, that Charles lost his head."[1]

[1] Carpenter, 213.

CHAPTER XXIX

LINCOLN ON HIS KNEES

As Paul established an analogy between Christianity and nature, so Abraham Lincoln illustrated in his life the possibility of divine companionship along with the essential religiousness of what men call the ordinary affairs of men and nations. By living Christianity, he made it more than a doctrine. It became a vital force in every day affairs. This is why much of the speculation and even academic discussions as to how far Lincoln was a Christian is beside the mark. He lived increasingly the life of faith and hope, and translated fate into purpose, benevolence into the Fatherhood of God, relationship with others into brotherhood of man. He harmonized the ideals of morals and the essentials of Christianity. He accepted Jesus' estimate of prayer as spiritual communion, as filial trust always necessary to the higher life. He spoke of prayer as "talking with God" and counted it so necessary that once he declared: "I have been driven to my knees over and over again because I have nowhere else to go." He would have everybody pray that his own faith might not fail him in the hour of trial and that the Union might be saved.

To L. E. Chittenden, one of his closest friends, he said: "It makes me stronger and more confident to know that all Christians in the loyal States are working to the same end; thousands of them are fighting for us, and no one will say that an officer or a private is less brave because he is a praying soldier."

A clergyman from New York, during a call at the White House, said: "I have not come to ask any favours of you, Mr. President; I have only come to say that the loyal people of the North are sustaining you and will continue to do so. We are giving you all that we have, the lives of our sons as well as our confidence and our prayers. You must know that no boy's father or mother ever kneels in prayer these days without asking God to give you strength and wisdom." His eyes brimming with tears, Mr. Lincoln replied: "But for those prayers, I should have faltered and perhaps failed long ago. Tell every father and mother you know to keep on praying, and I will keep on fighting, for I know God is on our side." As the clergyman started to leave the room, Mr. Lincoln held him by the hands and said: "I sup-

pose I may consider this as a sort of pastoral call?"
"Yes," replied the clergyman. "Out in our country," continued Lincoln, "when a parson makes a
pastoral call, it was always the custom for the
folks to ask him to lead in prayer, and I should
like to ask you to pray with me today. Pray that
I may have strength and wisdom." The two men
knelt side by side, and the clergyman offered the
most fervent plea to Almighty God that ever fell
from his lips. As they arose, the President
clasped his visitor's hand and remarked in a satisfied sort of way: "I feel better."[1]

At another time, when Mr. Lincoln was reminded that he was daily remembered by those
who prayed "not to be heard of men" as no man
ever had before been remembered, he caught at
the homely phrase and said: "Yes, I like that
phrase 'not to be heard of men,' and I guess it is
generally true as you say; at least I have been
told so, and I have been a great deal helped by
just that thought."[2]

As early as 1851 when Mr. Lincoln's father was
in his last illness, Lincoln, who could not go to the
bedside because of sickness in his own family,
wrote to his step-brother, John Johnston:

[1] *The True Abraham Lincoln*, pp. 383-4.
[2] Noah Brooks, *Harper's Magazine*, July, 1865, p. 226.

Tell father to remember to call upon and confide in our great and good and merciful Maker, Who will not turn away from him in any extremity. He notes the fall of the sparrow, and numbers the hairs of our heads. He will not forget the dying man who puts his trust in Him. Say to him, if it be his lot to go now, he will soon have a joyous meeting with loved ones gone before, and where the rest of us, through the help of God, hope ere long to join him.

Brigadier-General James F. Rusling in his work: *Men and Things I Saw in Civil War Days*, throws the following light on Lincoln as a man of prayer in the White House:

Bishop Edmund Janes testified that "many times during the war when I visited Lincoln in his private office in Washington, he said, 'Don't go, Bishop, until you have prayed with me. We need your prayers and the divine direction in these critical hours,' and so, time after time, I knelt with Mr. Lincoln in the White House when we two were alone, and carried the cause of the Union and the needs of the President's anxious heart and our distracted country, to the Lord in prayer."

Akin to this testimony is that of the Rev. Edgar DeWitt Jones in the *Homeletic Review* for 1909 (p. 156):

To Bishop Simpson who called once when the clouds were thickest, Lincoln said: "Bishop, I feel the need of prayer as never before; please pray for me." And the two men then fell on their knees in prayer to God for strength and guidance.

Noah Brooks, one of Mr. Lincoln's most trusted friends, who but for the assassination, would have become one of his confidential secretaries, in a letter to the Rev. J. A. Reed, states that Mr. Lincoln informed him "that after he went to the White House he kept up the habit of daily prayer. Sometimes," he said, "it was only ten words, but those ten words he had."[1]

Among the men whom Mr. Lincoln knew intimately, was John Nicolay, one of his private secretaries. Speaking of Mr. Lincoln as a man of prayer, Mr. Nicolay said ·

Mr. Lincoln was a praying man. I know that to be a fact and I have heard him request people to pray for him, which he would never have done had he not believed that prayer is answered. Many a time have I heard Mr. Lincoln ask ministers and Christian women to pray for him, and he did not do this for effect. He was no hypocrite; he had such reverence for sacred things that he would not trifle with them. I have heard him say that he prayed.[2]

Nicolay thus dispels the injustice of Herndon's testimony that as he knew Lincoln in his Spring-

[1] *Scribner's*, May, 1873, p. 333.
[2] Curtis, pp. 385-6.

field days, Lincoln's attitude toward prayer was "merely conventional." He could not pretend. Posturing was foreign to his self-respect. Deception was incongruous with his sincerity.

Much ink has been spilled, more may yet be spilled, in controversy about purely technical questions as to Lincoln's Christianity. It will always be enough for plain people that Lincoln lived the Christian life of prayer which Jesus lived, and made it the test of Christian theory and practice. If a man who prayed as much as Lincoln prayed was not a Christian, all churches might well question their potential usefulness to man. Lincoln in fact makes all controversy foolish by such words as he spoke to a friend after the second fatal battle of Bull Run: "I have talked with God. It is His cause, and the Union is His. As He willeth, so it will be. We can but follow and pray for its integrity and for mercy on the fallen." [1]

Upon one occasion, he was so absorbed in the issues of the battle which was being fought at Port Hudson that his soul, like the Psalmist, was cast down. Finally arousing himself from his depression, he exclaimed: "The Battle of Port Hudson is now going on and many lives will be sacrificed on both sides, but I have done the best I could,

[1] Chapman, p. 380.

trusting in God; for it will be unfortunate if they gain this important point, and on the other hand if we can only gain it, we shall gain much, and I think we shall as we have a great deal to thank God for; we have Vicksburg and Gettysburg already."

Mrs. Rebecca Pomeroy, who was present upon that occasion said: "Mr. Lincoln, prayer will do what nothing else will. Can you not pray?" "Yes, I will," he said, and while the tears were coursing down his haggard face, he said: "Pray for me," and he went to his room. At 12 o'clock at night, while the soldiers were guarding the house, a sentinel riding by halted with a telegram that was carried to the President. A few minutes later, the door opened, and the President standing under the chandelier holding the telegram in his hand, exclaimed: "Good news! Good news! Port Hudson is ours! The victory is ours and God is good." Mrs. Pomeroy said: "Nothing like prayer in time of trouble." "Oh, yes, yes, there is," responded Mr. Lincoln, "Praise; for prayer and praise go together."[1]

The editor of the *Advance* tells this memorable story which he had from the lips of James F. Murdock, elocutionist, lecturer, and actor.

[1] *Lincoln Scrapbook*, p. 54.

I spent three weeks in the White House with Mr. Lincoln as his guest. One night, it was just after the battle of Bull Run, I was restless and could not sleep. I was repeating the part which I was to take in a public performance. The hour was past midnight; indeed, it was getting near dawn, when I heard low tones proceeding from a private room near where the President slept. The door was partly open. I saw the President kneeling beside an open window. The light was turned low in the room, his back was toward me. For a moment I was silent, looking in amazement and wonder. Then he cried out in tones pleading and sorrowful: "Oh, Thou God that heard Solomon in the night when he prayed for wisdom, hear me. I cannot lead this people; I cannot guide the affairs of this nation without Thy help. I am poor and weak and sinful. Oh, God, Who didst hear Solomon when he cried for wisdom, hear me and save this nation." [Then, Mr. Murdock adds]: I think from that time the clouds which had long lain threatening over the affairs of our Government began to roll away. The skies were brighter; the smile of heaven was upon our President; God heard his prayer and sent deliverance.[1]

We often wonder whether the narratives in Holy Writ of the intimate communion of the prophets with God and their direct guidance, is not a touch of oriental imagination or illusion, or the vision of the night. But the incident related by General Rusling in his *Men and Things I Saw*

[1] *The Presbyterian*, April 5, 1893.

in Civil War Days, and corroborated by General Daniel E. Sickles, without any substantial disagreement as to the important facts involved, would help convince us that the Almighty still concerns himself with the affairs of men.

It was Sunday, July 5, 1863, the day following the great victory at Gettysburg where Gen. Sickles lost a leg. He had been removed to Washington and was occupying a room in a temporary hospital where President Lincoln called upon him early Sunday morning. In reply to a question from Gen. Sickles whether or not the President was anxious about the battle at Gettysburg, Gen. Rusling reports that Lincoln gravely said:

"No, I was not. Some of my Cabinet and many others in Washington were, but I had no fears."

Gen. Sickles inquired how this was, and seemed curious about it. Mr. Lincoln hesitated, but finally replied:

Well, I will tell you how it was. In the pinch of your campaign up there, when everybody seemed panic-stricken and nobody could tell what was going to happen, oppressed by the gravity of our affairs, I went to my room one day and locked the door and got down on my knees before Almighty God and prayed to him mightily for victory at Gettysburg. I told Him that this war was His, and our cause His cause, but we could not stand another Fredericksburg or

Chancellorsville. Then and there I made a solemn
vow to Almighty God that if He would stand by our
boys at Gettysburg, I would stand by Him, and He
did stand by you boys, and I will stand by Him. And
after that, I don't know how it was, and I cannot
explain it, soon a sweet comfort crept into my soul.
The feeling came that God had taken the whole business into His own hands, and that things would go
right at Gettysburg, and that is why I had no fears
about you.

As concerning Vicksburg, the news of which
victory had not yet reached him, he said:

"I have been praying for Vicksburg also and
believe our Heavenly Father is going to give us
victory there too."

Of course, he did not know that Vicksburg had
already surrendered the day before.

General Rusling says that Mr. Lincoln spoke
solemnly and pathetically as if from the depth
of his heart, and that his manner was deeply
touching.

The Confederacy reached its high-water mark at
Gettysburg. The battle started by mistake, and
the charge of the First Minnesota Regiment, with
its resultant losses, broke the record of the Civil
War for fatality. Pickett's charge and repulse
reached the bloody angle of pre-eminence. At
sundown, General Meade was bewildered, not

knowing what step to take next, when a strange and irresistible impression moved him to order up his reserves. At daylight, he was ready to meet the Confederate advance. He had a similar experience the second night with a similar result.

What was the secret of the President? Why was he rightly directed when the destiny of the nation was at stake? Whence the light in those days of darkness by which he moved with unerring instinct to victory? Draw what conclusions we may, there is ever in the normal mind the vision of the prostrate figure of the great war President, lying on his face on the floor of the White House, crying out of the deep of his anxiety: "Save, Lord, or we perish!" And Lincoln, at least, believed God answered prayer.

CHAPTER XXX

LIVING HIS RELIGION

SOME men seem naturally good. Lincoln has his proper place among all such. Yet it was reserved for Christianity to lift him up above all other good men of his time, to put the final elevating touch of Jesus Christ upon him, and to make him in the Christian sense a man of God. We have already seen how with his penetrating and inclusive mind, he worked out before he died a Christian theology singularly consistent and complete. We come now to consider the expression of his Christian faith in terms of everyday existence.

He once said in his Springfield days, "Whenever any church will inscribe over its altar as a qualification for membership the Saviour's statement of the substance of the law and Gospel, 'Thou shalt love the Lord thy God with all thy heart, and with all thy soul, and with all thy mind, and thy neighbour as thyself,' that church will I join with all my heart and soul."[1] In reply to a committee

[1] Curtis, 374.

from the Evangelical Lutheran, General Synod, Mr. Lincoln said: "You all may recollect that in taking up the sword, thus forced into our hands, this government appealed to the prayers of the pious and good and declared that it placed its whole dependence upon the favour of God. I now humbly and reverently, in your presence, reiterate the acknowledgment of that dependence."[1]

To the American Baptist Home Mission Society, he said: "I can only thank you for thus adding to the effective and almost unanimous support which the Christian communities are so zealously giving to the country and to liberty."[2]

In reply to an address from the Society of Friends, delivered to him at the White House, Sept. 28, 1862, he said: "I am glad to know I have your sympathy and prayers. In the very responsible position in which I happen to be placed, being a humble instrument in the hands of our Heavenly Father, as I am and as we all are to work out His great purposes, I have desired that all my works and acts may be according to His will and that it might be so, I have sought His aid."[3]

To a committee of sixty-five members of the General Assembly of the Presbyterian Church in

[1] Complete works of Abraham Lincoln. Nicolay and Hay.
[2] *Ibid.*   [3] *Ibid.*

the United States of America, he said: "Relying
as I do upon Almighty God and encouraged, as I
am by the resolutions which you have just read,
with the support which I receive from Christian
men, I shall not hesitate to use all the means at my
control to secure the termination of the rebellion
and will hope for success."[1]

In a letter of reply to a deputation of ministers
who presented to him resolutions adopted by the
General Conference of the Methodist Episcopal
Church, May 18, 1864, he said: "God bless the
Methodist Church, bless all the Churches—and
blessed be God who in this our great trial, giveth
u the Churches."[2] He never was formally attached to any church, though he had a passion
not merely for attending Sunday services but also
midweek prayer meetings.[3] Abraham Lincoln,
however, won from those whose judgment we all
value, tributes to his Christian character not
usually paid church members, perhaps if taken in
the large never paid before to any other soul save
Jesus Christ. Surely that devoted youthful secretary, John Hay, who lived to be at last himself a
model of high-minded statesmanship, spoke hon-

[1] Complete works of Abraham Lincoln.   Nicolay and Hay.
[2] *Ibid.*
[3] *Lincoln the Christian*, Johnson, p. 13.
    19

estly when he called Lincoln "the greatest man since Christ." Theodore Roosevelt, a student till the last of Lincoln, said: "If ever there was a man who practically applied what is taught in our churches it was Abraham Lincoln." Dr. J. G. Holland, while the world was still aghast at Lincoln's untimely taking off, predicted that "Mr. Lincoln will always be remembered as eminently a Christian President." Tolstoy pictured Lincoln as "a miniature Christ." And it was a devout Roman Catholic Priest, Father Chiniquy, who "found him the most perfect type of Christian."

In his own heart Lincoln was ever building up the Church of Jesus Christ. He was in fact a member of the Church invisible and indivisible. While he was working out a Christian theology altogether satisfying, he was also giving proof in all of his relationships with men that he did love his neighbour as he loved himself; that beneath all differences of opinion he perceived the Christlike in his fellows; that no incidental error, no petty jealousy, no subtle ambition, no overweening arrogance, no actual unfaithfulness to himself could blind him to the good inherent in all men or make him for a moment overlook the necessity of bearing all things and enduring all things, however disagreeable, to insure his country's profiting by the

best talent and experience that could be enlisted
in its service.

It is worth while to make a special study of
Lincoln's relationships with some of those nearest
to him from 1861 to 1865 in order to appreciate
his Christian attitude steadily maintained in spite
of every aggravation and insult.   William H.
Seward had expected to be President. He came
into the Cabinet assuming he was greater than
the man who had been great enough to call the
greatest to his side because the times demanded
the greatest to save the Union.   Seward was, indeed, a man of far higher education and of wider
reputation as publicist, orator, and statesman.
He had been Governor of the great Empire State
and United States Senator.   By common consent
he took intellectual precedence over any active
leader of his party in the movement that resulted
in the triumph of the Republican Party in 1860.

If Lincoln had any ground for resentment
toward Seward, it was not because Seward had
been his chief political rival, but because of his
patronizing arrogance and assumption of superiority, as when he submitted to the President, on
April 1, 1861, a remarkable state paper in which
he had the effrontery to declare at the end of a
month in office that the administration was as yet

without a policy, either foreign or domestic, and that the United States should demand a categorical explanation from Spain and France, with the alternative of a declaration of war against them in case their explanation was not satisfactory. "But whatever policy is adopted," Seward declared, "there must be an energetic prosecution of it. For this purpose it must be somebody's business to pursue and direct it incessantly. Either the President must do it himself and be all the while active in it, or devolve it upon some member of his Cabinet. Once adopted, debate on it must end, and all agree and abide. It is not in my special province, but I neither seek to evade or assume responsibility."

Seward's meaning would not have been plainer if he had suggested outright to Mr. Lincoln that he abdicate the functions of the Presidency and turn them over to the Secretary of State. Almost any other man in Lincoln's place would have taken Seward's arrogance as a personal insult, and promptly have ejected him from the Cabinet. Instead, Lincoln immediately sent Mr. Seward a reply couched in tactful but firm language, in which, by superior logic, he allowed his shrewd secretary to discover for himself wherein he had erred and what was his real place in the administra-

tion.   The hand of iron was covered with the glove
of velvet.   By quotations from his first Inaugural
Address, Lincoln proved that the administration
had a policy, and that it had been persistently
pursued, both in domestic and foreign matters.   In
regard to Seward's suggestion as to the person
who should be charged with the responsibility of
carrying out the policy that might be adopted,
Mr. Lincoln said:

> If this must be done, I must do it.   When a general
> line of policy is adopted, I apprehend there is no
> danger of its being changed without good reason, by
> continuing to be a subject of unnecessary debate.
> Still, upon points arising in its progress, I wish, and
> suppose I am entitled to have, the advice of all the
> Cabinet.

Severe as was the rebuke, Seward accepted it
in a becoming spirit, and remained in the Cabinet
without sacrifice of self-respect.   Never after did
he attempt to encroach upon the President's pre-
rogative, or to look upon him as in any way in-
ferior.   To his chief, he gave without reservation
his tireless industry and unstinted support those
four hard years, and when Lincoln died, it was
Seward who described him as the best man he had
ever known.

Toward Secretary Stanton, Lincoln's magnanimity was even greater. In the summer of 1857, Stanton had greatly insulted and humiliated Lincoln on the occasion of the latter's visit to Cincinnati as associate counsel with Stanton in the important case of McCormick *vs.* Manny. Lincoln expected to make one of the arguments in the case, and had prepared with unusual care. As the case was of national importance, Lincoln's prominent appearance in connection with it would have been of real value to him professionally. But Stanton professed to be shocked by Lincoln's uncouth appearance, treated him with rude contempt, and even spoke contemptuously of him, within his hearing, as an ignorant backwoodsman. Stanton made such protest against Lincoln's appearing prominently in the case that Lincoln waived his rights, took a back seat, and permitted Stanton to make the argument which he had himself expected to make.

Four years later it was Stanton who was called into the Cabinet as Secretary of War. Even this act was not the full measure of Lincoln's magnanimity. In June, 1861, Stanton gave currency in writing to his belief that the rebels would be in Washington "within thirty days," in consequence of the "painful imbecility of Lincoln." Frequently, throughout the remainder of Lincoln's

life, he was obliged to put up with insolence from
his Secretary of War. But he never abandoned
his patient and kindly attitude toward Stanton, or
failed to give him support in any policy or measure
that Stanton undertook for the good of the cause
for which they both laboured. It was Stanton
who, completely won at last by Lincoln, broke the
solemn silence of the death chamber with the sublime statement, made as Lincoln's last breath
failed,

"Now he belongs to the ages!"

Chase as Secretary of the Treasury proved difficult to handle. He too, had an exaggerated idea of
his own importance and popularity. His political
ambition was voracious. Not always was he
strictly loyal to his Chief. Every soldier who was
not promoted to his own satisfaction, and every
citizen who failed of appointment as postmaster,
when they came to Washington, drifted around to
Chase's Cave of Adullam. They comforted each
other by abusing Lincoln as "the old coward,"
"the old gorilla," etc., and were unanimously of
the opinion that "Congress ought to impeach
him." All of which was faithfully reported to
Mr. Lincoln. "Well, that does not make it so,
does it? Mr. Chase is a good Secretary. The

people believe in him and take his money. That is what we want, is it not? I think we will keep him at it." Such was always Lincoln's answer. It seemed to him of little consequence what Chase said about him so long as Chase served the public.

One day a man ran into Mr. Lincoln's office and said, "President Lincoln, do you know where Chase is?" "Yes." "Do you know that he has gone to the Republican Convention in Ohio?" "Yes." "Do you know that he is going to make a speech there?" "Yes." "Don't you know that he wants to be President, and that you ought to keep him at home?" "Oh, don't worry about Chase. He has just as good a right to want to be President as any man in America, and if the people want Chase to be President, then I want him to be President. When I was a boy I worked on a farm. We ploughed corn, and I rode the horse and a neighbour boy held the plough. The horse was lazy. I pounded him with my heels and the neighbour boy threw clods at him, but he would not go much, till one day a blue-headed fly lit on his back and began to get in his work. The horse could not switch him off, and started to run. The neighbour boy cried: 'Abe, Abe, knock off that fly.' I said: 'No you don't, isn't that just what we want?' If Chase has anything in his head that will make him work for the Republic, isn't that just what we want?"

Mr. Chittenden, the last survivor of the Lincoln Cabinet, is reported in his later years as remarking to an intimate friend: "I went over to Mr. Lincoln's office one morning and found Mr. Lincoln sitting there with his head bowed down, his chin on his chest, evidently much depressed.   He handed me a letter he had just read.   It was Chase's letter, resigning.   I read the letter and felt overwhelmed, and said, 'President Lincoln, you cannot afford to divide the party at such a time.   You *must* hold Chase to it.'   Mr. Lincoln said: 'Mr. Chittenden, Mr. Chase has determined the matter and I will hold him to that.'   After a few moments, lifting up his head he said: 'Mr. Chittenden, Mr. Chase will make a good Chief Justice, and I will appoint him.'"   Continuing, Mr. Chittenden said: "I had long known and loved Mr. Lincoln, but when I saw him in that hour, under the sting of personal insult, and under the shadow of threatened calamity, put that man into the highest place in the Nation, for the good of the Republic, he went up and up, into an atmosphere of which I had never dreamed.   He was the greatest man I ever saw."

The Postmaster-General, Montgomery Blair,

brought the President a problem quite as difficult to solve. Though loyal to the Union, Blair had incurred the hostility of nearly all the radical Republicans in the country. The Baltimore Convention which renominated Lincoln in 1864 adopted a resolution evidently aimed at the Postmaster-General calling for the reorganization of the Cabinet in the interest of harmony. Letters poured in upon the President urging outright the immediate removal of Blair. Henry Wilson, afterwards Vice-President, wrote: "Blair everyone hates. Tens of thousands of men will be lost to you or will give a reluctant vote, on account of the Blairs." Neither the political nor the military outlook was bright. Lincoln doubted for a while that he would win a second term. A division in the party was developing, and Blair was manifestly not with Lincoln. The Cabinet by this time realizing that Lincoln was—as John Drinkwater makes one of them admit—"the best man among them," were lining up with Lincoln and making Blair's position in the Cabinet difficult for him.

Lincoln, however, was not yet convinced that Blair could well be spared from public service. Nor was he of a mood to allow his Cabinet to drive out from the sacred circle by subtle indiscretion or by studied insult one who, if he was to go at all, should

go by Presidential wish expressed in Christian
courtesy. It was for this reason that Lincoln
read the Cabinet a lecture, when the moment for
it had arrived, which all could understand and
none would dare to answer.

I must myself [he said] be the judge how long to
retain and when to remove any of you from his position. It will greatly pain me to discover any of you
endeavouring to promote another's removal or in any
way to prejudice him before the public. Such en-
deavour would be a wrong to me and much worse, a
wrong to the country. My wish is that on this subject no remark be made or question asked by any of
you, here or elsewhere, now or hereafter.

Then with the field clear to deal with perfect
fairness with all in any way concerned, Lincoln
watched and waited. The evidence accumulated
that Blair was increasingly losing the public confidence on which his usefulness depended, and was
not likely to regain it. Meanwhile as the month
of September drew near its end, inspiring news
began to come of Union victories. The Peace at
any Price Platform adopted by the Convention at
Chicago which nominated McClellan in opposition
to the President was evidently not a winning cause.
The entire situation was now as bright as it had
been dark a few weeks earlier. The peril of seem-

ing to act under compulsion or menace had wholly disappeared. Forbearance under the intemperate utterances of Blair was no longer needful for the public safety.

Simply, sincerely, tenderly, like the Christian gentleman he was, Lincoln wrote to his Postmaster-General:

You have generously said to me more than once, that whenever your resignation could be a relief to me, it was at my disposal. The time has come. You very well know that this proceeds from no dissatisfaction of mine with you personally or officially. Your uniform kindness has been unsurpassed by that of any friend; and while it is true that the War does not so greatly add to the difficulties of your Department as to those of some others, it is yet much to say, as I most truly can, that in the three years and a half during which you have administered the General Post Office, I remember no single complaint against you in connection therewith.

That was Lincoln's way of Christian management of a complex case, and Blair not merely responded in kind, resigning without asking for an explanation, but in addition began to speak and work at once for Mr. Lincoln's re-election.

It was in dealing with McClellan that Lincoln's magnanimity attained its climax. Almost from the first he endured impertinence, ingratitude, and even questionable loyalty from McClellan. At the very time McClellan was writing his friends how he "despised the old dotard because he defers to me so much," Lincoln was refusing the demand of the Committee on the Conduct of the War for the removal of McClellan.

Once, in a perilous hour, Mr. Lincoln went to McClellan's headquarters to consult him. McClellan was out, attending the wedding of a member of his staff. Mr. Lincoln waited three hours. McClellan came in and went upstairs. Lincoln, thinking McClellan did not know the President was waiting to see him, sent a note to the General that he, the President, wanted to see him on important war matters. The servant returned with this message: "Tell Lincoln that General McClellan has gone to bed." Even this almost incredible insult Lincoln condoned, doubtless because he felt that the exigencies of the hour demanded that he should. He held the pompous little McClellan in the hollow of his hand, and had but to turn it edgewise to let the peacock of the Army fall into oblivion.

On another occasion, Mr. Lincoln had an engagement with McClellan and two other officers. McClellan paid no attention to the appointment. The other officers spoke their minds freely in regard to McClellan's treatment of the President. But Lincoln was not moved from his consistent purpose to think only of McClellan's value to the country.

McClellan had at last to go. He would not fight, and fighting after all was his official business. There was no other reason why he should be the Commander of the Army. But in his disposition of McClellan's case as in that of Seward, Stanton, Chase, and Blair, Lincoln was never thinking of himself, intent only on the fulfilment of his oath of office to preserve the Union, living out the words of the Man of Nazareth.

CHAPTER XXXI

THE CHARM OF SIMPLE GOODNESS

As a wilderness lad in Kentucky, as a youth in the wilds of Indiana, as a struggling man in Illinois, and finally, as bearer of the Nation's burdens, it could be said of Lincoln as Wordsworth wrote of Milton:

> So didst thou travel on life's common way,
> In cheerful godliness; and yet thy heart
> The lowliest duties on itself did lay.

There still lives in Springfield an aged woman who told a recent visitor that when she was a little girl waiting with trunk packed to take her first railway journey, Mr. Lincoln passed the house and finding her in tears lest she should miss her train, took her cheerily by the hand, flung her trunk upon his stalwart shoulder, and got her to the train in time.

Mr. Lincoln's visit to the Five Points Mission in New York can never be forgotten, if only to recall how little children gathered round him and called forth from the Great Commoner the quiet comment to his friend: "I have now a better understanding than ever before of what the Saviour meant when He said 'Of such is the Kingdom of Heaven.'"

Lincoln loved to play with children. When Miss Tarbell in the nineties was preparing her biography of Lincoln, she found still living in Washington men and women who as children there in the sixties had played with Lincoln. Said Mr. Francis P. Blair, "the boys for hours at a time played 'town ball' on the vast lawn at his grandfather's place near Washington, and Mr. Lincoln drove out there frequently and would join ardently in the sport. I remember vividly how he ran with the children; how long were his strides and how far his coat-tails stuck out behind, and how we tried to hit him with the ball as he ran the bases. He entered into the spirit of the play as completely as any of us."

An aged conductor of the Chicago and Alton Railroad tells a story which illustrates the mysterious distinction simple goodness gave to Lincoln. Many famous men were wont to travel on that road: Stephen A. Douglas, Norman Judd, Lyman Trumbull, David Davis, as well as Abraham Lincoln.

He was the most folksy of any of them [said the conductor to Mr. J. E. Edwards]. He put on no airs. He did not hold himself distant from any man; but there was something about him which we plain people couldn't explain that made us stand a little in awe of him. I now know what it was, but didn't then. It was because he was a greater man than any other we had ever seen. You could get near him in a sort of neighbourly way, as though you had always known him, but there was something tremendous between you and him all the time. I have eaten with him many times at the railroad eating houses, and you get very neighbourly if you eat together in a railroad restaurant. At least we did in those days. Everybody tried to get as near Lincoln as possible when he was eating because he was such good company, but we always looked at him with a kind of wonder. We couldn't exactly make him out. Sometimes I would see what looked like a dreadful loneliness in his face, and I used to wonder what he was thinking about. Whatever it was he was thinking all alone. It wasn't a solemn look, like Stephen A. Douglas sometimes had. Douglas sometimes made me think of an owl. He used to stare at you with his great dark eyes in a way that frightened you. Lincoln never frightened anybody. No one was afraid of him, but there was something about him that made plain folks feel toward him a good deal as a child feels toward his father, because you know every child looks upon his father as a wonderful man.

Frederick Douglass—not long up from slavery —became a man of consequence in Civil War days.

Regardless that Douglass was a negro, Lincoln more than once consulted him concerning public matters, and in later years Douglass said Lincoln was one of the few white men he ever knew who never in any way reminded him in conversation of his colour. [1]

There was no man in public life in Lincoln's time who more surely personified culture and exclusiveness than Charles Sumner of Massachusetts, and yet in his funeral oration on Lincoln in Boston, on June 1, 1865, he laid stress on the simple goodness of the man in the memorable words:

He was naturally humane, inclined to pardon, and never remembered the hard things said against him. He was always good to the poor, and in his dealings with them was full of those "kind little words which are of the same blood as great and holy deeds." With him as President, the idea of republican institutions, where no place is too high for the humblest, was perpetually manifest, so that his simple presence was like a proclamation of equality for all men.

No wonder William Cullen Bryant wrote of him when word came of his taking off:

> Oh, slow to smite and swift to spare,
> Gentle and merciful and just;
> Who in the fear of God did'st bear
> The sword of power, a Nation's trust.

[1] Carpenter, p. 204.

It was the goodness of the man that from the earlier days made first impression on each new friend. A Democratic lawyer in Chicago, Mr. U. F. Linder, said soon after Lincoln's death:

I was introduced to him at the hotel in Charleston, in this State, in the year 1835. There struck me then more than anything else in the man, the expression of goodness and kindness which gleamed in his eyes, and which sat there all the days of his life; and it has seemed to me a hundred times since I heard of his assassination, that no man would have looked in his face and assassinated him. [1]

Some people affect to love their fellowmen or have a spasmodic attack of good fellowship. Lincoln always, in every circumstance, showed the instinct of neighbourliness with high and low, rich and poor. This was now and then interpreted by the "highbrows" of the time as vulgarity. But none of these things moved Lincoln. He always lived up to the words he spoke to the Wisconsin State Agricultural Society at Milwaukee, in 1859: "To correct the evils, great and small, which spring up from want of sympathy and from positive enmity among strangers, as nations or as individuals, is one of the highest functions of civilization."

[1] Brockett, *Life and Times of Abraham Lincoln*, p. 701.

"The President of the United States has a multiplicity of duties not specified in the Constitution or the laws," said Mr. Lincoln to a friend who once found him counting some greenbacks. "This is one of them. This money belongs to a negro porter n the Treasury Department who is now in the hospital so sick that he cannot sign his name. According to his wish, I am putting a part of it aside in an envelope, labelled, to save it for him."

It was not enough that he should save the Union: he must also save the savings of a friendless coloured man.

Some shepherds of men have been too busy to be kind; Lincoln was so busy being kind that often he had little time for anything else. Arnold says that one day he was walking along the tree-covered path leading from the Executive Mansion to the War Office. He saw the tall form of the President seated on the grass under a tree. A wounded soldier, seeking back-pay and a pension, had met the President and sought his counsel. Taking the soldier's papers, Lincoln sat down upon the grass, examined the documents, and told him what to do, giving him a note to the proper bureau, and thus secured prompt attention for the wounded man.

On another occasion, a tax having been levied

upon oxen, the owner of a pair came to Lincoln, the most heavily burdened man in the world, hoping he might help him to get rid of the tax. Knowing the man, and remembering the oxen, the President, like an oriental patriarch, kindly said: "Are those the oxen I see standing at the corner whenever I go to the Treasury? I never see them move. Maybe they are not movable property. Perhaps we may get them put down as real estate."

On one of his visits to a hospital, Lincoln suddenly ordered the driver to stop. A man had walked directly in front of the horses, which were brought to a standstill just in time to save him from being run down. The President quickly discovered that the unfortunate, scarcely more than a boy, was a blind soldier, having been shot in both eyes. Taking his hand, Lincoln asked his name, his service and his home. The sightless face of the youth was all aglow with gratitude as he heard the words of sympathy spoken by the man who, on leaving, modestly said: "I am Abraham Lincoln."

Next day a commission, signed by the President, was placed in the youth's hands. He was made a first lieutenant in the Army of the United States, and was retired on three quarters pay for life.

He never seemed to think in terms of self: only of his country and his neighbours. Leaving the War Department at midnight of November 10, 1864, with the re-election fresh in mind, he said:

So long as I have been here I have not willingly planted a thorn in any man's bosom. While I am deeply sensible of the high compliment of re-election, and duly grateful, as I trust, to Almighty God for having directed my countrymen to a right conclusion, as I think for their own good, it adds nothing to my satisfaction that any other man may be disappointed or pained by the result. May I ask those who have not differed from me to join with me in this same spirit toward those that have?

But he was on record long before in those loving words to his good friend: "Speed, die when I may, I want it said of me by those who knew me best that I always plucked a thistle and planted a flower when I thought a flower would grow."

Goodness, to have charm, must be certain of itself. It must live above all concern for criticism. Lincoln never wasted time in answering attacks upon him save when silence would have hurt the cause he represented. He once said: "I do the very best I know how—the very best I can; and I mean to keep doing so until the end. If the end brings me out all right, what is said against me won't amount to anything. If the end brings

me out wrong, ten angels swearing I was right
would make no difference."[1]

The charm of his inherent goodness seemed
sometimes to shine out from his homely face. On
the word of Thaddeus Stevens, Lincoln once
granted the request of an aged woman whose son
had been convicted of a grave offence, and sent
her out of the White House with the pardon in her
pocket. Silent till she was half way down the
stairs, she suddenly broke out in furious indignation: "I knew it was a copperhead lie!" "What
do you mean," said Mr. Stevens? "Why, they
told me he was an ugly looking man," she answered
in excitement. "He is really the handsomest man
I ever saw."[2]

He had his convictions. Woe betide the man,
Douglas or anybody else, who thought that he
could shake them. Yet Lincoln saw the good
there usually is somewhere on the other side. One
of his old friends, who lived on till the nineteenth
century was at an end, reports this human comment Lincoln made on slavery: "We've been
wrong, North and South, about slavery. No use
to blame it all on the South. We've been in it,
too, from the start. If both sides had been willing

[1] Carpenter, 258.
[2] *Ibid.*, 173.

to give in a little, we might have worked it out, that is, if we had all been willing to admit the thing was wrong, and take our share of the burden in putting an end to it."[1]

Nothing pleased him more in his simplicity than for men to recognize that he was trying to do the will of God. At a White House reception a man from Buffalo said: "Up my way we believe in God and Abraham Lincoln." "My friend," replied the President, "you are more than half right."

A Southern woman besought the President to have her husband released from a Northern prison. Though his politics seemed pernicious, she emphasized the fact that he was a religious man. "I'm glad to hear that," said Mr. Lincoln, brightly; and the woman was filled with hope. Then the President went on: "Because any man who wants to disrupt this Union needs all the religion in sight to save him."

It is well known that military officials were constantly remonstrating with the President because he often interfered in cases of courts-martial. Once, when he refused to countenance the shooting of twenty-four deserters in a row, he said: "There

[1] Ida M. Tarbell, *Red Cross Magazine*, February, 1920, p. 68.

are already too many weeping widows; for God's sake, don't ask me to add to the number, for I won't do it."

One Thursday, looking at a great pile of sentences upon his desk, he said: "Tomorrow is butcher's day, and I must go through these papers and see if I can't find some excuse to let these poor fellows off."

A father besought him at night on behalf of his nineteen-year-old boy, who had fallen asleep at his post. The President sat up in his night-clothes as he wrote an order suspending sentence, and fearing lest his order might miscarry, he dressed himself and went in person to the War Department. His paternal heart was such that he could neither slumber nor sleep.

He was approached one day by a broken-hearted old man. His only son had been convicted of unpardonable crimes and sentenced to be shot. "I am sorry I can do nothing for you," said Mr. Lincoln, kindly. "Listen to this telegram I received from General Butler yesterday":

President Lincoln, I pray you not to interfere with the courts-martial of the army. You will destroy all discipline among our soldiers.

B. F. BUTLER.

Watching the old father's grief for a moment, Lincoln then exclaimed: "By jingo! Butler or no Butler, here goes!" Writing a few words, he handed the paper to the old man, reading:

"Job Smith is not to be shot until further orders from me.
"ABRAHAM LINCOLN."

"Why," exclaimed the father, disappointedly, "I thought it was a pardon. You may order him to be shot next week."

"My friend," answered Lincoln, "I see you are not very well acquainted with me. If your son never dies till orders come from me to shoot him, he will live to be a great deal older than Methuselah."

A woman, the wife of one of Mosby's men, called on the President. Her husband had been condemned to be shot, and she came, accompanied by a Senator, to seek the President's pardon. He heard her story, and then inquired what kind of man her husband was. "Is he temperate? Does he abuse the children and beat you?" "No, no," she replied, "he is a good man, a good husband; he loves the children and we cannot live without him. The only trouble is that he is a fool about politics. I live in the North, born there, and if

I get him home, he will do no more fighting for the South." "Well," said the President, after examining the papers, "I will pardon your husband and turn him over to you for safe keeping." Overwhelmed with joy the wife began to sob as if her heart would break. "My dear woman," said Lincoln, "if I had known how badly it was going to make you feel, I would never have pardoned him." "You do not understand me," she cried, between her sobs, "you do not understand me, Mr. President!" "Yes, yes, I do," answered Lincoln; "and if you do not go away at once, I shall be crying with you."

Another phase of Lincoln's great heart is manifested in the spirit of democracy of which he was the incarnation. A sham of any stamp could not live in the presence of his transparent soul. His horror of a lie was intense. As an illustration of Lincoln's honesty and hatred of pretence, Herndon relates that he once drew up a dilatory plea for the purpose of getting a case put over to another term of court. "Is this founded on fact?" Lincoln asked. Herndon replied that he had merely done it to safeguard their client's interests. Then Lincoln answered: "You know it is a sham, and a sham is very often but another name for a lie. Don't let it go on record. The cursed thing may come staring us in the face long after this suit is forgotten."

Morgan, in his biography, relates a memorable dream of Lincoln's. He thought he was in a vast assembly, and the people drew back to let him pass, whereupon Lincoln heard someone say: "He is a common-looking fellow." But in his dream Lincoln turned to the man and said: "Friend, the Lord prefers common-looking people; that is the reason why he made so many of them."

No wonder that on leaving Springfield for Washington, we hear this open-hearted illustrator of the charm of simple goodness saying to Herndon, his law partner: "Billy, over sixteen years together, and we have not had a cross word during all that time, have we?" "Not one." "Don't take down the sign, Billy; let it swing, that our clients may understand that the election of a President makes no change in the firm of Lincoln & Herndon. If I live, I'm coming back, and we will go right on practising law as if nothing had ever happened." Then they left the office, going down the stairs and across the town to the railroad station, Lincoln never to come back alive.

He was considerate of beast and bird as well as folk. One day when, as a country lawyer accompanied by friends he was going over the circuit, he got down from his horse in a heavy storm and soiled his boots and clothing in the deep mire to release a pig that had become painfully entangled in a fence. When his companions laughed at him for his kindly interest in the animal, Lincoln answered: "I could not stand the look in that pig's eye as we rode past; it seemed to say to me: 'There goes my last chance.'"

On another occasion, while riding the circuit in Illinois, Lincoln was missed by his fellow-lawyers. Joining them a few minutes later, he explained that he had caught two young birds which the wind had blown from their nest. "I could not have slept," he said, "unless I had restored those little creatures to their mother."

He never lost his special interest in the poor and the distressed. Located near the White House in Washington was a primary and intermediate school, the yard of which was separated by a fence from the rear end of the White House grounds. One of the events that stands out distinctly in the memory of some of those schoolboys is this: One day the teacher gave a lesson on neatness, asking each boy to come to school next day with his boots blacked. They all obeyed, excepting John S., a poor, one-armed lad, who brought down upon himself no end of ridicule, because he had used stove blacking, the only kind of polish which his humble home afforded. Boys are sometimes merciless in their ridicule. This boy, only nine years old, and doubly sensitive because of his lost arm, tried to be brave, but his lips were quivering and the tears were in his eyes, when the jeering suddenly stopped, for there, leaning upon the fence and listening, stood the President.

Uttering no word of reproof, but entering the schoolhouse, Mr. Lincoln made inquiry of the teacher. He learned that John was a son of a dead soldier, and that his mother, who had other children, was a washerwoman. Then he went away, and it was many days before he returned again; but the next morning John was at school in a new suit, and with new shoes radiant of the best blacking. The change was so great the boys hardly recognized their companion. John reported that the afternoon before, the President and Mrs. Lincoln and another lady called at his home, in their carriage; that the President had taken him to a clothing store and bought him two suits; and that while he was doing this, the ladies made inquiries of his mother, which later were followed by clothing for the two little girls and a supply of coal and groceries. In addition to this information the lad brought to his teacher a scrap of paper containing a verse of Scripture which Mr. Lincoln had requested to have written on the blackboard: "Inasmuch as ye have done it unto one of the least of these My brethren, ye have done it unto Me." Some weeks later, when Mr. Lincoln visited the school again, the verse was still on the blackboard and the teacher called his attention to it. Adjusting his spectacles, he read it; then, removing his eyeglasses and wiping them, the boys thought they saw tears in his kindly eyes. He quickly replaced his glasses, and, taking a crayon, said: "Boys, I have another quotation from the Bible, and I hope you will learn it, and come to know its truth as I have known and felt it." Then below the verse he wrote:

"It is more blessed to give than to receive."

CHAPTER XXXII

DISCIPLINED BY GRIEF

MR. LINCOLN's fondness for children was one of the most beautiful traits of his character. This trait doubtless accentuated his love for his own son Willie, whose death so rent the father's soul that for a time it seemed his mind would be unseated. But he emerged from his great sorrow disciplined into religious maturity.

Miss Ida Tarbell, in her excellent biography of Lincoln, says:

The protecting sympathy and tenderness of the President, extended to all children, became a passionate affection for his own. Willie and Tad had always been privileged at the White House, and their pranks and companionship did much to relieve the tremendous strain under which the President was suffering. Many visitors who saw him with the lads at this period have recorded their impressions how keenly he enjoyed their company, how indulgent and affectionate he was with them. When both children fell ill, when their father saw them suffering and when it became evident as it afterwards did, that Willie the elder of the two, would die, Mr. Lincoln's anguish was unspeakable. He would slip away from the visitors and the Capitol at every opportunity to visit the sick room.

During the last four or five days of Willie's life, when the child was suffering terribly and lay in an unbroken delirium, the father shared with the nurse the nightly vigils at the bedside. When Willie finally died, the President was so prostrated that it was feared by many of his friends that he would succumb entirely to his grief. Standing by the side of his boy, he said to the nurse, "This is the hardest trial of my life. Why is it? Why is it?" In the course of a conversation with her, he questioned her concerning her situation. She told him she was a widow and that her husband and two children were in Heaven, and added that she saw the hand of God in it all and that she had never loved Him before as she had since her affliction. "How was that brought about?" inquired Mr. Lincoln. "Simply by trusting in God and feeling that He does all things well," she replied. "Did you submit fully to the first loss?" he asked. "No," she answered, "not wholly, but as blow came upon blow and all was taken, I could and did submit, and was very happy." He responded, "I am glad to hear you say that. Your experience will help me bear my affliction." On being assured that many Christians were praying for him on the morning of the funeral, he wiped away the tears that sprang to his eyes and said, "I am glad to hear that. I want them to pray for me. I need their prayers."

As he was going out to the burial, the good woman expressed her sympathy with him. He thanked her gently and said, "I will try to go to God with my sorrow." A few days afterward she asked him if he could trust God. He replied, "I think I can, and I

21

will try. I wish I had the childlike faith you speak of, and I trust He will give it to me." And then he spoke of his mother, who so many years before had been committed to the dust among the wilds of Indiana. In this hour of his greatest trial the memory of her who had held him upon her bosom and soothed his childish griefs came back to him with tenderest recollections. "I remember her prayers," said he, "and they have always followed me. They have clung to me all my life."

Never perhaps was a human heart more sore than Lincoln's after Willie died. He drank the dregs of sorrow, and only religion could bring him any consolation. Those were not the days of shorthand interviews. Doubtless some entirely trustworthy witnesses who have reported Lincoln's outpoured grief to them are only substantially correct. But that is quite enough. He made on several the same impression Simon Peter must have made when he said to our Lord: "To whom shall we go? Thou hast the words of eternal life."

In the Episcopal Church of war times no man was worthier in reputation or mightier in words than the Rector of historic Trinity Church of New York City, the Rev. Dr. Francis Vinton. Being in Washington when Lincoln's mourning was almost melancholy, through Mrs. Lincoln whom he knew, he was invited to the White House. He spoke straight from the heart in pastoral consolation to the President as he would comfort one of his own flock.

"Your son is alive."

"Alive," exclaimed Mr. Lincoln. "Surely you mock me."

"No, sir: believe me," answered Dr. Vinton; "it is a most comforting doctrine of the Church, founded on the words of Christ Himself."

Mr. Lincoln threw his arms around Dr. Vinton's neck, laid his head upon his breast, and sobbed aloud, "Alive! Alive!"

Dr. Vinton greatly moved said: "My dear sir, believe this, for it is God's most precious truth. Seek not your son among the dead: he is not there; he lives today in paradise! God has called your son into His upper kingdom— a kingdom and an existence as real, more real, than your own. It is a part of God's plan for the ultimate happiness of you and yours. Doubt it not. Think of the full import of the words I have quoted. The Sadducees, when they questioned Jesus, had no other conception than that Abraham, Isaac, and Jacob were dead and buried. Mark the reply: 'Now that the dead *are* raised, even Moses showed at the bush when he called the Lord the God of Abraham, the God of Isaac, and the God of Jacob.

For he is not the God of the dead, but of the living, *for all live unto Him!*' Did not the aged patriarch mourn his sons as dead?—'Joseph is not, and Simeon is not, and ye will take Benjamin also.' But Joseph and Simeon were both living, though he believed it not. Indeed, Joseph being taken from him, was the eventual means of the preservation of the whole family. And so God has called your son into His upper kingdom—a kingdom and an existence as real, more real, than your own. It may be that he too, like Joseph, has gone, in God's good providence, to be the salvation of *his* father's household. It is a part of the Lord's plan for the ultimate happiness of. you and yours. Doubt it not."

Dr. Vinton then told Lincoln that he had a sermon on the subject. Mr. Lincoln asked him to send it to him as early as possible and thanked him repeatedly for his cheering and hopeful words. When Lincoln received the sermon he read it over and over, and had a copy made for his own private use. A member of the family said that Mr. Lincoln's views in relation to spiritual things seemed changed from that hour.[1]

Those who have studied carefully the Lincoln pictures have learned that it was about this time a

[1] Johnson, pp. 81–84; Carpenter, pp. 117–19; Barton, 206–8.

new gravity settled on his face.   A resigned sadness
began to look forth from his solemn eyes.   He had
found more of the peace that passeth understanding.   His confidence in immortality grew stronger.
But his mind dwelt more on death.   He talked
oftener of his own ending.   He gave the impression
that he knew he had not long to live.   Charles
Sumner, not prone to plunge into extravagance of
joy or grief, was deeply moved on one occasion by
Lincoln's reading and re-reading to a little group
of friends the familiar passage from *Macbeth:*

> Duncan is in his grave;
> After life's fitful fever he sleeps well;
> Treason has done his worst; nor steel, nor poison,
> Malice domestic, foreign levy, nothing
> Can touch him further.

With faith in God ever growing, and the rich
experience of consolation it brought, we are not
surprised to find Mr. Lincoln's interest in everything pertaining to Christianity deepening and
widening, manifesting itself in his attendance upon
public worship, in his regular habit of prayer, and
even more in his desire that the comforts and blessings of Christianity should be made the privilege
of the Army.   He even read the Bible to the
coloured "help" in the White House.   He kept in
close touch and sympathetic co-operation with the

Christian Commission. His official and personal approval of the workings of this charity was one of the greatest encouragements to those who were actively engaged in it. At a meeting of the Commission held early in 1864, Mr. Lincoln was a deeply interested spectator, and was particularly moved by the remarks of Chaplain C. C. McCabe, afterward Bishop of the Methodist Church, then just released from Libby Prison. The Chaplain gave a graphic description of the scene among the prisoners upon hearing the news of the victory at Gettysburg, when they took up Julia Ward Howe's *Battle Hymn of the Republic*, beginning with the lines, "Mine eyes have seen the glory of the coming of the Lord," and fairly made the old prison walls rock with the stirring melody. After the Chaplain had sung the hymn, Mr. Lincoln sent to the platform a request for its repetition. It was a song he could appreciate and it stirred him like a trumpet blast.

Like the saints and martyrs of earlier Christian history, he seemed to grow increasingly dependent on the consciousness of God. Like Dwight L. Moody and Henry Clay Trumbull he counted no trouble too great to take now and then to get close to some man he thought more richly endowed than he with spiritual gifts. After one public

disaster almost too grievous to be borne, he travelled by gunboat from Washington to West Point.
Returning by way of Brooklyn, he called late Sunday evening on Mr. Beecher, and without sending in his name, came muffled in a heavy dark cloak
into the room with even his face hidden.   Mrs.
Beecher was somewhat alarmed, mindful of the
many threats which had been made upon her
husband's life because of his stout loyalty to Lincoln and the Northern cause.   For hours with
anxious heart she heard her husband and his
mysterious visitor pacing the floor above and talking in low tones.   She was relieved when near
midnight, still muffled in his cloak, the visitor left
the home.   Not until twenty years later, just before his death, did Mr. Beecher confide to anyone
that his strange visitor was the President of the
United States, so bowed with care, so broken by the
sorrows of a nation, that he had to have the help of
one he regarded as a spiritual expert, whose words
and prayers would help him to "carry on" and to
understand a little better the discipline of sorrow.[1]

---

[1] Chapman, *Latest Light on Abraham Lincoln*, p. 535. This
story, sometime questioned, has received new confirmation in a
letter, dated April 29, 1919, written to the author and certifying
that the President was in New York in conference with General
Scott the very day he visited Mr. Beecher, as reported by Mrs.
Beecher to her grandson, Mr. Samuel Scoville, Jr.

These and many other incidents in the life of Lincoln show that he was ever learning from experience, ever growing under the chastisement of sorrow in spiritual discernment and in personal communion with God. The problems of the war itself assumed increasingly a religious aspect. What at first seemed to Mr. Lincoln in part a utilitarian question became so grave in its far-reaching influence, so fundamental in its relation to all civilization, that he made it not only the subject of constant private meditation and prayer, but upon one occasion, his heart became so heavy beneath the crushing burden that he hinted that he felt like Jesus in Gethsemane, and falling on his knees in the presence of his Cabinet, he asked them to join with him in prayer.[1]

This increased devotion to God was only the completion of the evolution of Mr. Lincoln's character. From the day he wrote to Parson Elkin, urging him to come and conduct the funeral service for his mother, on through his boyhood to manhood, then as a lawyer, as a member of the Illinois Legislature, and of Congress, through the exciting scenes of his political campaigns, while delivering addresses before Bible Societies and Sunday Schools, and in all the rapidly changing

[1] Carpenter (in Raymond), page 735.

phases of his life, he developed a growing sense of dependence on God, and an ever-enlarging Christian character founded on the Rock of Ages.   But never must it be forgotten that it was the discipline of suffering in his home circle and for the millions whom he loved as a father, that stopped at last all tendency to speculate or doubt and armed him with an irresistible and triumphant faith!

CHAPTER XXXIII

THE PROCLAMATIONS OF A CHRISTIAN PRESIDENT

MR. LINCOLN'S many proclamations to the people of the Union appointing days for thanksgiving and prayer reveal the absolute integrity of his religious life. For him to live was God. He harked back in each national as well as individual emergency to God. "It is"—as he once said—"my constant prayer that I and this nation should be on the Lord's side." His continuous dependence on God Lincoln revealed in his proclamation, July 12, 1863, for a day of national thanksgiving:

It has pleased Almighty God to hearken to the supplications and prayers of an afflicted people, and to vouchsafe to the Army and Navy of the United States victories on the land and on the sea, so signal and so effective as to furnish reasonable grounds for augmented confidence that the Union of those States will be maintained, their Constitution preserved, and their peace and prosperity permanently restored. It is meet and right to recognize and confess the presence of the Almighty Father and the power of His hand equally in these triumphs and sorrows

Inviting the people to assemble on the 6th day of August he recognized not only God but the Holy Spirit also in the impressive phrase:

To render the homage due the Divine Majesty for the wonderful things done in the Nation's behalf; to invoke the influence of the Holy Spirit to subdue the anger which has produced and so long sustained a needless and cruel rebellion; to change the hearts of the insurgents; to guide the counsels of the Government with wisdom adequate to so great a national emergency; and to visit with tender care and consolation, throughout the length and breadth of the land, all those who through the vicissitudes of marches, voyages, battles, and sieges have been brought to suffer in mind, body, or estate; and finally, to lead the whole Nation, through the paths of perfect enjoyment of Union and fraternal peace.

His proclamation of April, 1861, elaborated in detail his adherence to the Christian faith as follows:

It is fit and becoming in all people and at all times to acknowledge and revere the supreme government of God; to bow in humble submission to His chastisements; to confess and deplore their sins and transgressions, in the full conviction that "the fear of the Lord is the beginning of wisdom"; to pray with all fervency and contrition for pardon of their past offences and for a blessing upon present and prospective action.   When our beloved country, once by the blessing of God united, prosperous and happy, is now

afflicted with faction and civil war, it is peculiarly fit
for us to recognize the hand of God in this terrible
visitation, and in sorrowful remembrance of our faults
as a nation and as individuals, to humble ourselves
before Him and to pray for His mercy, to pray that
we may be spared further punishment, though most
justly deserved, that our arms may be blessed and
made effectual for the re-establishment of law, order,
and peace, throughout the wide extent of our country,
and that the inestimable boon of civil and religious
liberty, earned under His guidance and blessing by
the labours and sufferings of our fathers; may be
restored in all its original excellence.

Convinced that God answers prayer the
President continues:

In the midst of a civil war of unequalled magnitude
and severity, which has sometimes seemed to foreign
states to invite and provoke their aggressions, peace
has been preserved with all nations, order has been
maintained, the laws have been respected and obeyed
and harmony has prevailed everywhere except in the
theatre of military conflict. Needful diversions of
wealth and strength from the fields of peaceful industry to the national defence, have not arrested the
plow, the shuttle, or the ship. The axe has enlarged
the borders of our settlements, and the mines as well
of iron and of coal as of the precious metals, have
yielded more abundantly than heretofore. The
population has steadily increased, notwithstanding
the waste that has been made in the camp, the siege,
and the battlefield. No human counsel has devised,

nor hath mortal hand worked out, these great things.
They are the generous gifts of the Most High God,
Who, while dealing with us in anger for sins, hath
nevertheless remembered mercy.   It has seemed to
me fit and proper that they should be solemnly, reverently, and gratefully acknowledged, as with one heart
and one voice, by the whole American people.

It is not generally known that Lincoln national-
ized the New England observance of Thanksgiving
Day by his proclamation of a National Thanksgiving, followed yearly by every President since,
the governors of the various States regularly
awaiting the President's proclamation fixing the
date of Annual Thanksgiving, and then issuing
proclamations in conformity thereto.

But whenever the occasion seemed to require
Lincoln called his people to their knees in supplication or thanksgiving as on March 30, 1863, when
he announced a day of National Prayer and
Humiliation, the history, content, and spirit of
which are without parallel in the Presidential messages of the United States Government.   This
message was born of the bitter disappointments
and agonies of the dark days of 1863, days made
terrible by the crushing defeat at Fredericksburg.
The whole land was burdened with taxes, stricken
with sorrow, and harrowed by sentiments of trea-

son. The national debt had grown until, on February 2, 1863, the public credit reached the lowest point in our history. Many regiments in the army of the Potomac had not received pay for six months. Beaten under Burnside, decimated and penniless, the army of the Potomac had lost its morale and six hundred desertions were reported daily. Northern editors were clamouring for peace at any price and Greeley, too presumptuous a letter-writer, added to the burdens of the President the irrelevant note: "I venture to remind you that the bleeding, bankrupt, almost dying country longs for peace."

It was in this extremity that Senator Harlan of Iowa, not resting simply on confession of national sins and shortcomings, not expressing merely contrition through conscious guilt and supplication before God for pardon, peace, and national regeneration, called the Senate to the recognition of Jesus Christ Himself in the solemn resolution offered in the Senate at the crucial moment and adopted *without a dissenting vote:*

RESOLVED, That, devoutly recognizing the supreme authority and just government of Almighty God in the affairs of men and of Nations, and sincerely believing that no people, however great, in numbers and resources, or however strong in the justice of their cause, can prosper without His favour, and at the same time deploring the National offences which provoked His righteous judgment yet encouraged, in this day of trouble, by the assurance of His Word, to seek Him for succour according to *His appointed way, through Jesus Christ*, the Senate of the United States do hereby request the President of the United States by his proclamation to designate and set apart a day for National prayer and humiliation, requesting all the people of the land to suspend their secular pursuits and unite in keeping the day in solemn communion with the Lord of Hosts, supplicating Him to enlighten the counsels and direct the policy of the rulers of the Nations and to support the soldiers, sailors, and marines and whole people in the firm discharge of duty, until the existing rebellion shall be overthrown and the blessing of peace restored to our bleeding country.

Now we touch the crux of the religious faith of Abraham Lincoln. Would he endorse a resolution even though solemnly adopted by the Senate, confessing Christ before the world? In his proclamation, in response to the resolution of the Senate, Mr. Lincoln speaks for himself:

WHEREAS, The Senate of the United States, devoutly recognizing the supreme authority and just government of Almighty God in all the affairs of men and Nations, has by a resolution requested the President to designate and set apart a day for National prayer and humiliation and whereas, it is the duty of

Nations as well as of men to own their dependence upon the overruling power of God, to confess their sins and transgression in humble sorrow, yet with assured hope that genuine repentance will lead to mercy and pardon. and to recognize the sublime truth announced in the Holy Scriptures and proven by all history, that "those Nations only are blessed whose God is the Lord."

And, inasmuch as we know that by His divine law nations like individuals, are subjected to punishment and chastisements in this world, may we not justly fear that the awful calamity of civil war which now desolates the land may be but a punishment inflicted upon us for our presumptuous sins to the needful end of our National reformation as a whole people?

We have been the recipients of the choicest bounties of heaven; we have been preserved these many years in peace and prosperity; we have grown in number, wealth, and power as no other Nation has ever grown. But we have forgotten God. We have forgotten the gracious hand which preserved us in peace and multiplied and enriched and strengthened us, and we have vainly imagined, in the deceitfulness of our hearts, that all these blessings were produced by some superior wisdom and virtue of our own. Intoxicated with unbroken success we have become too self-sufficient to feel the necessity of *redeeming and preserving grace*, too proud to pray to the God who made us.

It behooves us, then, to humble ourselves before the offended power, to confess our National sins, and to pray for clemency and forgivenesss. Now, therefore, in compliance with the request, and *fully concurring in the views* of the Senate, I do by this my proclamation designate and set apart Thursday the 30th day of

April, 1863, as a day of National humiliation, to abstain on that day from their ordinary secular pursuits, and to unite in their several places of public worship and devoted to the humble discharge of the religious duties proper to that solemn occasion.

All this being done in sincerity and truth, let us then rest humbly in the hope authorized by the divine teachings that the united cry of the Nation will be heard on high and answered with blessings no less than the pardon of our National sins and the restoration of our now divided and suffering country to its former happy condition of unity and peace.

IN WITNESS WHEREOF, I have hereunto set my hand and caused the seal of the United States to be affixed.

Done at the City of Washington, this 30th day of March, A.D., 1863, and of the Independence of the United States the eighty-seventh.

ABRAHAM LINCOLN.

By the President,
WILLIAM H. SEWARD, *Secretary of State.*

Slavery was rapidly emerging out of politics into the realm of moral valuations. It was ceasing to be a question for discussion and becoming an ugly sin as Lincoln long had known and said. Now the Senate was coming over to his side, and the House was soon to follow. On June 9, 1863, Owen Lovejoy, who more than twenty-five years before had witnessed the martyrdom of his brother Elijah, offered in the House a resolution denouncing slav-

22

ery as a crime and calling for its abolition. This resolution was actually adopted by the Senate on June 9, 1863, concurred in by the House on June 17th, and signed by the President on June 19th. At last a penitent Republic had set itself right before God. All this had taken place in less than three short months and the North had now won the moral victory. Only the victory at arms remained for it to win.

Dark days followed before Gettysburg and Vicksburg came to confirm the judgment of Executive and Legislature that they were now on God's side, but Lincoln, with the majestic confidence of one who had never doubted the outcome, announced on July 4, 1863, the victory at Gettysburg with the expressed desire that "on this day He whose will, not ours, should ever be done, be everywhere remembered with profoundest gratitude." Not of him could it be said as of the lepers healed in the New Testament and forgetful to be grateful: "Were there not ten cleansed? but where are the nine?"

Lincoln's proclamations were pervaded with a tone of sincerity, of trust, of confidence, of prayerful dependence that never faltered, even when the clouds of discouragement rolled blackest. With all the intensity of a prophet's soul, he declared his faith in the divinity that shapes the course and destiny of nations in accordance with the unseen laws that rule the world.   "No human hand hath devised, nor hath mortal hand worked out these things," he said.

He attributed to God's goodness every gain the nation made, and it made many a gain during those four years in population, wealth, and power. When the nation's suffering in men, money, and prosperity in a war of unequalled magnitude is taken into account, it may well be questioned if a like experience has occurred in the history of any nation.   To other nations recuperation has usually come after war, not during war.   France after the Franco-Prussian War and Belgium after the World War are illustrations.   It is stranger than fiction, it is in fact a providence, that growth and increase seemed to go hand in hand with the enormous sacrifice of the national resources, which the Civil War exacted.   The loyal States had lost more men, spent more money, and drawn far more heavily upon their material resources than the Southern States, and yet their aggregate possessions in all that makes a people rich and powerful were actually increased at the close rather than at the beginning of the titanic struggle, while exhaustion overtook the South long before Appomattox.

As early as 1863 Lincoln foresaw this and with characteristic spiritual insight attributed it to the favour of Almighty God. His deep spirit of thankfulness to God found an echo in the hearts of his loyal people and inspired in them the courage to continue the struggle to a successful issue. Even in the darkest days when men like Greeley and McClellan were for making peace with recognition of the independence of the South, Lincoln carried with him the great masses because he lived a life of prayer, he depended upon God, and embraced every proper occasion to call upon the people to unite in thanksgiving to the Almighty, whose protecting arms were thrown around the imperilled nation. On December 7, 1863, he said:

Reliable information being received that the insurgent force is retreating from East Tennessee, under circumstances rendering it probable that the Union forces cannot hereafter be dislodged from that important position; and esteeming this to be of high national consequences, I recommend that all loyal people do, on receipt of this information, assemble at their places of worship and render special homage and gratitude to Almighty God for this great advancement of the National cause.

On May 9, 1864, when General Grant was hammering Lee's army hard, and immediately following the bloody battles of the Wilderness, in which the Army of the Potomac fully demonstrated the ability to fight under a commander who would fight, Lincoln issued the following:

To the friends of Union and Liberty; Enough is known of army operations within the last five days, to claim a special gratitude to God, while what remains undone demands our most sincere prayer to and reliance upon Him without Whom all our efforts is in vain, I recommend that all patriots at their homes, in their place of public worship, and wherever they may be, unite in common thanksgiving and prayer to Almighty God.

The prayers of Lincoln and the loyal people were needed, for although Grant never let go his bulldog grip upon the throat of the rebellion, there was still much fighting to be done and numberless sacrifices to be made. President Lincoln watched the struggle with great anxiety, but with his usual patient reliance on the will of God Who, he fully believed, was keeping watch over the Republic and holding its destiny in the hollow of His hand.

On July 7, 1864, the President in response to a concurrent resolution of Congress, issued a proclamation appointing a day of humiliation and prayer. Grant was fighting it out on the line he had chosen, and it was indeed taking all summer.

The Union losses were appalling, and while neither the President nor General Grant ever lost confidence, the day seemed dark and the issue doubtful. Lincoln, by his proclamation, requested his constitutional advisers, the members of Congress, all soldiers, sailors, and marines, with all loyal and law-abiding people, at their usual places of worship or wherever they might be—

To confess and repent of their manifold sins, to implore the compassion and forgiveness of the Almighty, that, if consistent with His will, the existing rebellion may be speedily suppressed and the supremacy of the Constitution and laws of the United States be established throughout all the States; to implore Him, as the Supreme Ruler of the world, not to destroy us as a people nor suffer us to be destroyed by the hostility or connivance of other nations, or by obstinate adhesion to our own counsels, which may be in conflict with His eternal purposes, and to implore Him to enlighten the mind of the nation to know and do His will, humbly believing that it is in accordance with his will that our people should be maintained as a united people among the family of nations; to implore Him to grant to our armed defenders and the masses of the people that courage, power of resistance, and endurance necessary to secure that result; to implore Him in His infinite goodness to soften the hearts, enlighten the minds and quicken the consciences of those in rebellion, that they may lay down their arms and speedily return to their allegiance to the United States, that they may not be utterly destroyed, that the effusion of blood may be stayed, and that unity and fraternity may be restored and peace and fraternity established throughout all our borders.

This was actually the language of the joint resolution passed by Congress but the President readily and gladly adopted it as his own, and appointed the first Thursday of the following month to be observed as a day of humiliation and prayer. Nine months and two days from the date of this proclamation every petition therein contained was answered. By the surrender of General Lee and his army, peace was restored, the Union preserved, and the insurgents saved from the "utter destruction" from which Lincoln prayed they might be spared.

Lincoln issued another proclamation on September 3, 1864, recommending thanksgiving for the

Signal success that Divine Providence has recently vouchsafed to the portions of the United States fleet and army in the harbour of Mobile, and the reduction of Fort Powell, Fort Gains, and Fort Morgan. and the glorious achievements of the army under Major Sherman in the State of Georgia, resulting in the capture of the city of Atlanta.

In his annual Thanksgiving Proclamation, dated October 20, 1864, the President said:

It has pleased God Almighty to prolong our life another year, defending us with His guardian care against unfriendly desires from abroad, and vouch-safing to us in His mercy many and signal victories over the enemy who is of our own household. It has pleased our Heavenly Father to favour as well our citizens in their homes as our soldiers in their camps and our sailors on the rivers and seas, with unusual health. He has largely augmented our free population by emancipation and by immigration, while He has opened to us new sources of wealth, and crowned the labour of our working-men in every department of industry, with abundant rewards. Moreover, He has been pleased to animate and inspire our minds and hearts with fortitude, courage, and resolution sufficient for the great trial of civil war into which we have been brought, by our adherence as a nation to the cause of freedom and humanity, and to afford us reasonable hopes of an ultimate and happy deliverance from all our dangers and afflictions.

The numerous proclamations Lincoln issued realized their highest point in the Emancipation Proclamation even though it was by no means his last or even his most avowedly religious. It belongs among those few State papers like Magna Charta and the Declaration of Independence which for a blending of intellectual, moral, and religious meaning will be remembered when others are forgotten.

Years before he became President, Lincoln was

convinced that slavery was a moral not a mere
political issue.   He was still a young man when he
determined, if the opportunity ever came, to hit
it hard.   He sacrificed his chance to be Senator
of the United States when in his debates with
Douglas he convinced his hearers that slavery was
not after all debatable, because it was a moral
wrong.   But he took the oath of office as President
pledged not either to maintain or to destroy slavery but to preserve the Union.   While others
missed the issue he singled it out and held firmly
to it amid all the babel of discordant voices, and
even went so far in the earlier days of his administration as to insist that he had no right at that
time to interfere with slavery in the States where
it was, by law, established.

His words to Greeley cannot be kept out of mind
in understanding his sincerity in dealing with the
matter: "What I do about slavery and the coloured
race I do because it helps to save the Union: and
what I forbear, I forbear because I do not believe
it would help to save the Union."   And yet with
a foresight almost supernatural he foresaw that
slavery would ultimately have to go and long before had said: "I believe the time will come when
the sun will shine, the rain fall, on no man who
goes forth to unrequited toil.   When that time

will come, how it will come, I do not know, but that time will surely come."

For its coming he was ever watching. While the war was still young he began evidently to suspect that the salvation of the Union would prove to be bound up with the emancipation of the slaves. But he was not the man to be hurried by the unthinking prematurely into action. Nothing more definitely proves his perfect understanding of the complexity of his problem than his recorded interviews with those who saw but one side of the question or whose minds proved to be single-track.

On the 13th of September, 1862, in reply to a delegation of Chicago clergymen who sought to convince Lincoln that the disasters the Union Army had recently suffered were tokens of God's displeasure at his failure to proclaim the freedom of the slaves, he said sarcastically that if it was probable that God would reveal His will to others on a point so intimately connected with the President's duty, it might be supposed that He would reveal it to the President himself; and that it was a little strange that if the Lord had a special communication for him, He would send it way round through the wicked city of Chicago. However, before he dismissed the delegation, he assured the clergymen that he had the matter under con-

sideration, thanked them for the suggestions they
had made, and expressed the hope that nothing he
had said had hurt their feelings. He also told
them that the time was not yet ripe for the action
they urged, and that to "issue a document that the
world would see must necessarily be inoperative
would be like the Pope's bull against the comet."

To another delegation of ministers determined
to hasten his action he said:

Gentlemen, suppose all the property you possessed
were in gold, and you had placed it in the hands of a
Blondin to carry across the Niagara River on a rope.
With slow, cautious, steady steps he walks the rope,
bearing your all. Would you shake the cable and
keep shouting at him; "Blondin, stand up a little
straighter; Blondin, stoop a little more; go a little
faster; lean more to the south; now lean a little more to
the north?" Would that be your behaviour in such
an emergency? No, you would hold your breath
every one of you, as well as your tongues. You would
keep your hands off until he was safe on the other side.
This Government, gentlemen, is carrying an immense
weight. Untold treasures are in its hands. The
persons managing the ship of state in this storm are
doing the best they can. Don't worry them with
needless warnings and complaints. Keep silence; be
patient, and we will get you safe across.

The hour struck at last, and he was ready for it.
In fact Emancipation had been definitely decided

348 ABRAHAM LINCOLN—MAN OF GOD

weeks before Antietam was fought. Lee's army
was driven back across the Potomac from Maryland into Virginia. Immediately following this
victory Mr. Lincoln summoned his Cabinet to the
usual meeting-place. "Gentlemen," he said, "I
want your attention." He laid the historic paper
down upon the table. To what he then remarked
to them they all felt it would be futile to object.
"Gentlemen," he declared, "I do not want your
advice as to whether I shall issue this document or
not, for that I have determined myself. If you
have suggestions concerning minor points, when
you have heard it read, I will hear them." He
then added in a lower tone of voice: "I have not
consulted any one; I promised myself, I told the
Lord."

Secretary Seward turned to Lincoln and asked:
"What did I hear you say?" Mr. Lincoln faced
full upon the Secretary and replied: "Secretary
Seward, I told the Lord that if He would drive the
rebels out of Maryland, I would emancipate the
slaves, and I will do it."

The effect of the proclamation was both more
firmly to consolidate the South, and to create some
division among the Unionists of the border States
and among the conservatives of the North. But
it also crystallized about the President all the

forces that made for victory and intensified their purpose to continue the war to a successful issue. What the administration lost in numerical support was more than compensated by the new flame of spiritual enthusiasm, which burned with a steadily increasing fervour to the very end of the struggle. No wonder Lincoln said: "God bless the churches." He now had them all with him. He had at last killed slavery without violation of his oath of office to maintain the Union.

CHAPTER XXXIV

INSPIRED UTTERANCES

PROOF of the strong vein of piety that ran like a golden thread through Lincoln's nature abounds in the utterances made during the last few years of his life. All through his trying experiences he was pondering the problem of the mysterious ways of the Almighty in dealing with human affairs. In 1862 he wrote down on a slip of paper some of his musings:

The will of God prevails. In great contests, each party claims to act in accordance with the will of God. Both may be, and one must be, wrong. God cannot be for and against the same thing at the same time. In the present Civil War, it is quite possible that God's purpose is something different from the purpose of either party, and yet human instrumentalities working just as they do are of the best adaptation to effect His purpose. I am almost ready to say that this is probably true, that God wills this contest, and wills that it shall not end yet. By His mere great power on the minds of the now contestants He could have either saved or destroyed the Union, without a human contest; yet the contest began, and having begun, He could give the final victory to either side any day, yet the contest proceeds.

One of Lincoln's biographers says:

As time went on, and his conviction that his cause was right grew stronger, in spite of the reverses he suffered, he began to feel that God's purpose was to wipe out slavery, and that war was a divine retribution on North as well as South, for the toleration of slavery.

In a letter dated April, 1864, Lincoln wrote:

At the end of three years' struggle, the Nation's condition is not what either party saw or any one expected. God alone can claim it. Whither it is tending seems plain. If God now wills the removal of a great wrong, and wills also that we of the North as well as you of the South shall pay for our complicity in that wrong, impartial history will find therein new cause to attest and revere the justice and wisdom of God.

It is not strange that with such a habit of mind Abraham Lincoln came at last into a full recognition of spiritual truth in all its phases and practical application. Proof of his growing appreciation of Christian ideas and institutions is found in his manifest desire to secure the proper observance of the Sabbath, so far as war conditions would permit. On his visits to the various commands he had been pained to see that Sunday was scantily observed by the men in camp, while much profanity was indulged in by the men and officers. These observations led him to issue the following remarkable order:

The importance for men and beasts of the prescribed weeky rest, the sacred rights of Christian soldiers and sailors, a becoming deference to the best sentiment of a Christian people, and a due regard for the Divine Will, demand that Sunday labour in the Army and Navy be reduced to the measure of strict necessity. The discipline and character of the national forces should not suffer, nor the cause they defend be imperilled by the profanation of the day or the name of the Most High.

Lincoln went so far as to admonish a certain general who was addicted to the habit of profanity to abandon the habit himself and to use his authority to discourage it among the soldiers. Thus the Christian type of Lincoln's character was increasingly manifest. He had in his heart the fire of a reformer and a martyr, the mysticism of a prophet, the vision of an enthusiast, and the solemn sense of duty characteristic of the devotee. Of him it has well been said:

To a hope which saw the delectable mountian of absolute justice and peace in the future, to a faith that God in His own time would give to all men the things convenient to them, he added a charity which embraced in its deep bosom all the good and bad, all the virtues and infirmities of men, and a patience like that of nature, which, in its vast and fruitful activity, knows neither haste nor rest. A character like this is among the precious heirlooms of the Republic, and by a special good fortune every part of the country has an equal claim and pride in it.

In 1864, after Lincoln had been elected to a second term by an overwhelming majority, in spite of the organized opposition in the North to the conduct of the war, and despite the call for 500,000 men to fill up the depleted ranks of the armies which some of his friends had vainly besought him to postpone until after the election, he said to a party that came to congratulate him on his victory: "If I know my own heart, my gratitude is free from any taint of personal triumph. I do not impugn the motives of any one who opposed me. It is no pleasure to me to trample over any one. But I give thanks to the Almighty for this evidence of the people's resolution to stand by free government and the rights of humanity."

To the congratulations of a personal friend, he replied:

"I should be the veriest shallow and self-conceited blockhead upon the footstool, in my discharge of the duties that are put upon me in this

23

place, if I should hope to get along without the wisdom that comes from God and not from man."

In his second Inaugural Address—another masterpiece of literature—he said:

On the occasion corresponding to this, four years ago, our thoughts were anxiously directed to an impending Civil War. All dreaded it; all sought to avert it. While the inaugural address was being delivered from this place, devoted altogether to saving the Union without war, insurgent agents were in the city seeking to destroy it without war, seeking to dissolve the Union and divide effects by negotiation. Both parties deprecated war, but one of them would make war, rather than let the Union survive, and the other would accept war rather than let it perish, and the war came. One eighth of the whole population were coloured slaves, not distributed generally over the whole Union, but localized in the Southern part of it. These slaves constituted a peculiar and powerful interest. All knew that this interest was somehow the cause of the war. To strengthen, perpetuate, and extend this interest was the object for which the insurgents would rend the Union, even by war; while the government claimed no right to do more than restrict the territorial enlargement of it. Neither party expected for the war the magnitude or the duration which it has already attained. Neither anticipated the cause of the conflict might cease with, or even before the conflict itself should cease. Each looked for an easier triumph and a result less fundamental and astounding. Both read the same Bible and prayed to the same God, and each invoked His aid against the other. It may seem strange that any man should ask a just God's assistance in wringing his bread from the sweat of other men's faces, but let us "judge not that we be not judged." The prayers of both could not be answered. That of neither has been answered fully. The Almighty has His own purposes. "Woe unto the world because of offences, for it needs be that offences come, but woe to that man by whom the offence cometh." If we suppose that American Slavery is one of these offences which in the Providence of God must come, but which having continued through His appointed time, He now wills to remove, and that He gives to both North and South this terrible war as the woe due to those by whom the offence came, shall we discern therein any departure from those divine attributes which the believers in a living God always ascribe to Him? Fondly do we hope and fervently do we pray that this mighty scourge of war may speedily pass away; yet if God wills that it continue until all the wealth piled up by the bondman's two hundred and fifty years of unrequited toil shall sink, and until every drop of blood drawn by the lash shall be paid by another drawn by the sword, as was said three thousand years ago, so still it must be said, "The judgments of the Lord are true and righteous altogether." With malice toward none, with charity for all, with firmness in the right as God gives us to see the right, let us strive on to finish the work we are now in, to bind up the nation's wounds, to care for him who shall have borne the battle, and for his widow and orphan, to do all which may achieve and cherish a just and lasting peace among ourselves and with all nations.

Marvellous revelation of inspired utterance! No wonder the French minister said: "No such document as that ever before came to the French Court." How impersonal, how impartial, how balanced in its judgments, how charitable, how lofty in its inspiration this remarkable document, breathing the spirit of Holy Writ itself! It was addressed to the whole Nation, and not only to this Nation, but to the world. In it we see the clear reflection of Lincoln's religious faith, his broad charity, his magnanimity, his unquestioning submission to the Divine Will, his implicit belief in the righteousness of his cause, his assent to the justice of retribution exacted for the sins of which all the people were directly or indirectly guilty, and his sublime confidence that in the final arbitrament, the Lord of all the earth would do right.

An eminent French ecclesiastic, Monseigneur Du Pannoup, Bishop of Orleans, in a letter to a friend, thanking him for a copy of the address characterized it as "a beautiful page of the history of a great people," and said that he read it with the most religious emotion and sympathetic admiration.

Mr. Lincoln [he added] expresses with solemn and touching seriousness the sentiments of, I am certain, the noble and best souls of the North as well as the South.   What a beautiful day, when there will be a union of these souls in the true and perfect light of the Gospel, but what a beautiful day we behold already when the twice-elected chief of a great nation strikes a lofty Christian note too much absent in Europe, and in official language befitting large affairs,   announces the end of slavery and prepares the way for the triumph of justice and mercy in the very spirit of the Holy Scriptures.

But it remained for Walt Whitman to pay perhaps the most memorable tribute yet on record to the mingling of the intellectual and the spiritual in Lincoln.   He wrote:

One of the best of the commentators of Shakespeare makes the height and aggregate of his quality as a poet to be that he thoroughly blended the ideal with the practical or realistic.   If this be so, I should say that what Shakespeare did in poetic expression, Abraham Lincoln essentially did in his personal and official life.   I should say that the invisible foundations and vertebræ of his character, more than any man's in history, were mystic, abstract, moral, and spiritual.   He seems to have been a man of indomitable firmness on rare occasions, involving great points: but he was generally very easy, flexible, tolerant, respecting minor matters.   As to his religious nature, it seems to me to have certainly been of the amplest, deepest-rooted kind.

CHAPTER XXXV

LINCOLN'S CHRISTIAN VIEW OF LABOUR

WHEN Lincoln was beating out the music of a soul as just as it was kind, there was no labour problem such as confronts us today. There was at most an isolated and grotesque aberration of the problem furnished by the fact of slavery which had become so ingrained in legality as to blind most people to its awful immorality.

Lincoln was the first American to set himself to disentangle the wrong of slavery from the status given it by history and legislation. He believed slavery an insult to the soul of man and to the heart of God. He said if slavery was not wrong, nothing was wrong. He regarded it not merely as unchristian but also as an inescapable menace to American democracy. "This nation cannot remain half slave and half free," "A house divided against itself cannot stand," were his very words. While others were seeking the way out by compromise and concession, Lincoln though putting paramount the preservation of the Union was making ready for the time to come—as come he knew it would for the redemption of the promise made to himself long years before in the slave market at New Orleans to "hit that thing hard."

Yet as one looks back on Lincoln's record and his writings, the conclusion is inevitable that almost from the first he saw slavery as but one aspect of the labour problem and applied to it the same fundamental principles of Christianity by which labour at all times must be tested.   These words from a speech which he delivered in 1847 are as true today as when they first were spoken:

In the early days of our race the Almighty said to the first of our race, "In the sweat of thy face shalt thou eat bread," and since then if we except the light and air of Heaven, no good thing has been or can be enjoyed by us without having first cost labour.   And inasmuch as most good things are produced by labour, it follows that all such things of right belong to those whose labours have produced them.   But it has so happened in all ages of the world, that some have laboured, and others have, without labour, enjoyed a large proportion of the fruits.   This is wrong and should not continue.   To secure to each labourer the whole product of his labour, or as nearly as possible, is a worthy object of any good government.

Here is a concise declaration of essentials. Labour is the law of life.   The labourer is worthy of his hire and is entitled to the product of his toil. Slavery aroused Lincoln's indignation because it violated this first principle. It allowed some to live on the toil of others. "It may seem strange," he declares, "that any man should dare to ask a just God's assistance in wringing bread from the sweat of other men's faces."

In a letter to Dr. Ide and others, in 1864, he gives more elaborate utterance to this thought:

To read in the Bible as the Word of God Himself, that "In the sweat of thy face thou shalt eat bread," and to preach there from that "In the sweat of other men's faces shalt thou eat bread" to my mind can scarce be reconciled with honest sincerity. When brought to my final reckoning, may I have to answer for robbing no man of his goods; yet more tolerable even this, than for robbing one of himself and all that was his. When a year or two ago those professedly holy men of the South met in the semblance of prayer and devotion, and in the name of Him Who said, "As ye would all men should do unto you, do ye even so unto them," appealed to the Christian world to aid them in doing to a whole race of men as they would have no man do unto themselves, to my thinking, they condemned and insulted God and His church far more than Satan did when he tempted the Saviour with kingdoms of the earth. The devil's attempt was no more false and far less hypocritical.

Here Lincoln indicates the principle that he would have applied to the solution of economic problems; namely, "As ye would all men should do unto you, do ye even so unto them," thus substituting the Golden Rule for the rule of gold, the only guarantee of industrial tranquillity.

Lincoln never dodged an issue. To him it was evident that Christianity and slavery were contradictory. One had to perish. In Cincinnati in 1859, he said:

Our government was not established that one man might do with himself as he pleased, and with another man, too. I hold that if there is any one thing that can be proved to be the will of Heaven by external nature around us, without reference to Revelation, it is the proposition that whatever any one man earns with his hands and by the sweat of his brow, he shall enjoy in peace.

From this clear view of the necessity of labour and the right of the individual to enjoy what he earned by labour Lincoln moved logically and steadily along to appreciation of the capitalistic system of industry which unmistakably excludes slavery. Capital and slavery could not live long side by side. As the capitalistic method of industry developed, the planter found himself more and more threatened by an agency of industry which he could not use. Industrial leaders everywhere, except in the South, were using the most modern appliances, increasing masses of capital and encouraging the development of skilled free labour. The planter was in slavery using an instrument as ancient as man. In the fields of industrial change, therefore, the unseen hand was pushing slavery on to its doom.

But unfortunately this was not the end of the labour problem. In Europe, its broader aspects had been widely and intensely discussed. Karl Marx, a repudiated Jew, had sounded the note of war on capital and private ownership in his *Communist Manifesto* of 1848. Cabet in France had heralded a new industrial heaven until bleeding Icaria had sobbed out its doom. Louis Blanc was able to induce revolutionary France to adopt a radical scheme in 1848, only in six months to run on the rocks. Proudhon with raucous voice thundered the immortal lie that "Property is robbery." Maurice, Kingsley, and Carlyle had sounded in more delicate tones the discontent of British labour. In America, however, little discussion occurred, absorbed as we were in the social problems of slavery and states rights. For fifty years the tides of social controversy had swept the continent of Europe, yet had scarcely touched our shores. Such alien literature reached us as Marx's correspondence. Arthur Brisbane's exposé of Fourierism and Greeley's harmless utterances feebly echoed alien views.

Lincoln was not widely read. There is no evidence that he understood much that was being said and done across the sea. He dug out of his own consciousness and conscience illuminated by Christianity what he knew concerning labour, capital, and property. It is a marvellous instance of clear thinking led by loyalty to righteousness. In bold contrast Lincoln stands out against Marx and his followers who distorted Ricardo's sayings to support the Marxian view that labour, meaning physical labour, produces all wealth, that rent and interest are therefore merely robbery and exploitation, that property and capital have no right to exist.

Lincoln evidently perceived the irrepressible industrial conflict. He was clearing the ground for the final struggle. He was weaving general principles into the technical discussion that was on. He was going straight to the point. To workingmen themselves he was defending property in such pregnant utterances as are found in the speech made March 1, 1864, to the Committee of the Workingmen's Association in New York:

Property is the fruit of labour. It is desirable. It is a positive good to the world. That some should be rich shows that others may become rich, and hence it is just encouragement to industry and enterprise. Let not him who is houseless pull down the house of another, but let him labour diligently and build one for himself, thus by example assuring that his own shall be safe from violence when built.

These calm, conservative, and rational words of Lincoln on the question of property stand in striking contrast with the lawless methods advocated and adopted by the agitators and revolutionaries of the present day. The existing industrial system of America, largely the fruit of Lincoln's practical wisdom and action, constitutes the Gibraltar of economic stability upon which the wild dreams and lurid experiments of Syndicalism, the I. W. W., and Bolshevism, are utterly shattered as unpractical and unworkable schemes.

But at the same time with his inclusive mind Lincoln recognized the responsibility of capital to labour. He saw that they depended on each other, that the relation was reciprocal. In a speech in Cincinnati, in 1859, he said:

That there is a certain relation between labour and capital I admit. That it does exist and rightfully exist, I think is true. That men who are industrious and sober and honest in the pursuit of their own interests should after awhile accumulate capital and after that should be allowed to enjoy it in peace, and also, if they should choose, when they have accumulated it, to use it to save themselves from actual labour, and hire other people to labour for them is right.   In doing so they do not wrong the men they employ, for they find men who have not their own land to work upon, or shops to work in, and who are benefited by working for others—hired labourers, receiving their capital for it.   Thus a few men who own capital hire others, and these establish the relation of labour and capital rightfully—a relation of which I make no complaint.

Thus Lincoln proclaims this reciprocal relation between capital and labour, and indicates it cannot be too strongly emphasized.   The moment you deny labour the hope of acquisition, you degrade it to slavery.   To destroy or do away with capital would produce universal poverty.   Capital must reap in order to replenish itself.   Profits are nothing more than replacement fund.   Abolish profits and the wheels of industry must stop.

Understanding as he did the right relation between capital and labour Lincoln had sympathy with labour because labour appears to be more dependent than capital.   To preserve a just balance between these two is to solve the riddle of the ages. For the abuse of capital which is the temptation always incident to capital, Lincoln never held a brief.   He understood that human nature is prone to take advantage of those easy opportunities which come more readily to capital than to labour. Speaking in the Legislature of Illinois as early as 1837 he said with this tendency in mind: "These capitalists generally set harmoniously and in concert to fleece the people, and now that they got into a quarrel with themselves, we are called upon to appropriate the people's money to settle the quarrel." But he was as quick to warn against unjust attacks on capital, and at New Haven, March 6, 1860, he said:

I like the system which lets a man quit when he wants to, and wish it might prevail everywhere. One of the reasons why I am opposed to slavery is just here. What is the true condition of the labourer? I take it that it is best for all to leave each man free to acquire property as far as he can. Some will get wealthy. I don't believe in law to prevent a man from getting rich; it would do more harm than good. So while we do not propose any war upon capital, we do wish to allow the humblest man an equal chance to get rich with everybody else.

Perhaps no man has ever been more conscientious in maintaining the even balance between labour and capital. In his second message to Congress, December 3, 1861, he said: "Labour is the superior of capital and deserves the much higher appreciation. Capital has its rights which are as worthy of protection as any other rights. Nor is it denied that there is, and probably always will be, a relation between labour and capital producing mutual benefits."

Had he lived today doubtless his keen mind would have cut through the Marxian theory of "class struggle," which re-enforced by the rifle and the bomb is not only the terror of Russia but the peril of the world. It is at least reassuring to find in his second Inaugural these words: "It is not forgotten that a considerable number of persons mingle their labour with capital, *i. e.*, they labour with their own hand, and also buy or hire others to labour for them; but this is only a mixed and not a distinct class. No principle is disturbed by the existence of this mixed class." And again: "As has already been said, there is not, of necessity, any such thing as the free hired labourer being fixed in that condition for life."

Lincoln's Christian view of labour included also education for all grades of labour. In his agricultural address, delivered in Milwaukee in 1859, he analyzed the situation as follows:

By the "mudsill" theory it is assumed that labour and education are incompatible, and any practical combination of them impossible. According to that theory, a blind horse upon a treadmill is a perfect illustration of what a labourer should be—all the better for being blind, that he could not kick understandingly. . . . A Yankee who could invent a strong-handed man without a head would receive the everlasting gratitude of the "mudsill" advocates.

But free labour says:

No. Free labour argues that as the Author of man makes every individual with one head and one pair of hands, it was probably intended that head and hands should co-operate as friends, and that particular head should direct and control that pair of hands. As each man has one mouth to be fed, and one pair of hands to furnish food, it was probably intended that particular hands should feed that particular mouth, inseparably connected with it; and that being so every head should be cultivated and improved by what will add to its capacity for performing its charge. I suppose, however, I shall not be mistaken in assuming as a fact that the people of Wisconsin prefer free labour with its natural companion.

Lincoln once invited criticism in a misquoted phrase calling labour a commodity. Even if fairly credited to Lincoln it would not be inapplicable, for labour was so described by some authorities at that time. The following paragraph, however, shows the meaning Lincoln gives the phrase:

If the negro were not deported, the same amount of labour would still have to be performed. The freed people would surely not do more than their own proportion of it, and very probably for a time would do less. With deportation, even to a limited extent, enhanced wages would be mathematically certain. Labour is like any other commodity in the market, increase the demand for it and you increase the price of it.

Radicals of various types have been eager to get Lincoln on their side at any cost. John Nicolay listed over a dozen spurious quotations, among them one which gained wide vogue, representing Lincoln as prophesying the ruinous reign of the money power. Of this his daughter, Helen Nicolay, writes:

This alleged quotation seems to have made its first appearance in the campaign of 1888 and it has returned with planetary regularity ever since. Although convinced by internal evidence of its falsity, my father made every effort to trace it to the source, but could find no responsible nor respectable clue. The truth is that Lincoln was no prophet of a distant day. His heart and mind were busy with the problems of his own time. The legacy he left his countrymen was not the warning of a seer, but an example and an obligation to free their own dark shadows with the sanity and courageous independence he showed in looking upon those that confronted him.

Lincoln is insistent that labour be free to acquire property. Again and again he recognizes

24

the right of "getting rich." Our government itself is built on the idea of the equal opportunity of
everybody to become all that is in him. Democracy would give a chance to every man to do the
best he can. If he has the ability to rise, he will
rise. If he happens to be born into a higher level
on which he has not the capacity to sustain himself,
he will naturally sink by the gravitation of his
natural ability to a lower level. Lincoln himself
is a living example of the priceless opportunity
which democracy affords even to the lowliest.
July 1, 1854, he said: "There is no permanent
class of hired labourers amongst us. Twenty-five
years ago I was a hired labourer. Advancement
is the order of things in a society of equals."
Born in obscurity, reared in poverty, he exempli-
fied by his elevation to the Presidency how a
real democracy may work under the checks and
balances of an ordered Constitution operating in a
Christian commonwealth.

CHAPTER XXXVI

JERUSALEM

As the war dragged to its end, Lincoln grew unutterably weary both in soul and body. "I think I shall never be glad again," he confided to a friend. Out of sunken eyes—so pitiful as one perceives who studies the life mask Clark Mills made a while before he died—there looked not merely brooding sadness, but something like unspeakable despair.

The morning of April 14th dawned soft and sunny on the Nation's Capitol. The lilacs were in eager bloom. The willows clothed their graceful boughs with a new green. Spring had come. For ten days news of victory after victory had been flashing over every wire, and even nature seemed determined men should know the winter's discontent was blossoming into a glorious summer of reunion and of reconciliation. The war was over. There was no longer any doubt of that.

Early in the morning came the final word. Everyone rejoiced. Even the countless many who were mourning their dear dead felt the common thrill of a new joyousness. James Russell Lowell wrote his good friend Norton: "The news, my dear Charles, is from Heaven."

Lincoln was happiest of all. There was a new spring in his step. The bowed shoulders were up-lifted. His tired face was all agleam with serene cheeriness. At the Cabinet meeting held soon after breakfast someone showed concern because no word had been received from Sherman. It was Lincoln who bade them be of good courage. They would soon have news from Sherman—news that all was well. He had dreamed the night before—as often during those four years when something gratifying was about to happen—that he saw a vessel "moving with great rapidity toward a dark and indefinite shore." He had learned to trust that dream. It never failed him.

In the afternoon he took Mrs. Lincoln out into the country for a drive and talk that only wife and husband know the meaning of at such a time. They planned far into the future. "Mary," he said, "we have had a hard time in Washington; but the war is over and with God's blessing we may hope for four years of peace and happiness, and then we will go back to Illinois."[1]

[1] Arnold's *Life of Lincoln*, p. 429.

They were going home. To go home is the best thing any one can do. The call home is the one urge to which all normal men respond who have been beaten by the storms of life till the power to go on seems almost broken. The home-going instinct is world-wide.

That evening the President's box at Ford's Theatre was to be occupied. The party came in late. The play was well worth seeing. Laura Keene was at her best. The attention of the crowded house was divided between the play and the President. All were glad with him and glad for him.

For him at such a time the theatre had no glamour, the play no allurement. He was thinking of the better days to come, of going home, of God and His unfailing mercy, of Jesus Christ and His redeeming grace. Among the plans flitting through his mind was one to go as soon as circumstances would permit to Palestine. A yearning had come over him to tread "those holy fields over whose acres walked those blessed feet . . . nail'd for our advantage on the bitter cross."

He said to Mrs. Lincoln there was no place he wished so much to see as Jerusalem. The word was but half finished on his lips. Mary heard him whisper, "Jeru—!" Then the most cruel and

most senseless bullet ever fired in history sped
too surely to its mark.   The man of God started
for Jerusalem, but it was,

> Jerusalem, the golden,
> The home of God's elect.[1]

[1] *Lincoln Scrapbook*, p. 52.   From Rev. N. W. Miner's conversation with Mrs. Lincoln soon after the assassination.   Dr.
Miner had been a pastor in Springfield and assisted also in the
burial service at Springfield on May 4, 1865.

APPENDIX I

PETER CARTWRIGHT was the forerunner of Abraham Lincoln. This was the order of Providence. Religious emotion would precede political commotion. The heart had to be warmed before the mind could be convinced. A flame of love had to be kindled before the conscience could be converted.

Peter Cartwright was born in Virginia in 1785 of impecunious parents. His father was a soldier in the Revolutionary War; his mother was a devout Methodist. In 1793 his parents settled in Logan County, Kentucky, near the Tennessee border. Here it was that Jacob Lurton, a travelling Methodist Preacher, one day asked permission to preach in the Cartwright cabin. Peter was in his ninth year and was sent out to invite his neighbours to hear the preacher, thus paralleling the memorable experience in the life of Lincoln at the age of nine, when he went out to invite the neighbours to hear the sermon at his mother's grave.

When the Cartwrights settled in Logan County, there was not a mill within forty miles and no schools. Sunday was a day set apart for hunting, fishing, horseracing, cardplaying, dances, and all kinds of amusement.

"We killed our own meat out of the woods," says

Cartwright in his *Autobiography*, "and beat our meal
and hominy with a pestle and mortar"; "we stretched
a deerskin over a hoop, burned holes in it with the
prongs of a fork, sifted our meal and baked our bread.
We gathered out of the woods sage, bohea, cross-vine,
spice, and sassafras, and other herbs; we raised our own
cotton and flax and our garments we made out of what
we wove."

It was at a place called Cane Ridge in Kentucky in
1800, that, to use Cartwright's words, "the unex-
pected happened and the power of God was displayed
in a very extraordinary manner; many were moved to
tears and a bitter and loud crying for mercy. The
meeting was protracted for weeks. Ministers of all
denominations flocked in from far and near. Thousands came on foot, on horseback, in carriages, and in
wagons. The attendance numbered from twelve
to twenty-five thousand. Hundreds fell prostrate
under the power of God, as men slain in battle. Stands
were erected in the woods from which preachers of
different denominations preached. It was not unusual for two, three, four, or seven preachers to be
addressing the meetings at one time from different
stands, and the Heavenly fire spread in every direction. Thousands broke out into shouting all at once
and the shouts could be heard for miles around."

This was the first camp meeting ever held in any
country and its fame must now be counted historic.
From this point the news spread through all the
churches and over all the land. Peter Cartwright was
converted later on at another meeting of the same
kind, when in his sixteenth year. This religious
movement had begun twelve years before the birth
of Lincoln.

In 1804, Cartwright was famous in Kentucky as the "Boy Preacher," but he never lost his head. Never was he sidetracked into vain ambitions of worldly and material power. Never did he covet fine homes and large tracts of land. Never was his imagination obsessed with the idea of becoming a Bishop. His was the simple life, and, like Lincoln, he would live and die a practical Christian.

In 1824, the great preacher moved with his family from Kentucky to Illinois, having been appointed by Bishop Roberts to travel the Sangamon Circuit. Springfield was then the new seat of Government. The circuit rider describes the place as "having a few smoky, hastily built cabins and one or two very little shanties called stores, and, with the exception of a few heavy articles, I could have carried on my back in a few loads all they had for sale."

Peter Cartwright was appointed in 1826 to the position of Presiding Elder of a district that extended from the Kaskaskia River to the extreme Northern settlements, and even to the Pottowattomis Nation of Indians on Fox River. In the whole of Illinois there were not more than three thousand of the Methodist Episcopal Church. The Forerunner had to travel up and down a district several hundred miles long, covering on the west side of the Grand Prairie fully two thirds of the geographical boundaries of the State.

"The year before I moved to Illinois," says the preacher, "there had been a strong move by a corrupt Legislature to call a Convention, with a view to alter the Constitution so as to admit slavery into the State. I had left Kentucky on account of slavery, and, as I hoped, had bid a final farewell to all slave institutions; but the subject was well rife throughout the country;

for although the followers of human liberty had sustained themselves and carried the election by more than one thousand votes, yet it was feared that the advocates of slavery would renew the effort and cause this abomination of desolation to stand where it ought not. I entered the lists to oppose slavery and without any forethought went into the agitated waters of political strife. I was strongly solicited to become a candidate for a seat in the Legislature of our State. I consented and was elected as a Representative from Sangamon County. I found that almost every measure had to be carried by a corrupt bargain and sale which would cause honest men to blush for their country. My sentiments placed me in a minority in my county and I retired from politics."

Like Lincoln, the great preacher had an extraordinary experience on the Mississippi River. In April, 1828, Cartwright and two companions, Thompson and Dow, met at St. Louis to take passage on board a steamboat to the Methodist Episcopal General Conference at Pittsburgh. "We had," he says, "never been on a steamboat before. Our boat was named *The Velocipede* with Mr. Ray, captain. Before we went aboard, Brothers Dow and Thompson, with the kindest feelings imaginable, thought it their duty to coach me to be very quiet, for those steamboat fellows, passengers and all, were desperadoes. They knew I was outspoken, loved everybody, and feared nobody. They were afraid I would get into some difficulty with somebody. I thanked them very kindly for their special care of me; 'but,' said I, 'Brethren, take care of yourselves, I think I know how to behave myself and make others behave themselves, if need be.'

"When we got aboard we had a crowded cabin, and a

mixed multitude: Deists, Atheists, Universalists, a great many profane swearers, drunkards, gamblers, fiddlers, and dancers. We dropped down to the barracks below St. Louis, and there came aboard eight or ten United States officers, a jolly set, I assure you. They drank, fiddled, danced, swore, played cards, men and women too. I walked about, said nothing, but plainly saw we were in a bad snap. But there was no way to help ourselves. Brother Thompson came to me and said: 'Lord, have mercy on me, what shall I do?'

"'Go to your berth,' said I, 'and stay there quietly.'

"'No,' said he, 'I'll reprove them.'

"'Now, Brother,' I said, 'Do not cast your pearls before swine.'

"'Well,' said he, 'I won't stay in the cabin, I'll go on deck.'

"Up he started, and when he got there, behold they were playing cards from one end of the deck to the other. Back he came and said:

"'What shall I do? I cannot stand it.'

"'Well,' said I, 'Brother Thompson, be quiet and behave yourself. You have no way to remedy your condition unless you jump overboard and swim to shore.'

"So things went on for several days and nights. At the mouth of the Ohio there came aboard a Captain Waters. He had a new fiddle and a pack of cards. He was a professed infidel. Card-playing was renewed all over the cabin. The captain of the boat was as fond of dancing and card-playing as any of them. There was a lieutenant of the regular army, and although he was very wicked, he had been raised by religious parents. His wife, as he told me, was a good Christian. In walking the guard, this lieutenant whose name was Barker and myself fell into conversation, and, being by ourselves, I took occasion to remonstrate with him on the subject of his profanity. He readily admitted that it was wrong and said, 'I have been taught better.' There was also a Major Biddle on board, a professed infidel, but gentlemanly in his manner. I talked with him in private. I remonstrated against his profanity. He agreed with me in all I said. Presently they gathered around a table and played cards. I walked carelessly by and looked on. Lieutenant Barker and Captain Waters looked up at me. I know they felt reproved.

"Said one of them to me: 'We are not blacklegs. We are not playing for money, but just to kill time.'

"I affected to be profoundly ignorant of what they were doing and asked them what those little spotted things were.

"Mr. Barker said: 'Sit down and I will show you what we are doing and how we do it.'

"'No use,' said I, 'my friends, I am afraid it is all wrong.' They insisted there was no harm in it at all.

"'Well,' said I, 'Gentlemen, if you are just playing for fun or to kill time, would it not be better to drop all such foolishness and let us talk on some topic to inform each other? Then we could all be edified. As it is, a few of you enjoy all the pleasure, while the rest of us are not benefited. Come, lay those little spotted cards that are only calculated to please children of a larger size and let us talk on history, philosophy, astronomy; then we can all enjoy it and be greatly benefited.' ·

"Captain Waters said, 'Sir, if you would debate

with me on the Christian religion, we will quit all our cards, fiddles, and dances.'

"'I will do it with pleasure, Captain,' said I, 'I have only one objection to debate with you for you swear and use oaths and I can't swear back at you. I fear a debate mixed up with oaths would be unprofitable.'

"'Well, sir,' said he, 'if you will debate with me on that subject, I will pledge you my word and honour I will not swear a single oath.'

"'Very well, sir,' said I, 'on that condition I will debate with you.'

"By this time a large crowd had gathered around us. Lieutenant Barker said: 'Now, Gentlemen, draw near and take notice of the terms on which this debate is to be conducted, take your seats and listen to the arguments and by the consent of the two belligerent gentlemen I will keep order.'

"We both agreed to this proposition. The Captain opened the discussion by a great flourish of trumpets expressing his happiness at having one more opportunity of vindicating the religion of reason and nature in opposition to the religion of an 'illegitimate.' To all of these flourishes, I simply replied that the Christian religion was of age and could speak for itself and that I felt proud of an opportunity to show that infidelity was born out of holy wedlock and therefore in the strictest sense of the word was an illegitimate, and I thought it ill became the advocates of such a spurious progeny to heap any reproaches on Christ.

"These exordiums riveted the attention of all the passengers, the Captain, ladies, and all. My opponent proceeded to lay down his premises and draw his conclusion. When his twenty minutes expired, I replied,

quoting a passage of Scripture. 'Hold, sir,' said my
opponent, 'I don't allow a book of fables and lies to
be brought in, nothing shall be admitted here but
honourable testimony.'

"Very well, sir,' said I, 'the Bible shall be dispensed
with altogether. I shall introduce testimony drawn
from the book of nature.' And proceeded with the
argument.

"In his second replication, he quoted Tom Paine
as evidence.

"'Hold, sir,' said I, 'such a degraded witness as Tom
Paine can't be admittted as testimony in this debate.'

"My opponent flew into a violent passion and swore
profanely that God Almighty had never made a
purer or more honourable man than Tom Paine. As
he belched forth these horrid oaths, I took him by the
chin, and worked his jaws together until his teeth
rattled. He rose to his feet. So did I. He drew
his fist and swore that he would smite me to the
floor.

"Lieutenant Barker sprang in between us and said:
'Cartwright, stand back. You can beat him in arguments and I can whip him; if there is any fighting to
be done, I am his man, from the point of a needle to
the mouth of a cannon, as he pledged his word and
honour that he would not swear, and he has broken his
word and forfeited his honour.' Then I had to fly in
between them to prevent a bloody fight, for they both
drew deadly weapons. Finally this ended the argument. My valorous Captain made concession and all
became pacified.

"From this on Barker became my fast friend and
would have fought for me any time, and my infidel
Captain Waters became very friendly with me, and

when we landed at Louisville wanted me to go home with him and partake of his 'very best hospitalities.'"

The advent of Peter Cartwright was not a coincidence.

The moral and religious world is guarded by law and not by chance.

The Methodist converts in Illinois formed a nucleus around which Lincoln worked with success from the start. What class of people gave Lincoln the closest attention and most respectful hearing? The early followers of Cartwright and his co-workers. All who were converted by his preaching and example knew his views regarding slavery and when Lincoln appeared, his sentiments did not shock them by their strangeness. The soil had been ploughed by the intrepid preacher and Lincoln would cultivate and reap, his mission being so far-reaching that a special preparation was necessary, and in considering his life we have to abandon our preconceived notions about politicians and statesmen.

Too many books have been devoted to the dry details of his life. Too many writers have missed the mark when dealing with it. The time is at hand when the dry facts must yield the proofs of the spiritual will behind them and the noble character of Peter Cartwright, the Forerunner, must shine out above all superficial speculation, as the yellow corn shines in the sunlight when stripped of the husks. We can no more separate the work of Cartwright from that of Lincoln than we can separate Bonaparte from the French Revolution or slavery from the War of Secession.

The same inquiry must now be made into the impelling forces behind the character and career of Peter Cartwright as in the case of Lincoln. Let the materialist explain why both moved from Kentucky into Illinois; why both opposed slavery; why both were militant on the same moral grounds; why both belonged to the common people; why both were self-educated and both had mothers who were deeply religious.

Take Peter Cartwright on any ground and his gifts will stand out unsurpassed except by those of Lincoln. On moral grounds he was the great President's equal and feared no man. He was very robust physically and his Christianity was manual when it was necessary, muscular on occasion and militant always.

Cartwright was unconscious that he was the Forerunner of Lincoln. To the contrary, he regarded himself as the political antagonist of Lincoln and took pride in the thought that he was working against Lincoln when, in fact, he was preparing the way for him. Two such representatives of a great, divine idea could not long be kept apart. Separated as partisans, they were united as patriots and reformers, Cartwright opening the way for Lincoln as they both advanced, step by step, toward the promised land of freedom.

The workmen on the Parthenon were so blinded by the dust of the blocks at which they were chiselling, that they could not see the symmetry and glory of the temple which sprang from the brain of Ictinus and crowned the hills of Athens. They saw it when it was completed. Peter Cartwright's eyes were so blinded by the dust of partisan prejudice and controversy that he could not catch the divine inspiration of Lincoln's life nor behold in full outline the vastness of his soul; neither could he discern the great purpose which fired the consciousness and sustained the ambition of Lincoln, a purpose with which Cartwright not only held kinship but which, in fact, he pioneered.

This knowledge, however, gradually dawned upon Peter Cartwright, and when it reached its full fruition, he was ready to take the witness stand and openly champion the prophet of whom he was the herald.

In his *Personal Recollections of Abraham Lincoln*, Mr. Henry B. Rankin, of Springfield, Illinois, who before the war was a law student in Lincoln's office, has put on record a startling and vivid account of Peter Cartwright's experience at a dinner party given in his honour by James Harper, the senior member at that time, of the Harper Publishing Company in New York City.

It was in the winter of 1862 when Cartwright visited the East and addressed many large audiences in the leading cities. "After his return,"[1] says Mr. Rankin, "he spent several days with my parents and I shall repeat the account he gave us of that dinner party. The company at the Harper reception given in his honour was composed, he said of representative merchants, bankers, lawyers, and a few ministers. The ministers seemed less desirous of meeting him than were the others. He said that they met at an hour earlier than usual for such functions because he had previously made an engagement with a Brooklyn pastor to address a meeting for him at 8.30 the same evening and had accepted Mr. Harper's invitation subject to this earlier engagement. Cartwright said that 'he felt like a cat in a strange garret' on 'meeting so many celebrated men for the first time' and that when he was introduced to the guests he was 'all doubled up' but (using a favourite expression when endeavouring to be cautious and conventional) that

[1] *Personal Recollections of Abraham Lincoln*, Henry B. Rankin, p. 276.

25

he 'poised himself' so as not to reflect discredit upon his backwoods raising."

He said he had hoped to play the inconspicuous part of a quiet listener among these eminent men whom he regarded as superiors. Instead, for an hour or more, he was forced to take the most prominent part, answering their questions concerning the frontier life, his experiences as a preacher at camp-meetings, and on other occasions among the rough characters of the Far West. At length he succeeded "in directing the conversation to the sad condition of national affairs." Having diverted the attention from himself, he lapsed into silence in order that he might learn the attitude of such a representative company of New York men toward Abraham Lincoln and his efforts to crush the Rebellion. He knew how seriously the loss of Southern trade had affected the business of some of the guests; and he expected to find their sympathies were influenced by this condition of their pocketbooks; but he did not expect to find any one there whose sympathies were strongly with the Southern Confederacy.

To Cartwright's great surprise, he heard nothing but criticisms of President Lincoln's course since his inauguration; or the milder view of "anything for peace," and a compromise guaranteeing whatever conditions the South might demand. "The consciences of the entire company" said Cartwright—to use his exact words—"were choked with cotton and cankered with gold." He said that he had never felt his blood so hot with indignation as it was while sitting there as the guest of honour and listening to such conversation.

Looking at his watch, he saw that it was nearly time

for him to be on his way to Brooklyn. Holding his
watch in his hand, he addressed Mr. Harper, asking
to be excused since, making allowances for delays in
transit, he had only sufficient time to meet his appointment. Mr. Harper protested: "No, no, Father Cartwright, not until after the next course, which is the
best and rarest to be served."

Cartwright replied: "That is very kind and considerate, Brother Harper, very kind indeed, and I
thank you for your forethought. But instead of sharing the next course with you, I beg your attention
before I leave to hear from me a few parting words of
admonition and counsel." The request was granted,
and I repeat what he said as nearly as I can recall his
report of the startling words with which he addressed
them:

"I am an old man; the sands in the hour-glass of my
life have nearly finished their flow. What I can say
and what I can do in this world, if accomplished at all,
must be done promptly. So I wish to speak very
plainly to you tonight. If I had known I would meet
such a nest of tories and traitors here, I would not
have put my legs under your table.

"My father," continued Cartwright, "was a Revolutionary patriot. He gave the best years of his life
to this country as a soldier in wresting from the British Crown the independence of the Colonies and
winning the West for these United States. Since
then, as boy and man, first in 'the dark and bloody
battleground' of Kentucky's Indian strife, and later
as a pioneer in the frontier settlements of Illinois, I
have kept most sacred, by personal service in an humble way, my faith and loyal devotion to the priceless
legacy of these United States, left me by my patriot

father. I know what his united country is worth to us now. I have seen and rejoiced in its growth; I have lived its glorious life. I have been baptized with the blood that won, and have had a part in the labours that cemented together these United States which now span the land from ocean to ocean with more happy and prosperous homes than God's sun ever shone on before.

"As I near the sunset days of my life I behold, with none of your dollar-blurred vision, what is to be our country's future if we hold these states united as our fathers bequeathed them to us. At the same time I see in anticipation and horror fully as clearly, through what would be my blinding tears of wrath and dismay, the huge hell of jealousy and discord that can be opened up within our country's boundaries if the secessionists succeed in rending the Union of our States. You, their sympathizers on this side of the Mason and Dixon line, are accomplishing here today more for those secessionists, by your criticisms and lack of sympathy for President Lincoln's noble labours for the Union, than you could do were you down South this hour, enrolled in the ranks of Jeff Davis's Confederacy.

"As I have tonight listened to such unpatriotic censures by you of the President, allow me to express to you from first-hand knowledge, my opinion of his personal capacity and patriotism. As the crow flies, I have lived within a score of miles of Abraham Lincoln for a third of a century. Until shortly before he took the oath of office as President of the United States, we had trained in different political camps, he a Whig and I a Democrat. I remained a Democrat until the firing on Fort Sumter. Since then I know no party save that of my undivided country and Abraham Lincoln its President.

"Once we were opposing candidates for a seat in Congress. I went down to defeat. But it was defeat by a gentleman and a patriot. I stand here to-night to commend to you the Christian character, sterling integrity and far-seeing sagacity of the President of the United States, whose official acts you have, in your blind money-madness, so critically assailed.

"When you go from here to your homes, I want you to bear with you the assurance of his neighbour and once political opponent that the country will be safe in his hands. I wish to have you understand that back of him will stand an unflinching host of Western men, who have no financial ghosts that terrify them, and who are destined to rescue this nation from the perils now before us. Why stand ye here, idle critics? May God send patriotic light into your stingy souls!

"I am through. I may have said too much, and said it too harshly, for I am not a man of smooth, soft words. I was born in a cane-brake, where my mother was hurried and secreted to escape the tomahawks of savage Indians; I was rocked in a bee-gum for my cradle; and my graduation degrees were taken from, and in, life's thunderstorms. I may be considered by you a very rude guest; but in such national distress, when I feel so intensely my country's perils, I could not speak less strongly than I have spoken. I could not withdraw in silence and go sneaking from this company without feeling that I had been a coward and false to my country.

"In a last word and as my farewell, I shall give you a toast. In this glass of Heaven-brewed 'Adam's

Ale' I proclaim and admonish you with the sentiments uttered by the great Webster in the United States Senate, and its patriotic companion piece announced by Senator Douglas the last time he stood before an Illinois audience."

Cartwright said that as he spoke this last sentence he reached before him for a glass of water by his plate and, holding it high above him, repeated the words of the two illustrious senators: "Liberty and Union, now and forever, one and inseparable." "There are now but two parties—Patriots and Traitors!"

Nothing more vivid rises up out of my memories of more than half a century past than those earnest words as he repeated them to us with that intensity and emotion so characteristic of that veteran hero of Western Methodism, that life-long Jacksonian Democrat of the stalwart, old school type of partisanship.

This conversation occurred in the latter part of 1862, ten years after Cartwright's autobiography had been published. In that book he had made no mention of his candidacy for Congress with Lincoln as his opponent, though that campaign was made ten years before his autobiography appeared. This omission seemed to me at the time peculiar; and I was all the more at a loss to account for it on hearing him speak so favourably of President Lincoln. So I ventured to mention this omission and to ask him whether there had not been some very interesting matters connected with the Congressional campaign of 1846 between himself and Lincoln well worth the telling in his autobiography.

Cartwright replied that I should remember that when he published his autobiography in 1856, Lincoln had

not attained national prominence; but stated that the
principal reason for this omission was that he thought
his own political ventures the most unsatisfactory
part of his life to him and to many of his friends, and
that this was a portion of his past that he referred to
in the closing pages of his book, where he asked forgiveness for all the shortcomings and imperfections
without number in his eventful life. He added:
"That 1846 campaign cured me of all political hanker-
ings for office, and I hope the good Lord will forever
save me from getting any more political bees in my
bonnet."

It was at this point in the conversation that my
mother referred to the campaign story of 1846 in regard to Lincoln's being an avowed infidel when at
Salem. She put the direct question to him whether
he was not now convinced that the charge was false;
and that the story circulated at that time, that Lincoln wrote a book at Salem attacking the Bible—
which manuscript was burned by Samuel Hill—was
not a gross fabrication based upon the burning of
another paper having no relation to the Bible, or any
religious subject.

Cartwright replied that he had learned as much as
that from an intimate conversation he had with Men-
ter Graham some years after that campaign. From
him he learned the facts concerning that unfortunate
story. He found that he had been wonderfully mis-
informed and misled by the account he had received,
believed, and circulated about the infidel book said to
have been burnt by Hill. He said that he was so
chagrined and abashed by the discovery of the political purpose in that story, that it was one of the
inducements that caused him to ignore in his book

everything connected with his candidacy against Lincoln in 1846.

"I did not wish," he said, "to embalm in my history a story that nobody since has ever referred to. It was dead. It was very silly in me not to have verified the whole story at the time and found how false it was." "A short time after Lincoln's nomination for the Presidency by the Republican Party in 1860," he went on to say, "I found more substantial reasons than any I ever had before, to assure me that Lincoln was not what my party friends and I, relying upon them, had charged him with being in 1846. This came from my meeting Dr. Smith, the pastor of the First Presbyterian Church of Springfield, and spending an evening in his company at the home of a mutual friend in Springfield. I found him a pleasant Christian gentleman and the evening in his society was a profitable one. He was a college man, but I found he had roughed it on the frontier as well, and got the college starch out of him. Dr. Smith told me that Lincoln and his family were regular attendants at his church, and that at some time he expected Lincoln to unite with his church, as Mrs. Lincoln had done. Dr. Smith said that Mrs. Lincoln had been brought up an Episcopalian, and previous to their marriage had attended that church; but that in deference to Lincoln's Baptist views against so many formalities in church worship, she had joined the Presbyterian Church as a compromise, expecting Lincoln at some future time to come into that church."

Jacquess also assured me that during the year he was stationed in Springfield, he had spent many hours with Lincoln in the State Library, and by their conversations, was well satisfied that Lincoln's attitude toward religion was not that of an infidel.

Cartwright said that his being a member of the State Legislature had put such political ambitions into his head that it was not hard for his friends to get him into the canvass for Congress in 1846,[1] that hereafter, if the Lord and the good people would forgive him for the political campaigning of his life in the past, he felt proof against being tempted into any political strife again in his few remaining days. He believed that Lincoln was fitted for political life and knew how to keep his eye on the laurel while he played the game; but for himself, he had tried and most ingloriously failed in it, and knew that for Peter Cartwright hereafter, it would be better to stick to Methodism and fighting the devil and his imps, and when no longer able for that work, he should settle down on his farm at Pleasant Plains until God should call him home.

We are now so far removed from that period that we are no longer unable to "see the woods for the trees." The distance necessary to true perspective has been measured in history, and we can now see that

[1] In this campaign Lincoln attended a preaching service of Peter Cartwright, after having spoken in the same town in the afternoon. Cartwright, observing the presence of Lincoln, after delivering an intensely evangelistic sermon, called upon all desiring to go to heaven to stand up. All arose but Lincoln. Then he asked all to arise who did not want to go to hell, Lincoln still remained seated, whereupon Cartwright exclaimed: "I am surprised to see Abe Lincoln sitting back there unmoved by these appeals. If Mr. Lincoln does not wish to go to heaven and does not want to escape hell, perhaps he will tell us where he does want to go." Lincoln slowly arose and replied, "I am going to Congress."—Ida Tarbell, in *Red Cross Magazine*, Feb., 1919.

while Cartwright and Lincoln were adherents of different political parties, they occupied common ground in relation to human freedom and the preservation of the Union. Their political differences were merely superficial. Their political faith was essentially the same, and, while upon different political paths, they were moving toward the same goal.

The initial battles of freedom were being fought out in Illinois, Lincoln beginning as a Whig and ending as a Republican; Cartwright, a Jacksonian Democrat, born and baptized into that party by his father, who was a Revolutionary hero, ceased his partisan subserviency when Sumter was fired upon and knew no party save that of his undivided country and Abraham Lincoln, its President.

It is a significant fact that the Forerunner defeated Lincoln for the Legislature. This was Lincoln's only defeat by popular vote. Lincoln's time had not yet arrived. The soil was not yet prepared. The influence of Cartwright was necessary in the Democratic party and, as a member of the Legislature, that influence was preparatory to the coming of Lincoln. Single-handed and alone, Cartwright stood in that Legislative body striking with all his might against the institution of slavery. A little later Lincoln appeared as a member of that body and took up the fight where Cartwright laid it down, finally joining with Dan Stone in a protest against slavery which sounded the prelude of its death-knell. Cartwright had been the prophet of this dawn. He had "left Kentucky on account of slavery." Upon reaching Illinois, he found "there had been a strong move by a corrupt Legislature to call a convention with a view to alter the constitution so as to admit slavery into the State; and he had entered the list to oppose slavery and without any forethought he went into the agitated waters of political strife," and being "strongly solicited" to become a candidate for a seat in the Legislature, he ran against Abraham Lincoln and was elected Representative from Sangamon County.

"My sentiments placed me in a minority in my county," he declares, and yet he stood practically alone against the majority, lifting his voice like the thunder of Sinai against the institution of slavery which cursed the soil and soul of the nation.

Cartwright retired from politics. He felt that his clerical garments were bedrabbled with the contamination. Lincoln was better qualified from the standpoint of political sagacity and strategy to fight the battle than the preacher; and so Cartwright is supplanted by Lincoln, Lincoln to carry forward the work which Cartwright had begun, their paths diverging to meet in 1846 when, after a heated contest, Lincoln defeated Cartwright and went to Congress.

The Forerunner had done his work. Lincoln was now fairly launched in the arena of national politics. Cartwright had now to say: "I must decrease, and you must increase." He had pioneered the way for Lincoln to the State Legislature and had been his opponent in a Congressional campaign which opened for Lincoln the path to the White House. Cartwright goes back to the pulpit, Lincoln continues to ascend the heights of political preferment, and thus Lincoln was prepared for the crisis when it broke, and the country was prepared for Lincoln when he arrived.

It is worth while to note here how Lincoln, standing alone in the White House, ridiculed, maligned, and

obstructed, was championed by his Forerunner,
Peter Cartwright, who journeyed to New York during the war, as Lincoln had journeyed there before
the war and, at the opportune moment, pointed to
Lincoln as the man of the hour.

That Harper dinner was a scene sacred and historic.
There, in the midst of the brains and wealth of the
great Metropolis, the Forerunner appeared, grim,
gaunt, and grotesque, carrying with him the manners
of the frontier, his dislike for conventionality pronounced, his abhorrence of sham and hypocrisy, apparent, his devotion to flag and country paramount,
his attitude toward Lincoln loving and loyal.

At last, with eyes undimmed by partisan prejudice,
emancipated from the thraldom of tradition, stepping
out into the clear light of duty and patriotism, joining hands with the "Rail-splitter of the Sangamon,"
even as Douglas had held his hat at his Inauguration,
he hails him as the conservator of democracy, signals
him as God's man for the crisis, and crowns him as
the Heaven-inspired saviour of the Union!

APPENDIX II

THE hand of Providence is apparent in the direction of the Abolition Movement. Lincoln, who saw things in what Bacon called the "dry light" did not fail to recognize the vital significance of the work, the mission and the sacrifice of Elijah P. Lovejoy, the first martyr to the cause.

At the beginning of the Nineteenth Century a few young men received the "call," each in a separate walk of life. Peter Cartwright was called while yet a youth; Lovejoy, William Lloyd Garrison, and Wendell Phillips responded in early manhood. Cartwright's influence radiated from the pulpit, Lovejoy's from his own printing press, that of Garrison and Phillips from the rostrum and the public market place. No position of vantage was left unoccupied. The divine call was heard in various sections of the country by ears attuned to the whisperings of conscience, of religion and the higher command. The "still small voice" spoke to these men in accents that left no room for misgivings or evasions. In every case the call was imperative, the command absolute. These men, like Lincoln, indulged in no compromises, cherished no illusions, offered no half measures. Their Christianity was unyielding. With them agnosticism was unknown. They could not conceive a state of mind in

which doubt held the spirit in a condition of mental
bondage. They looked upon slavery as a positive
evil and they determined upon its destruction by
positive speech and drastic action. They put principle above politics, and trust in the moral law above
fear, right above might, justice above wrong. Because of this attitude the example of Lovejoy and his
supporters ought to be kept conspicuously before the
American public at this critical juncture. As the
Lovejoys and the Garrisons fought the tyranny of
slavery we have to fight the tyranny of autocracy in
every form.

The Reverend Malvin Jameson who was long a
resident of Alton says in his book, *Elijah P. Lovejoy as
a Christian*: "On November 6, 1837, the city was quiet.
Mr. Gilman, the owner of the warehouse where the
Lovejoy press was stored, intending to stand guard
there all night asked some of his friends to remain with
him; nineteen responded. About ten o'clock they
became aware that a crowd had gathered. Soon the
demand was made for the surrender of Lovejoy's press
and shots were fired on both sides. A man was killed.
Threats were made to set the warehouse on fire. A
ladder was placed against the building and a man began to ascend it to carry out the threat. Volunteers
were called for from the defenders inside the warehouse to go out and fire upon this man. Mr. Lovejoy
was one of the three who responded. Two of the
three were hit by shots from the mob. Mr. Lovejoy
was shot fatally, five balls being lodged in his body and
he had only strength enough to run upstairs into the
counting room where he immediately expired. This
was November 7th. The next day he would have
been thirty-five years old." Soon after this tragedy

John Quincy Adams described it "as a shock as of an earthquake throughout the continent which will be felt in the most distant regions of the earth."

On December 8, 1837, William Ellery Channing called an indignation meeting at Faneuil Hall, Boston, when resolutions were presented which were opposed by the Attorney-General of the Commonwealth of Massachusetts in a violent speech, in which he declared that Lovejoy "died as the fool dieth."

Sitting in the audience there was a young man whose name was as yet unknown, whose talents were as yet untried. His name was Wendell Phillips. Over his thin, pale face and long, Roman nose his forehead loomed like a bastion above a watchtower. His eyes had the look of the prophet, his mouth the firmness which nothing can move nor change. As this unknown young man rose to give his judgment, a profound silence fell on the vast assembly. For now he was about to deliver, offhand, a speech which would rank with Patrick Henry's "Give me liberty, or give me death," and Lincoln's supreme tribute to the fallen heroes at Gettysburg. Young Phillips had not been speaking long before the people who crowded Faneuil Hall saw in him all the elements of the natural orator, recognized the penetrating logician, and the master of polished and disconcerting invective. A star of the first magnitude had appeared above the horizon of slavery whose course pointed to democratic freedom and the advent of Lincoln.

His was the oratory of a great and solemn day. On this, his first public appearance, justice triumphed, and Channing's resolutions were carried, and obloquy began to pursue slavery to its death.

Two years after Appomattox Mr. Phillips lectured

in Alton. The following day his visit to Lovejoy's grave inspired a letter to the *Anti-Slavery Standard* in which he stated: "Hitherto the name of this city brought but one idea to my mind and I could not hear it or see it in print without a shudder, but I have had a cordial welcome here and I can now think of Alton as the home of brave and true men. The gun fired at Lovejoy was like that of Sumter—it shattered a world of dreams! Looking back, how wise as well as noble his courage seems! Incredible that we should ever have been obliged to defend his imprudence! What world-wide benefactors these imprudent men are— the Lovejoys, the John Browns, the Lloyd Garrisons, the saints and martyrs! How prudently most men creep into nameless graves, while now and then one or two forget themselves into immortality!"

John Quincy Adams in a memoir to Lovejoy uses these words: "That one American citizen, in a State whose constitution repudiates all slavery, should die a martyr in defence of the freedom of the press is a phenomenon in the history of the Union. It forms an era in the progress of mankind toward universal emancipation. The incidents which preceded and accompanied and followed the catastrophe of Mr. Lovejoy's death, point it out as an epoch in the annals of human liberty. He was the first American martyr to the freedom of the press and the freedom of the slave."

This tragic circumstance must have been burned indelibly into Lincoln's mind. It made Owen Lovejoy, brother of the murdered man, his lifelong friend and counsellor. Lincoln did not always agree with him in matters of policy, but ever after his brother's death the man was an uncompromising Abolitionist, and Lincoln never forgot that Elijah Lovejoy, as John Quincy Adams said, was the first American martyr to the freedom of the press and of the slave.

The transcendent importance attached by Lincoln to the death of Lovejoy might have escaped attention but for the publication by W. C. MacNaul in 1865 of the volume *The Jefferson-Lemen Compact*. Lincoln's views on this subject have received wider circulation recently also through the publication of Gilbert A. Tracey's *Uncollected Letters of Abraham Lincoln*, in which appears a letter written by Lincoln dated Springfield, Illinois, March 2, 1857, to the Reverend James Lemen, regarded by many as the most remarkable letter he ever wrote.

"REV. JAMES LEMEN,
    "Friend Lemen:
    "Thanking you for your warm appreciation of my view in a former letter as to the importance in many features of your collection of old family notes and papers, I will add a few words more as to Elijah P. Lovejoy's case. His letters among your old family notes were of more interest to me than even those of Thomas Jefferson, written to your father. Of course, they (the latter) were exceedingly important as a part of the history of the Jefferson-Lemen anti-slavery pact, under which your father, the Rev. James Lemen, Sr., as Jefferson's anti-slavery agent in Illinois founded his anti-slavery churches, among which was the present Bethel Church, which set in motion the forces which finally made Illinois a free State, all of which was splendid; but Lovejoy's tragic death for freedom, in every sense marked his sad ending as the most important single event that has happened in the New World.

26

"Both your father and Lovejoy were pioneer leaders in the cause of freedom, and it has always been difficult for me to see why your father who was a resolute, uncompromising, and aggressive leader who boldly proclaimed his purpose to make both the territory and the State free, never aroused nor encountered any of the mob violence which both in St. Louis and Alton confronted or pursued Lovejoy and finally doomed him to a felon's death and a martyr's crown. Perhaps the two cases are a little parallel with those of John and Peter. John was bold and fearless at the scene of the crucifixion, standing near the cross and receiving the Saviour's request to care for his mother, but was not annoyed, while Peter, whose disposition was to shrink from public view, seemed to catch the attention of members of the mob on every hand until finally, to throw public attention off, he denied his Master with an oath though later the grand old apostle redeemed himself grandly, and like Lovejoy, died a martyr to his faith. Of course, there was no similarity between Peter's treachery at the temple and Lovejoy's splendid courage when the pitiless mob was closing around him. But in the cases of the two apostles at the scene mentioned, John was more prominent or loyal in his presence and attention to the great Master than Peter was, but the latter seemed to catch the attention of the mob; and, as Lovejoy, one of the most inoffensive of men, for merely printing a small paper devoted to the freedom of the body and mind of man, was pursued to his death, his older comrade in the cause of freedom, the Rev. James Lemen, Sr., who boldly and aggressively proclaimed his purpose to make both the territory and State free, was never molested a moment by the minions of violence. The madness and pitiless determination with which the mob steadily pursued Lovejoy to his doom mark it as one of the most unreasoning and unreasonable in all time, except that which doomed the Saviour to the cross.

"If ever you should come to Springfield again, do not fail to call. The memory of our many 'evening sittings' here and elsewhere, as we called them, recalls many an hour, both pleasant and helpful.

"Truly yours,

"ABRAHAM LINCOLN."

Lincoln declared the assassination of Lovejoy to be "the most important event that had happened in the new world." This statement was made at an epoch when things truly astounding were happening in the world of politics, science, and commerce. Invention was revolutionizing industry. Railroads were transforming commerce, Darwin was re-casting science and humanitarians were belting the world with love. Yet none of these "as single events" weighed heavily in his mind compared with the memory of the pale-faced Congregational preacher dying for an ideal, the freedom of the press, and the freedom of the slave, at the hands of the pro-slavery mob in the little city of Alton in November, 1837. He weighed carefully every word both in speech and in writing.

This letter of Lincoln should be framed and displayed in every public library and home as a fitting testimonial to the moral fibre and spiritual faith of Elijah Lovejoy, the prophet of Abolition, and as a vivid expression of the vital relation of free institutions to human liberty. It also illuminates the Christian faith and character of Abraham Lincoln;

it reveals his familiarity with the Scriptures and his admiration for Peter and John. He declares that Peter redeemed himself "grandly" after he denied his Master with an oath and styles him as "the grand old Apostle." He appreciates the influence of the church, declaring that Bethel Church had "set in motion the forces which finally made Illinois a free State." His reference to Jesus as "the Saviour"; his exaltation of the martyrdom of Lovejoy "as one of the most unreasoning and unreasonable in all time, except that which doomed the Saviour to the cross," glorifies the cross as the centre of all world events. Abraham Lincoln was the type of Christian who not only followed in the footsteps of the Master, quoting His words, citing His works, emulating His deeds and breathing His spirit, but he also climbed Golgotha's brow and under the very shadow of the cross, depicted with consummate skill the supreme tragic fact of history.

BIBLIOGRAPHY

HUNDREDS of books and thousands of pamphlets and addresses are in print concerning Lincoln. From every point of view he has been treated as a publicist. This book has pictured him as a man of heart as well as head who grew in grace as well as wisdom till at last he stood forth a true man of God, more and more as years went by endeavouring to pattern his life after that of Jesus Christ in Whose uniqueness he came increasingly to believe, trying to live up to his oath of office to preserve the Union Washington had established, and to do good to his fellow-man, rich and poor, white and black, whenever and wherever the way opened. That was Lincoln.

In consequence the author, though reading many books on Lincoln, has in preparation of this volume made actual use of comparatively few. He has largely based the book, which began years ago with a lecture, on the results of travel, observation, interviews with people who knew Lincoln and also with credible informants who have passed on to him much first-hand information about Lincoln. He, therefore, believes the book will in general prove self-authenticating as indeed the personality of Lincoln has already proved itself in history. They that have eyes to see will see. To no others will the work have any meaning.

A few of the sources of information may be listed as follows:

Abraham Lincoln: Complete Works. Edited by John G. Nicolay and John Hay. In two volumes. New York: The Century Company, 1894.

Life of Abraham Lincoln. By J. H. Barrett. Cincinnati: Moore, Wilstach, Keyes & Co., 1860.

The Life of Abraham Lincoln. By J. G. Holland. Springfield, Massachusetts: Gurdon Bill, 1865.

Life and Public Services of Abraham Lincoln. By Henry J. Raymond. New York: Derby & Miller, 1865.

The Life of Abraham Lincoln. By Ward H. Lamon. Boston: James R. Osgood & Company, 1872.

Abraham Lincoln: The True Story of a Great Life. By William H. Herndon and Jesse W. Weik, New York: D. Appleton & Company, 1892.

Personal Traits of Abraham Lincoln. By Helen Nicolay. New York: The Century Company, 1912.

Abraham Lincoln. By John T. Morse, Jr. In two volumes. Boston: Houghton, Mifflin & Company, 1893.

The Life of Abraham Lincoln. By Ida M. Tarbell. In two volumes. New York: The Doubleday and McClure Company, 1900.

Abraham Lincoln: The People's Leader in the Struggle for National Existence. By George Haven Putnam. New York: G. P. Putnam's Sons, 1909.

Abraham Lincoln. By Noah Brooks. New York: G. P. Putnam's Sons, 1882.

Abraham Lincoln. By Lord Charnworth. Henry Holt and Company, 1907.

Latest Light on Lincoln. By Ervin Chapman. New York: Fleming H. Revell & Company, 1917.

The True Abraham Lincoln. By William Eleroy
Curtis. Philadelphia: J. B. Lippincott & Company, 1903.

Abraham Lincoln. By Carl Schurz. Boston:
Houghton, Mifflin & Company, 1909.

The Life of Abraham Lincoln. By Isaac N. Arnold.
Chicago: A. C. McClurg & Company, 1916.

Abraham Lincoln. By Charles Carleton Coffin.
New York: Harper & Brothers, 1893.

Personal Recollections of Abraham Lincoln. By
Henry B. Rankin. New York: G. P. Putnam's
Sons, 1916.

Six Months at the White House. By Frank B. Carpenter. New York: Hurd & Houghton, 1866.

Diary of Gideon Welles. *Atlantic Monthly,* 1909.

Abraham Lincoln the Christian. By William J.
Johnson. New York: Eaton and Mains,
1913.

The Wisdom of Abraham Lincoln. Selected and
edited by Temple Scott. New York: Brentanos,
1918.

Abraham Lincoln. By Joseph H. Choate. New
York: T. Y. Crowell & Company, 1901.

Abraham Lincoln. By Phillips Brooks. A sermon
preached in Philadelphia, April 23, 1865.

*Recollections of President Lincoln and His Adminis-
tration.* By L. E. Chittenden. New York:
Harper & Brothers, 1891.

The Life and Times of Abraham Lincoln. By L. P.
Brockett. Philadelphia: Bradley & Company,
1865.

The Soul of Abraham Lincoln. By William E.
Barton. New York: George H. Doran & Company, 1920.

"Washington and Lincoln." By Lyman P. Powell. New York: *The Review of Reviews*, February, 1901.

The Valley of the Shadow. By Francis Grierson. John Lane Pub. Co., 1908.

Abraham Lincoln. By Bishop C. H. Fowler. Patriotic orations. Eaton & Mains.

Lincoln's Scrap-Book. Library of Congress, Washington, D. C. Men and Things I saw in Civil War Days. Gen. James F. Rustling.

INDEX

A

Abolitionism, 90
Adams, John Quincy, quoted, 399, 400, 401
Advance, editor of, quoted, 282, 283
Æsop's *Fables*, 33
Age of Reason, Paine, Lincoln's criticism of, 63
Akers, Dr. Peter, 51
Allies and America in World War, 209
Alton, 398, 400
American Baptist Home Mission Society, Lincoln's message to, 288
Antietam, battle of, 205, 215, 348
Appomattox, 206, 339,
Army of the Potomac, 210; at Arlington Heights, 210; morale, 334; in battles of the Wilderness, 341
Ashmun, George, Lincoln's letter to, 143–144
Atlanta, 206; capture of, 343

B

Baker, Edward D., 62, 221, 222
Baltimore Convention, 1864, 298
Barker, Lieutenant, prevents fight, 380–382
Barry, Wm., 41
Bateman, Newton, conversation with Lincoln, 229–234
Bates, Mr., of Chicago, 140
Battle Hymn of the Republic, 326

Bayard, Chevalier, 220
Beauregard, 210
Beecher, Henry Ward, sent to England, 194; criticized administration, 195; Lincoln's visit to, 327
Belgium, 339
Bell, John, candidate for president, 144
Berry, Rev. Richard, 10
Bethel Church, 404
Bible, Lincoln's mother read it to him, 31; a favorite of Lincoln's, 33; his belief in, 98–100, 248, 318, 319; he read it every day, 256–257; he quoted it to school children, 319; he read it to coloured help, 325
Black, Jeremiah S., Attorney-General, 157
Black Hawk War, Lincoln in, 39–40
Blaine, James G., candidate for president, 214
Blair, Montgomery, Postmaster-General, 'oses confidence of the public, 297–299; letter from Lincoln to, 300
Blanc, Louis, 362
Bloomington speech, 124–125
Bolshevism, 364
Breckinridge, candidate for president, 144
Breckinridge Democrats, principles of platform, 1860, 143
Brisbane, Arthur, 362–363
British labour, 362
Brooks, Noah, describes a waking vision of Lincoln's, 150–151

409